THE THREE
HALVES OF
INO MOXO

THE THREE

Teachings of the

HALVES OF

Wizard of the

INO MOXO

Upper Amazon

CÉSAR CALVO

Translated from the original Spanish by
Kenneth A. Symington

Inner Traditions International
Rochester, Vermont

Inner Traditions International
One Park Street
Rochester, Vermont 05767

First published in English in 1995 by Inner Traditions

First published in Spanish under the title *Las tres mitades de Ino Moxo* by Proceso Editores, Iquitos, Peru, 1981

LIBRARY OF CONGRESS CATALOGING-IN-PUBLICATION DATA

Calvo, César.
    [Tres mitades de Ino Moxo y otros brujos de la Amazonía. English] The three halves of Ino Moxo : teachings of the wizard of the upper Amazon / César Calvo ; translated by Kenneth Symington.
        p.   cm.
    ISBN 0-89281-519-1
    1. Indians of South America—Peru—Religion and mythology.   2. Córdova-Ríos, Manuel, 1887–1978.   3. Amahuaca Indians.   4. Hallucinogenic drugs and religious experience.   I. Title
    F 3429.3.R3C3413   1995
    299.895–dc20   94-30522
                                                                         CIP

Printed and bound in the United States

10 9 8 7 6 5 4 3 2 1

Text design and layout by Charlotte Tyler
This book was typeset in Cheltenham, with Middleton as a display face

Distributed to the book trade in Canada by Publishers Group West (PGW), Toronto, Ontario
Distributed to the book trade in the United Kingdom by Deep Books, London
Distributed to the book trade in Australia by Millennium Books, Newtown, N.S.W.
Distributed to the book trade in New Zealand by Tandem Press, Auckland

And this, which is nothing, is everything.

Ino Moxo

To Maestro Ino Moxo, two of whose three bodies disappeared blowing smoke.
To the sorcerers Don Javier, Don Hildebrando, Don Juan Tuesta, and Juan González.
To Manuel De Bernardi, in the high Cusco, Navel of the World.
To Esteban Pavletich, who taught us the courage and joy of living and writing books in freedom.

To Eduardo Portugal, Fernando Llosa, and Juan Carlos Domenack.
To Moises Lemlij.
To Gustavo Valcarcel, Juan Gonzalo Rose, Arturo Corcuera, and Reynaldo Naranjo.
To Turati and to Alfredo Gonzalez Teja.
Because without their counsel and friendship, I would not have been able to begin this book.
Because of more than that, much more than that.

César Calvo S.
Barcelona, June 1979

Contents

III. INO MOXO

IV. THE AWAKENING

Translator's Note

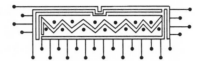

It was a humid November day in Taropoto, Peru, and I looked through the bookshelves of my friend Dr. Jacques Mabit before heading out to collapse in a hammock for what was left of that hot afternoon. I had gone to the Amazon following my intuition, an invitation from the young Peruvian healer Jose Campos, and my affinity for anything related to plants, especially those which have a history of ritual or shamanic use—the teacher plants—and I had not been disappointed. The sheer vitality, diversity, and size of the Peruvian Amazon, in the shadow of the Andes, was overwhelming.

In those bookshelves, I found it: *Las Tres Mitades de Ino Moxo: The Three Halves of Ino Moxo,* this book, in one of the out-of-print early Spanish editions. I noticed that it had been published only in Spanish and in a later Italian translation. I thought I would leaf through it before dozing off in the heat.

Not only did I not go to sleep that afternoon, but I slept very little in the following days: the book had me entranced as I went on its wild journey of vision, adventure, insight, and poetry. Reading the book at night reflected and deepened the sights and experiences I was living during the days. César Calvo's inimitable poetic descriptions of *ayawaskha* lore are far beyond anything else I have ever read on the subject: they contain a deep sense of the human and of the transcendental. My own visions were enormously enriched by the masterful prose, its fullness, its heart.

Gradually, over time, the thought of translating the book emerged. No one was exactly aware of where César lived, or even whether he was still alive. In a moment of inspiration, I wrote to him in Iquitos, in care of the publisher from nine years earlier. I heard nothing for over a year; the thought of the translation receded. Then I received an unexpected letter from César, who was in Lima and had just then received my year-old note. Things, including mail, go slower in the Amazon. We connected. I went again to Peru to meet César personally. The man in person far exceeded my expectations in vitality, heart, and imagination.

This imagination is evident in his treatment of the many "halves" of Peru: the Amazon jungle, the blacks, the Peru of the Incas, and the caucasian component, but all of them seen through the point of view of the first: that of the huge and forgotten Amazon rain forest. Viewed from that observatory, conventional notions of time are displaced and discarded. The masterful creation of a double by introducing two Césars (Calvo and Soriano), one a fictional cousin, parallels the sensation of having two bodies, an image related to altered states of consciousness and to a drive for integration.

César Calvo is a poet, a journalist, a man of heart, and a dynamo of unceasing energy, controversy, and sheer enjoyment of life, with all the good and the bad it has to offer. I am proud to call him a friend. He is now working on the sequels to *The Three Halves,* the first part of a trilogy to be named *The Invisible Colors.*

From that meeting in Lima came this book. The work of translating, without missing out on the beauty, pathos, and sheer exuberance César Calvo has instilled into the Spanish original, has been a demanding task but also a work of joy: I was transported every day to the Amazon locales that have become so meaningful and important to me in my own life. You have in your hand the result of that work. May you enjoy this magnificent story, with all of its marvelous insights, as much as I have.

Kenneth A. Symington
Sierra Madre, California, 1994

Prologue

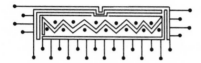

Not too many years ago, when the natives of the Amazon forest were being exterminated by the rubber collectors, the chief of the Amawaka nation, a sorcerer later famous as Ximu, the all-powerful, became aware that his people would not survive unless they were to oppose the white mercenaries with firearms, not just with lances and arrows. Since at that time it was forbidden to sell guns to natives, Ximu, the Amawaka chieftain, ordered the kidnapping of the son of a rubber collector and appointed the youth his successor, renaming him Ino Moxo, which means "Black Panther" in the Amawaka language. In that way those feared man-eaters came to be led by a white man and managed to survive. Ino Moxo, disguised in his prior identity, exchanging his Indian dress for the shirt and pants of some dead foreigner, infiltrated the cities, secured firearms, and taught Amawaka males how to use them.

When my cousin César Calvo, who was born in that region, told me the story, he made me become a part of it. Not only did he open up my curiosity while increasing his own, but also we both became captives of the same obsession: to do what no one had been able to do in over two decades—interview Ino Moxo, legendary chief of the Amawakas. With César I traveled from Lima to Pucallpa, from Pucallpa to Atalaya, and on from Atalaya, under the caprice of climate and rivers, in canoes, until we reached the territory hidden beyond the Mishawa River. During that journey we met other sorcerers—Don Javier, Don Juan Tuesta, Don Hildebrando, Juan González—and we gathered together other stories, events, and personalities, all of which began to overflow the originally intended boundaries of our report.

Even so, if someone suspects seeing in these pages anything other than just pages, I must say, as Ino Moxo said, "The miracle is in the eyes that see, not in what is seen." Because truthfully, this book is not a book. Nor a novel, nor a chronicle. It is barely a snapshot: the memories of a journey I completed while sleepwalking, magnetized by untamable forebodings and by ayawaskha, sacred drug of the Amazon sorcerers. Perhaps because of that, this story begins with my first ayawaskha visions, those images which made clear the route of our travels, the trails that Ino Moxo wished to reveal to us.

"It is unfair that people should suffer from diseases such as diabetes and several types of cancer, which are ailments we know how to stave off," said Ino Moxo when we said goodbye. "Everything that I have told you about me, about so many other things," he would say, "I have done so thinking about those people. Perhaps someone lost somewhere, without remedy, victim of a disease that doctors believe to be incurable, may read what you write and come to us and recover the joys of his existence. That is why I have told you what I have told you."

And that is why I have here joined together *the three halves*. If there is something of value in them, it is what Ino Moxo dictated to me, more through visions than through words, during the full length of a session with ayawaskha mixed with *tohé,* that other powerful and disconcerting hallucinogen.

"But I have not dictated this to you, but rather to your other self, to one of those persons inside you who surfaced during the visions, during the *mareación. . . .*"

I will only add that everything, absolutely everything contained in this text, is stored in seventeen magnetic tapes, in photographs, in the vocabulary at the end of this volume, in a booklet written by the rubber collector Zacarías Valdez, published in 1944 as "The Real Fitzcarrald in History," a copy of which I found in the library of the Maynas Municipal Council, and finally in the patience of the Green Magicians, who agreed to unveil some of their mysteries and ministries to us.

César Soriano C.
Iquitos, Peru, January 1979

As A Preface, Ino Moxo
Enumerates the Attributes of Air

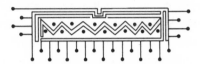

"It is a long story, I've told you. If I were to tell you everything, you would not believe anything. One can never believe everything. Do you know that? Never never can you listen to everything. . . ."

"I'm ready to do so, Maestro Ino Moxo," I hear myself say almost as a bribe; "that is why I have come."

"Could you? No, I don't believe you could." And his head leaning to one side, his eyes bringing it back up:

"To give you only one example, look at the jungle. If you try to listen to all of the sounds of the jungle, what do you hear? . . ."

And as if he had just caught himself, as if he himself were simultaneously the blowgun and the dart and the hunter and the prey and the burning wood waiting in the kitchen, Ino Moxo raised his voice:

"Not only the scream of the alert monkeys, not only the humming of the mosquitos, of the *arambasa,* which is the darkest and fiercest bee, of the *chinchilejo,* which you call dragonfly, of the *chushpi,* which infects you as it bites, of the *carachupaúsa,* which bleeds without warning; you not only hear the *ronsapa* hissing in the wind, and the *mantablanca,* which drinks your hair, and the *quillu-avispa* of yellow flights, and the *papási,* which is born from worms but is not a worm, and the *wairanga,* which never touches ground. Not only do you hear the flute bird, the *firirín,* which can't fly and has wings, nor the *ushún,* nor the *tabaquerillo,* nor the *shánsho,* nor the *piurí* nor the grayish *timelo,* nor the whitewhite *tibe,* nor the *taráwi,* which eats snails and is too black, nor the *sharára,* which knows how to live under the water very well, and even better above the wind, nor the blue *zui-zúi,* nor the great *yunguráru,* whose eggs are of the *zui-zúi* color, nor that giant red and white stork called *tuyúyu.* Not only will you listen to the all-knowing *urkutútu.* Nor the *quichagarza,* loose in excrement. Nor the *ucuashéro,* nor the *tiwakuru,* which only eats ants and sings in the top of the *wimbras,* nor the *páwcar,* which imitates all of the songs of the other birds, with its yellow and black plumage, nor the *unchala,* the same as a wine-red dove, nor the *paujil,* which you may have tasted, with flesh more flavorful than that of the *makisapa* monkeys, more flavorful than meat from the small white lizards, more pleasant than the giant plum of the *tageribá,* nor the *tatatáo,* which is a bird of prey that some call *virakocha.* You not only hear the *mariquiña* duck, the *locrero,* the *pinsha,* the *montete,* which in certain places is called *trompetero,* the *tuhuáyu,* the *pipite,* the *panguana,* which always lays five eggs and then dies, those blue macaws they call *marakána,* nor the carnivorous *wapapa* (surely you've seen it in the Mapuya River); not only do you hear its cousin the *wankáwi* giving the alarm when a human being approaches, nor the *chinwakullin,* nor the *korokóro,* nor the *ayaymáman,* which weeps like an abandoned child, nor the *camúnguy,* nor that man-sized stork with gray feathers called *mansháku,* so many birds. . . . Not only do you hear fat clouds of insects, chirping out after dusk, deep into the labyrinth of the jungle. Not only does the distrustful snake sound out, the *túnchi* forecasting a death, the sly quiet *otorongo* seeking warm flesh, nor the sticky *ronsoco* in the *yuca* patches, nor the huge fish with big heads in tricky nets.

"Not only do you hear fish: the *akarawasú,* the *gamitana,* the *tamborero,* the *paiche,* three meters long with a bony tongue, which lays creatures, not eggs, the *peje-torre,* which inflates itself with air and floats like a buoy, the *dorado,* which has a single spine, the *chállualagarto,* the *kunchi,* the *añashúa,* the eel that kills you with just one electric discharge, the *manitóa,* the *shitári,* the *doncella,* framed in black fringes, the *chullakaqla,* orphan without scales, the *tiríri,* the *fasácuy* in the bottom of lakes, the *shirúi,* the *maparate,* the *shiripira,* the *bujúrqui,* the *makána,* which looks like a sword with three edges, the *shuyu,* which knows how to walk on land, a fish of the road, and the *canero,* which enters your anus and eats your guts, the *demento-chállua,* which almost flies through the air, almost— and more incredible, the *saltón,* that giant fish that jumps several yards above the surface, weighs more than two hundred pounds, and measures over two meters long.

2

"Not to speak of the *paña,* which you know about as *piraña,* which consumes you in a few moments without reluctance. And the *kawára,* huge, and the *palometa,* tasting almost like a dessert, and the *bujéo,* also called river dolphin, the female being more delicious in love than a woman, more tasty, according to the fishermen who have tried it, and it has a vagina and breasts like a woman, and delivers its young just like a woman. Cutting out the labia of a female bujéo and curing them, some *shirimpiáre* make infallible bracelets for the love affairs of rejected lovers, as is well known. And you also hear the great *carachama,* with a stone mouth, which lives out of the water for a week or more, and which comes from long ago, from before the deluge, before the tiger came and dispersed our first Ashanínka ancestors. So many fish . . .

"Not only do you hear snakes, the innocent *afanínga,* harmless among the pastures, barely defending itself by swishing its tail, and the *aguaje-machácuy,* which breathes in the water and has skin like the surface of the fruit of the palm, and the deadly, small *naka-naka,* stalking in the rivers, and the *mantona,* with its useless length of ten meters, harmless to anyone, ten yards of strident colors, pure naive ornament, and the poisonous five-meter-long *chushúpe* biting its prey several times, and the *yanaboa,* reaching fifteen meters in length, as thick as a man, whom it first hypnotizes and then devours. And the *sachamáma,* a boa with ears, distinct from the *yakumama,* which lives only in the water. The sachamáma is a land boa; it inadvertently undergoes mimesis: grass grows freely on its body. The *jergón,* instead, undergoes mimesis but with a purpose: As it grows, its skin turns to a reddish color, mottled, like brilliant leaves, and you can only spot it by its aura, by that brilliance that the jergón leaves in the places through which it will pass, as a signal, as a soul.

"You hear so many existences, you hear so many silent wisdoms, when you hear the jungle. And that is even without being able to hear any longer the song of the fishes that once brightened the waters of the Pangoa, the Tambo, and the Ucayali Rivers, musical animals that foresaw the arrival of the great black otorongo and fled days before his arrival and were saved. You must know that the otorongo, with its giant paws, produced an avalanche of rocks that killed life in the rivers. Only those singing fish, which in their songs spoke and listened to the future, could survive the mud of those paws. Even though today they may no longer know how to sing, or perhaps if they still know how to sing, they must do so in secret, with sounds our ears are not accustomed to, perhaps in another dimension. . . .

"You should know that everyone, even human beings, when they are very

3

young, can hear the future, just as the fish could do before the deluge, as so many present-day animals can do. So many lives that know what will happen and cannot speak to us, warn us. Children, in general, have nine senses, not five, and I have seen some that have access to eleven. As they grow their bodies gradually become poisoned with foods and miseries, and as their souls become home to stained thoughts and dreams, the bodies and the thoughts of men lose their senses, their forces. That is why the sorcerers, the great shirimpiáre, in order to fully exercise the powers of air, to fully develop their powers of seeing, use the spirits of children, souls like new little families occupying the abodes of their body, the ruinous dwellings. . . .

"Not only do you hear animals: the *awíwa,* the worm one can eat like the *zúri,* another tasty worm of many colors, and the noisy toad that weighs more than a kilogram and is called *wálo,* and the *bocholócho,* which knows how to sing, and in its song knows only how to say its own name, "Bocholóchooooo," calling always to itself, from afar, and the *manacarácuy,* a fighter, invincible among birds, and the *cupisu,* small water turtle, which eats its own eggs and flesh, and the fierce *wangána,* wild pig that lives in herds of savage fangs, and the *tokón,* that monkey with a huge and hairy tail, and the *allpacomején,* an ant sentenced to live in the ground, and the *bayuca,* poisonous worm covered with blue, yellow, red, and green hairs, and the large ant without poison that feeds on mushrooms and is called *curuínce,* and the *añuje,* almost like a hare of some size, and the *isango,* which we can't see and bites us, getting into our flesh like a punishment, and the *anañawi,* the eye-of-the-dead, which others call firefly or glowworm, and the *achúni,* sought after because it has a bony phallus, which when powdered is used to season potions used by impotent men, and that other wild boar with coarse hair and a snowy collar named *sajino,* and the *ronsoco,* perhaps the largest rodent in nature, one meter long and one hundred kilos in weight, and the *apashira,* whose name is used by villagers as a synonym for a woman's sexual parts.

"The sounds come from so many animals that you've seen, that you haven't seen, that no one will ever see—creatures that learn how to think and converse just as human beings do. . . . The sound also comes from plants, from vegetables: the *katáwa,* with poisonous sap, the *chambira,* which lends us its leaves to make rope, the breadfruit tree, which they call *pandisho,* the tall *makambo,* with big leaves and fruit resembling a man's head, the spiny *ñejilla,* which grows in the lowlands, the rugged *pashako,* the *machimango,* with impossible odors, the *chimicúa,* whose branches tear with the slightest breeze, the *wakapú,* with harder heartwood than the bloodwood, the *itininga,* the *witino,* the *itahúba,* the *wikungu,* with its black spines, and the straight tree called *espintana,* which when fallen is good to sit on and talk, and the *wakapurána,* better for firewood, and *chonta,* the heart-of-palm: from *wasái, cinámi, pijuáyu,* and *hunguráhui* palms. And the *hunguráhui,* from whose fruit flows an oil that makes hair grow. And the creeping *wayúsa,* whose leaves contain a powerful tonic to erase weakness, and the *sapote,* with a fruit the color of green shade. And the very hard *tawarí.* And the *shiringa,* the rubber tree that unwillingly brought us disgrace. And the *quinilla,* and the *timaréo,* and the *shapája* of oily fruits, and the *wiririma,* and the giant *shebón,* offering leaves to thatch roofs with, and the vegetable marble we call *tágua,* and the *sitúlli,* that rarest banana with great red flowers, and the *wingu,* a bush whose fruit becomes a cup to hold drinks and is called *tutúmo,* and the *pitajáy,* the black and hard *pona,* and the giant *aguaje,* and the *andiroba,* and the *caimito,* with fruits like a virgin's breasts, and the *waqrapona,* waisted palm, and the delicious *anona,* and the *cashú,* which is an almond on the outside, and on the inside more sweet and juicy, and the *apasharáma,* with a leather-curing sap, and the *barbasco,* with a poison root, and the citrus *camucámu,* semiaquatic, and the *capirona,* matchless as firewood and charcoal, and the *aripasa,* with its small green-gray round fruit not to be eaten, and the *curmala,* and the *punga,* and the *cumaréba,* and the *cashirimuwéna,* and the *ashúri,* which protects teeth from caries, and the *catiríma,* whose fruits are fought over to the death by some fish, and the beatiful *cocona,* and that tuber, eaten raw, called *ashipa,* and the *pucaquiro,* with very hard red heartwood, and the leafy *punqúyu,* under whose shadow nothing can live because it expels venom from its branches, and the leafier *parinári,* with a large red fruit called *súpay-oqóte,* devil's ass, and the *lupuna* in the river banks, with its immobile wings, red on white, just above ground, the biggest of the trees in all of this Amazonia. And the other one that rains like a winter roof. And the other one that inflates and explodes worse than a hundred bullets in the night, deep in the forest, and the *renaco,* growing more than forests without leaves and without flowers, and the *garabatokasha,* which cures several types of cancers and dissolves the torpor of aging joints, and the *tamshi,* which distances you from the cold, and the *coca* used with ayawáskha for divination, and the *kamalonga* is used also for diagnosis, and the *renaquílla* entertains the lame, and the *wankawisacha* cures alcoholics forever, and the *chamáiro* helps in chewing coca, and the blackscrew, floating beneath water, halfway down thin rivers, which betray better than the juice of tohé when the moon is green and the time is good to cut cedars without splitting their bark, and the *paka,* which also sounds like a tunnel along vanished rivers, and the *zarsaparrilla* cures syphilis, and the green papaya eliminates the mange and bad breath and its leaves cover the toughest meats and turn them into tender little animals. And the *wenaira,* with a poisonous shadow as the juice of the flowers of tohé. And the tohé, which makes you see the worlds of today and the worlds of tomorrow that form those of today. And the *para-pára,* better known as *hiporúru:* That leaf never loses its shape, as if it were made of rubber, stubborn; you cut it from its stalk, crumple it, bend it, and it returns to the original shape in the branch, always returns to how it was, to its size, to the size and form of its two births. And it is not for that reason but from the powers that flow to it from afar that the leaf of the hiporúru knows how to return sexual youthfulness to men. And the *quino-quina,* which centuries ago learned how to wash rotting wounds. And the vine of the dead, ayawaskha, sacred, the Mother of the Voice in the Ear. With ayawaskha, with oni xuma, if you deserve it, you can pass from dreams to reality, without leaving the dream. . . . So many, so many plants, all of them producing sounds. The *abuta*—pay attention—the *abuta,* a medium-height tree whose reddish root is boiled and when the liquid is drunk, in a few days the sugar in the blood is erased; diabetics no longer suffer. And the *mariquita,* half lover and half flower, which knows how to open only in the purest shade. And the *tzangapilla,* orange and large, an only daughter, a flower warmer than a feverish forehead. All of them, all of them produce sound, as the stones do.

"And above all, you hear the sound of the steps of animals one has been before being human, the steps of the stones and the vegetables and the things every human being has previously been. And also what he has heard before, all of that you can hear at night in the jungle. Inside, each one of us hears, throughout life, dances, and fifes, and promises, and lies, and fears, and confessions, and war shouts, and moans of love. Voices of the dying that one has been, or that one has only heard. True stories, stories of tomorrow. Because everything that one will hear, all of that, sounds beforehand in the middle of the night, in the jungle. It is the jungle that sounds in the middle of the night. Memory is much, much more, do you know? The truthful memory also remembers what is to be—and what will never come about; it also retains that. Imagine. Just imagine. Who could hear everything? Who could hear everything, at once, and believe it?"

I

THE
VISIONS

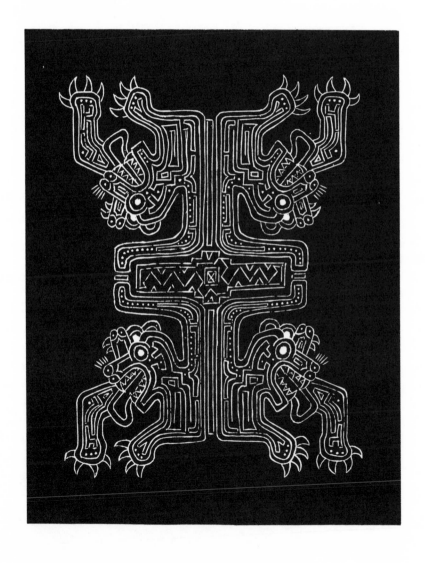

I

How Some Sorcerers Create People

"The first man was not a man," Don Javier tells me, entangled in deep laughter. "The first man was a woman."

"Not all of the *maestros,* by the mere fact of being one, are able to create *chullachakis,*" explains Don Juan Tuesta, half-reclining against this unpolished espintana, a tree lying on top of two stumps, which promote it to the status of a bench, as he concedes his eyes to Rumania Plaza, which extends before him here in the village of Muyuy Island.

Just a little farther, where a broad, dusty street begins, parallel to the currents of the Amazon, a mute board stuck on top of a stick proclaims "Calvo de Aráujo Avenue." The dose of ayawaskha that the sorcerer gave me last night has not yet returned to the air; it persists in my blood even though dawn is so white as to almost be indigo blue. In the adjacent huts begin rustles, fryings, body washings, rumors of breakfast. At our back the Amazon passes on, deafening and illuminating the sky. I hear an airplane, raise my face. I see it descend and shrink, turn into that colorful macaw, a *wacamayu,* and perch with scintillating plumage in the branches of an apasharáma tree. I don't know why I remember what I have never known. Perhaps the sorcerer Don Juan Tuesta may be informing me from afar, from behind the ayawaskha, twenty-five years ago when I ingested the drug the first time, last night. The wakamayu is a god of another time, two emeralds burning in place of its eyes, and there is no one behind those green and evanescent lights. The soul of the wakamayu is ornament without reason or passion, an empty place, and the great spirits are great because instead of annihilating the wakamayu in its vanity, they sustain it in their absence. They exchange the emeralds for corn kernels, and the wakamayu looks then

9

at objects of endearment, is distracted from its eyes and teeth, and only eats the hungers of affection. I'm looking at it now. It opens its eyes; it is no longer a wakamayu. It sings with sealed voice. A transparent wapapa is the airplane I've seen, which has fallen, and its body dissolves in the song, transformed into such a drizzle of colored leaves, so slow and silken. And each leaf is of diverse music, each leaf slides in a note, and their bottomless fall is their sound, none of them reaching the ground. The roar of the Amazon rubs them out, erases them against the warm air. I close my eyes, try to tame the latter effects of the vine-of-the-dead. I can see that the hand of the Amazon is rugged and grayish. I again half-open my eyelids; there is nothing. Only the voice of Don Juan Tuesta scintillates to my right, over the reclining espintana tree, reclining at the edge of Rumania Plaza, while it imposes itself over the blue-red hand, leading that five-headed serpent which the river-sea extends toward us.

"Maestro Ino Moxo, however, can himself invent chullachakis, invested as he is with power enough. Not only that, he invents them in a place and a time of his own choosing."

I decide to ask (I don't know if I quite do so), seeing the voice of Don Juan Tuesta replying:

"A chullachaki is more, not only a demon of the woods, that horror people believe in—no. There are other types. A chullachaki is like a person. It is more than and less than: scarcely appearing as a person. Would you understand me when I say appearance? Maestro Ino Moxo can thus create persons who are and are not persons, too much and not enough, always considering the excess and the lack in people within the normal. That is his habit—are you really understanding me? Ino Moxo is dextrous in the powers and wisdoms of sculpting chullachakis, I am certain. There are two main types of these chullachakis, and both are inventions, efforts of a sorcerer, authorized by the denizens of the air. The chullachaki that is created to deliver harm, lackey of the Evil One, can be identified by the lameness of a tiger or deer in its right foot. None of them can succeed in hiding that malformation if they have been created for evil, even if they are disguised in the body of a friend. In turn, the other type of chullachaki, a deceit in the service of truth, is a person of the good, and no one, no one can limit it. It is perfect in its feet, perfect in everything, humanly human.

"That second type of chullachaki cannot be identified," continues Don Juan Tuesta. "It has the appearance of a person, of a complete person. There is nothing to suspect. Only the trained eye sees that its body is not singular. More than several persons, several lives, seem to inhabit it—as if each part of its body had a divergent existence, and these divergent existences were harmonized into a single one in the eyes of others. Those chullachakis ignore evil and do not despise people or things. They only exist, while they exist, for the gentle, to help the good."

The hand of the Amazon retreats, I see, in the midst of colored fogs, and I remember the night that Oscar Ríos, jungle man and psychiatrist, defined the primary sensation of ayawaskha: "Inside the vine of the soul, everything is right, absolutely everything is very right, everything is good."

"In Don Juan Tuesta's cabin," says my cousin César Calvo, "around 1953, I was thirteen years old then," he says, "and participated for the first time in a session with ayawaskha, that hallucinogenic potion which the jungle magicians use as a reactant, and with its powers gaze at past and future times, and divorce bodies and souls from damage. Probably there, drinking the ayawaskha juices, sacred drug extracted by wizards from the vine of the dead, I also imbibed the restlessness that much later led me to . . ."

"Everything is all right, very right," repeats Oscar Ríos.

And that is precisely what I breathe now. Everything is all right, it is that which flows from those plantings and from the apasharáma tree, which shades one side of Rumania Plaza. It is that which is offered by the village church: wooden, calm, a toy, doorless and with a crown of silvery, copper-stained plates, green from oxide of rain and irreverent weeds. It is that everything is all right, which is repeated by the first sounds from the village, the early risers returning with full nets and canoes and baskets, by the assurances given to my memory, by Don Juan Tuesta. Everything is all right, absolutely everything is very right.

"Don Javier's wife—do you know her?—has a brother who is a chullachaki. That one—do you see?—is another class, another type of chullachaki."

The first time I took ayawaskha, I had an identical but more lasting sensation: the certainty of having two bodies, seeing them and touching them, two Césars lying on the floor of the sorcerer's house. It was here in Muyuy Island, and in this very house of Don Juan Tuesta, when I was thirteen years old, when ayawaskha was presented to me. And it happened. There were other images, other colors, but the unfolding resembled the one tonight, which does not want to leave me. Now there are not just two of my bodies which I succeed, for an instant, in verifying, only to lose them in the next. I see myself by lightning, on the right side of Don Juan Tuesta, seated on the fallen espintana tree, and at the same time on his left side, but with a face that appears to be mine, then doubts it, then begins to grow fuzzy, later to re-form with features that I recognize yet do not belong in my face. Nevertheless, I accept it as mine in the same way I accept that I will never be able to explain this fully to myself with words. I see myself, in two bodies, at either side of the sorcerer of Muyuy Island. And I receive his voice in two places, two existences. We are in 1953—two memories, already so foreign that they seem familiar.

"It's just that some sorcerers, perhaps lacking training, perhaps without enough time to accumulate merits, do not succeed in completely inventing a chullachaki. That is why they kidnap people, usually children, and enchant them into their service. If they charge the one they kidnap with evil powers, their right foot is altered. It hates itself, taking steps that contradict themselves always, leaving a human track with one foot when they walk, and the track of a tiger or a deer with the other one. And if it shows itself as an animal, depending on the size of the selected species, its right foot leaves the track of a boy, or a woman, or a man."

Perhaps it was here, when I was thirteen years old, where I imbibed the restlessness that later led me to discover the true identity of Ino Moxo. Because that night, Don Juan Tuesta also spoke of him, in his cabin by the river, when dawn began to attenuate the effects of the drug on me, and I was not hearing the sound that grew on me at the beginning of that initiatory session, that roar of rainbows tumbling from on high and transforming the Amazon into a mangled piece of jewelry.

"I can't tell you any more about him" says Don Juan Tuesta, "any more than I have already told you."

"But you haven't told me anything!" I protest.

"I have indeed told you. Perhaps without you being aware of it inside your head, without you realizing it in your mind, deep down, in your memories, is well stored what I have told you tonight about Ino Moxo. If ayawaskha does not let you remember, just keep going. The rope of the dead is never wrong. It knows. . . .

"Be advised that chullachakis love lupuna trees," Don Juan Tuesta is now telling me. "In the shade of the lupuna, the chullachaki is happy and lives under it, awaiting the moment to act. Sometimes, in the deep forest, have you ever heard the rumble as of a *manguaré* struck by no one? Maybe it was a kind chullachaki, tired of being alone, calling and wanting to be your friend. Maybe it was his feet drumming against the flank of the lupuna. If you had come and entered the shade of that tree, and if the tree was a white lupuna, surely the chullachaki would have appeared dressed in the body of your loved one, or even in a less defined shape, occupying an unexpected appearance, hateful, challenging you to fight him, without justification any greater than his insolence. Because if a chullachaki appears and says he wishes to be your friend, first you have to fight him. And you have to win. It is not difficult. Even more: it is inevitable. The chullachaki will allow himself to be overcome, as long as he becomes your friend. Once he achieves that, he takes you everywhere, makes the animals follow you if you go hunting. He will make gifts to you, farms with good soil, gentle rivers, generous and paunched. And he will give you the families you want, a heap of happy children, all of the lives you need to be free, all of the knowledge and powers, nothing but wonderful feelings. He gives you useful lives and generous deaths, and more resurrections to your life. He can give you more than anything. The chullachaki, created for good, is master of the world and time, is the master of time and the worlds. In exchange, though not always, the chullachaki demands that you do not smoke, that you not damage yourself by hurting others, that you not go to church, that you only go to the chullachaki's house. That itself isn't difficult: he makes sure that your paths, whether going to the forest or the village, in old age or in sleep, lead to the house that awaits you. This class of chullachaki has an indissoluble agreement of love with lupuna trees. Even the red lupuna submits, makes itself an accomplice—the same lupuna he used as a magnet for your friendship—and continues to serve him. Drumming on its rugged buttresses, he brings to you fortunes and kindnesses as nourishment. This chullachaki is pure kindness. He is even funny, so good, almost hilarious by just being so good. Those who have seen him while sober, without the help of the rope of the soul, say that he appears small, high on two huge red shoes, and with a red shirt, a red scarf, and red pants and hat. He shows himself thus the first time, not so later. Later, he grows taller or tinier depending on his intentions and can take the shape of a wild boar, a tame boar, a cougar, a butterfly, or a deer. He can surface as a fish, or as the song of a little bird, within the container he chooses. And he takes you with him without capturing you or forcing you to do anything: he starts running only to have you follow him. They're just like girls, these chullachakis: they do not escape *because* someone is chasing them, but *in order to* have someone chase them. And you, whether you like it or not, imagining rebellion, instead obey him. As if it had to do with happiness, thus you go after him. You do well. No matter how mistaken you may be, you do well: it always has to do with happiness."

Again the sensation has vanished. Hearing Don Juan Tuesta, I lodge again in a single body, here, on the espintana bitten by the mosses, to the right of the sorcerer of Muyuy Island. I don't know which nostalgia it is that encumbers me. It is almost a widower's sadness, remembering that other one that I was for an instant, who has folded again under the ayawaskha hallucinations.

"The brother of Ruth Cárdenas," Don Juan Tuesta tells me, "her youngest little brother, that is, the smallest brother-in-law of Don Javier, is himself another type of chullachaki. When you go to Iquitos, go look for Ruth Cárdenas, the wife of Don Javier. Ask her to tell you about Aroldo Cárdenas. Ask her in my name, and she will tell you more—everything you need to know."

2

All of the Campas Are Assassinated, but None of Them Die

"The *virakocha*—that is to say, the whites—long ago lived in a lagoon," ponders Don Juan Tuesta, with eyes closed, in the full of an ayawaskha night. Somebody who is not Don Juan Tuesta, but is Don Juan Tuesta, has occupied his body, overflows it without containment, and comes out through his dreamwalker mouth.

Near the virakocha lived the Campa—in other words the Ashanínka.˙On a certain day, a Campa heard barking noises coming from the lagoon. "Well, I'll fish that dog," and to do that he took some bananas with him. But since bananas are food for human beings, the dog was offended and refused to eat them. In turn, all of the virakocha came out of the lagoon and began to pursue, then kill, the Campa. They killed all of the Campa. The lagoon dried out. A single Campa survived, a sorcerer, one of those sorcerers called shirimpiáre: a Campa who used tobacco. Because you should know that not all sorcerers use tobacco, only shirimpiáre do. The other sorcerers have other spaces and a different name; they are called *katziboréri*. The surviving shirimpiáre invoked Tziho, the buzzard, and said, "Come, help me—the virakocha have killed all my brothers." "Where?" asked Tziho. "Everywhere," the Campa shirimpiáre answered, "but mainly in the Great Pajonal." You should know that the Great Pajonal, Don Juan Tuesta tells me, is the territory of the Campa nation, more than one hundred thousand square kilometers of pure flat jungle, an infinite plateau in the middle of the great forests and rivers that adjoin the High Amazon jungle, in the direction of Cusco. It was there, in the Great Pajonal, that the Campa resisted the Inka conquerors, repelled the Spanish conquerors. Even today they do not allow any Western church, nor police station, nor soldiers, nor school of the virakocha style. It was then that Tziho, the buzzard, when he learned of the massacre committed by the whites, gave the shirimpiáre the *ivénki,* the magic herb also called *piri-piri.* And with the ivénki, the Campa sorcerer could kill all of the virakocha in revenge. Only one escaped and went down river to the Ucayali. This is why, since then, there have been many virakocha in the Ucayali, and who knows where else. Meanwhile, in the Great Pajonal, Tziho was eating the dead virakocha. He cooked them first, and then ate them.

Don Juan Tuesta rears himself up, leaning toward me in the blackness of his hut, sits again, his body in vibration with the palm board flooring. I can see his blue sound, orange, ascending in thin transparent columns, brushing past my hair as a fresh breath of tobacco, cleansing my perspiring brow. The hand of the Amazon extending, skin of a tremendous snake, surrounding the cabin, a fearful and feared embrace. It is my first ayawaskha night; I am again thirteen years old. The hand of the Amazon peers through the doorway, opens the blue-orange mouth of its two heads, as a *koto-machácuy,* the giant bicephalous boa that lives in the bottom of eternal lakes and in the mouth of the Amazon River. From its two mouths comes the voice of Don Juan Tuesta in my visions.

Pachamakáite is Páwa, Father and God, who lives down river. He is not a virakocha, neither is he a man of the Andes, whom we call chori. Pachamakáite is Son of the Sun, and his wife is Mamántzike. Pachamakáite creates everything: machetes, bowls, gunpowder, shells, salt, guns, ammunition, hatchets. Because long ago the Ashanínka were poor. They had nothing; they had no machetes, hatchets—nothing. Where did the Ashanínka get all these things? They went to Pachamakáite and received everything. That is the way it was, long ago. Now, we don't know. Then, the Ashanínka did know. They went down the river from the Great Pajonal, and they took gourds to put over their heads so that Piri, the bat, would not bite them. Because in order to reach Pachamakáite, you have to pass through caves full of immense bats—vampires—which come out at night as far as the beaches in the river, seeking warm blood. Then you meet Oshero, the great crab, large as an Ashanínka. Oshero is in the middle of the path and blocks the way. To get through, you have to carry, you give him achiote, and only then will he let you pass. Then the Ashanínka arrives where Pachamakáite lives, but he cannot sit down. And Pachamakáite asks him, "What do you want?" And there, in Pachamakáite's house, there is everything: machetes, guns, ammunition, hatchets. And the Ashanínka, still without sitting down, says, "I want this, I want that," choosing. If he were to sit down, when he tries to leave he must get up and he can't. He is stuck to the floor. The Páwa Pachamakáite doesn't let him go. Then there is a tremor. All of the sorcerers' houses tremble. . . . Along the way also lies Pokinantzi the measles, who wishes to find a husband, and seeks the Ashanínka. One has to carry feathers of several birds, Hankatzi feathers, Itamiri, Herotzi, Wapapa feathers—especially Wapapa feathers—and leave them along the way. Pokinantzi, the measles, which is not far behind, wants to get the Ashanínka, but then sees the showy feathers and begins to gather them, allowing the Ashanínka to escape.

"And where is the god Pachamakáite now?" asks someone I hear within me.

"Pachamakáite is far, far away," answers the voice of Don Juan Tuesta, without moving his mouth or his body, as if he were receiving what the air dictated:

"Pachamakáite is farther away than Iquitos, but the way is obstructed with the woodwork of the virakocha rafts and those of the men of the Andes, the choris. In old times, the Ashanínka knew how to get to the place where the god Pachamakáite lives. Now all of the Ashanínka, all of the Campa, are dead. Now the things brought by the virakocha and the chori—machetes, hatchets, ammunition—are given by Pachamakáite, we know. He gives them for us so that the sons of the Ashanínka can hunt, can create farms and plantings. But the virakocha and the chori sell these things to us, saying that it will cost money to get them, that they buy these things, that they pay for them. It is a lie. Their owner gives these things to them for us, for the Ashanínka.

"I did not know you were a Campa, Don Juan."

"I am a descendant of the Ashanínka, the same as Don Javier, the same as Don Hildebrando, from both bloods, father and mother. We come from the first men of this era, who were Campa, who were Ashanínka, the first humans, sons of the sons of Kaametza and Narowé, who, obeying the god Pachamakáite, founded the nations, long ago and far away, when the Great Pajonal was not yet the Great Pajonal but an island surrounded by oceans of ashes. Maestro Ino Moxo, on the other hand, descends from Urus and virakochas. His mother was an Uru, his father a virakocha, in his two bloods. You should know that the Urus came from the first epoch, very distant in time. The Urus, who have now disappeared, were the grandfathers of the grandfathers of the Inkas. That is why Maestro Ino Moxo has queer little eyes, dark skin, and hair the color of earth from the river's edge, and his wise soul comes to him from his mother, from the Urus it comes. My first ancestors certainly were Campa, legitimate Ashanínka, those that knew long ago, when the Campa were not dispersed as they are now but lived together in towns, in huddled villages, families that made one single family, a single place. In that first beginning, a great cat fell from high in the mountains that surround the Great Pajonal, a black otorongo, a black panther, as huge as a big mountain. That tiger, that otorongo, was what dispersed the Ashanínka and forced them to live separated and distant and forever moving, changing places with houses and lives, families with a single family, fleeing each year to protect themselves. The virakocha, the whites, say that it was a deluge. What do they know. There was no deluge. It was an otorongo, a black tiger. . . . But you are scarcely listening, my friend Soriano, you look as if you were elsewhere, far away."

3

The Boy Aroldo Cárdenas Is Transformed into a Goblin

"I dislike talking, I really dislike talking about this," says Ruth Cárdenas, displeased, the wife of Don Javier, here in Iquitos, "and I'm going to tell you about it only because Don Juan Tuesta asks me to." She is in her house at 385 Napo Street, half a block away from the central square. "I have never spoken about this," she says, "except this time. Look: my brother who is now a chullachaki was named Aroldo—Aroldo Cárdenas—or is named, I don't know. He was four years old when it happened to him, when it happened to us."

"Was he the youngest?"

"No, my mother had already given birth to another child, who was then only about fifteen days old. We lived in a small town called Lieutenant Cornejo, near the city of Contamana. My father had bought a farm in exchange for two bottles of rum from the sorcerer Julio Valles, who was our neighbor. I remember my father worked hard on that farm, cleaning it, planting things; it was very nice. When the sorcerer Julio Valles saw that the farm was all prepared, ready to produce, he wanted it back. He proposed to return the bottles of rum to my father as the only payment, ignoring the cost of seeds, time, fertilizer, labor. Sensibly, my father refused. The sorcerer Julio Valles said nothing, but his face changed and his soul turned sour toward my father. He said nothing in the presence of my father, but he swore vengeance to other people around.

"My father was also a sorcerer. As a very young man he had taken enough ayawaskha. As a boy he had fasted and learned. He warned us that the sorcerer Julio Valles wanted to hurt him, so he prepared to defend himself.

"How did he prepare to defend himself?"

"He protected himself with the means at his disposal. And the sorcerer Julio Valles, seeing himself thwarted and without the capacity to hurt my father, decided to seek revenge on his children. He did not choose the weakest, but chose the most appropriate one, since the youngest one was not suited for evil. He was too small, he was almost nobody yet, he could not have induced the Evil One to hurt or steal him.

"That very day we had laborers working in the farm. My mother could not take food to them, since she was caring for her baby, and sent my sister and I, who were older. I remember Aroldito wanted to follow us, and my mother refused, saying that we would not take good care of him. Go yourselves alone, she ordered. And Aroldito remained, unaware that we would never see each other again. Just at that time torrential rains came. My mother was bathing the youngest one and had to stop, ignoring everything including Aroldo because of the rain. She went to take down clothes drying on a line to avoid getting them wet, and to take away the pieces of salted paiche that were spread out in the patio to dry in the sun, to put everything away. Because my father was also a good fisherman. Involved in those chores, my mother momentarily didn't realize where my little brother was heading. She finished putting things away in the house and went to look for Aroldito. He was nowhere to be found. And it was raining heavily. She looked for him all around the village. Nothing. When we returned to the farm, we found my mother desperate, weeping because the young one was missing. Thus in tears, she sent us to look for him. Under the rain we went. We warned our father, and the three of us went to search the hill, the lake, with the help of the laborers who by then didn't even want to eat.

"Some people told us that they had seen Aroldo walking toward the woods just when the rain began. Since we affectionately called him Negrito, these people called out to him 'Hey, Negrito, where are you going? go back home!' And Aroldo told them, 'I'm going to my mother.' And those people said they had told him 'But your mother is at home, we've just seen her,' and Aroldito had replied, 'No, my mother is in the woods; she's just called me and is waiting for me.' And he kept going. He went. Everyone saw him going deep into the woods, saying he was going to my mother, when in fact my mother was precisely in the opposite direction, getting things out of the rain. No one saw him return. The afternoon passed, the night passed, and nothing—the child was absent. My father traveled to Contamana and notified the police. Guards and even soldiers came, searching the woods, trying to find Aroldito, or if they couldn't find him, at least to find something—some sign that he was eaten by a tiger, because that is a zone frequented by big black otorongos, or at least evidence that my brother had drowned. They also searched the river for him—the whole river— diving, digging around the abutments of the shores far up. Nothing. They desisted after several weeks of searching. He was given up as hopelessly lost.

"Two years later we met a Campa, an Ashanínka, who lived beyond the village. I think his name was Severo. Yes; his name was Severo Quinchókeri. He told us that in his visions during times he took ayawaskha he had seen how the sorcerer Julio Valles had trapped my brother with the chullachaki. Severo Quinchókeri made it known to us that the sorcerer, disguised as a chullachaki identical to my mother, fraudulently costumed in the body and in the mind of my mother, had stolen Aroldito. Severo Quinchókeri, the Campa, also advised us that at night, since Aroldito was still a very young child and missed my mother and wept, the sorcerer Julio Valles brought him near our house to calm him down. At night, he brought him hidden in the darkness, and the child heard the voice of my mother or her weeping, because my mother wept day and night, and listening to her seemed to calm my brother. Even just hearing her weep calmed my brother. That house was made of palms, yarinas. It was open; you could walk freely to it. And the neighbors went in turn to talk with my mother, to console her in the evenings, to accompany her, to avoid leaving her alone. But my mother's solitude was not related to people but to her son Aroldo. And to think that during those same days, the chullachaki came in hiding with my brother, very near the house, between the yarina palms, and my mother wept not knowing that her tears returned happiness to Aroldito. I don't know—maybe she did know, without hope. In time, of course, as he grew older my brother became used to walking alone. That is why the sorcerer Julio Valles moved. He took my brother far away once he began to forget, once he became accustomed to forgetting my mother."

"Was it the sorcerer Julio Valles who brought your brother under cover?"

"No. The chullachaki brought him, that is to say, the devil who stole him disguised as my mother. Severo Quinchókeri, that Campa, also told us that thanks to ayawaskha he had seen that the child was neither eaten by a tiger nor drowned, but that a chullachaki had kidnapped him—not the sorcerer Julio Valles (or perhaps it was the sorcerer Julio Valles, but in a body that was not the body of the sorcerer Julio Valles). And the Campa Severo Quinchókeri said that he had not told us the truth before then, because he had looked into my father's eyes

21

and had seen the intent of vengeance. Under the effects of ayawaskha, Severo Quinchókeri had in his vision seen my father cutting the throat of the sorcerer Julio Valles with a stone knife.

"I also remember there was a prisoner in Contamana named Juan González, who sometimes invited the guards, the policemen, to drink ayawaskha in his prison cell. 'Do you want to find that lost little boy? I will make you see,' he said. And they all took it, because only when you drink ayawaskha can you see. And that sorcerer, who was in prison because of the accusation of an envious doctor, I believe—that same Juan González started to sing in ayawaskha and to call my brother by name. And my brother came. In everyone's vision he came clearly, already older. And truthfully, all who took ayawaskha saw Aroldo. 'There is the young son of Cárdenas,' they said the imprisoned sorcerer Juan González used to tell them. My dad found out and went to visit him in jail, asking him for help by joining forces, so that perhaps by joining both of their visions they might bring Aroldo back. But Juan González said he was sorry. He could not *work* while in prison; he was allowed to take ayawaskha only occasionally, and in order to concentrate, he would need a lot more dedication and have to do so outside of jail. He said he would need to work full time for two or three months, exclusively, doing nothing else but asking and asking the rope of the dead."

"When Julio González saw your little brother Aroldo in his ayawaskha visions, could he clearly see where your brother was?"

"Not clearly, clearly. He only said that Aroldo was living outside the jungle next to some hills. He saw him come from the foot of some unknown hills. He had to call him for many hours, he was so far. He also said that on that rainy day when the chullachaki stole Aroldo, my sister and I walked right past our little brother without noticing him. He said the chullachaki hid him from view so we couldn't see him, even though we almost stumbled over him several times in our search. Juan González said that if we had smoked a cigarette empowered by a sorcerer, we certainly would have been able to see Aroldo in spite of the strength and the knowledge of Julio Valles's chullachaki. But how were we to know? Neither did our dad. He didn't think of empowering a cigarette with an *icaro* song, he was so—so dejected. We never again heard from Aroldo. We only know that he was transformed into a chullachaki himself."

"Who *transformed* him into a chullachaki? Was it not the sorcerer Julio Valles?"

"Of course it was Julio Valles who turned him into a chullachaki. Look, a chullachaki is no longer what he was before, what he was once. A chullachaki is no longer a person; he is the appearance of a person. A chullachaki like that, for example Aroldo, is no longer Aroldo. Chullachakis are empty containers, which the sorcerers fill at their convenience, superimposing on them the appearances of the bodies they want to deceive with. Inside of the emptiness that constitutes a chullachaki, endowed nevertheless with great powers, they place the people they want, the people they want us to believe in. I don't know if you're understanding me. . . ."

"The sorcerer Julio Valles turned your brother into a chullachaki in order to put him at his service? at the service of the Evil One?"

"No. In the service of . . .

And the eyes of Ruth Cárdenas are lowered down to the level of my tape recorder, flee again, hesitate:

"Surely at the service of his souls, or of his other sorcerers. Because years ago we found out that the sorcerer Julio Valles had died. But my brother hasn't returned. My brother Aroldo has not turned back to become Aroldo again."

4

Don Juan Tuesta Says Things Are Not as They Are, but as What They Are

"I would like you to tell me your visions of last night, the last of your visions," Don Juan Tuesta requests, talking to the wind, in his cabin, which has now begun to shake.

"The last thing I saw," I tell him, "was Don Javier in Cusco. I dreamed that I was in Pisacq, high up in the Inkaic citadel of Pisacq, and that I, César Soriano, was not myself, but my cousin César Calvo, who was looking from the heights at the Urubamba River, the Sacred River, silvery and youthful, meandering like a snake between golden corn plantations, blue and orange gold, toward the jungles.

And Don Juan Tuesta, forever alert to the air, looking to the other side, losing himself in his eyes that drift toward the Amazon:

"Nothing else?"

And I, forced by more than my mouth:

"I dreamed that Don Javier lived in Cusco, not in Pisacq but in Pawkartampu, in a place called Three Crosses. I dreamed that Pisacq was at the same time Pawkartampu, and that Don Javier was a condor hunter in the time of the Inkas. I saw him in my vision."

"Tell me how you saw him," says Don Juan Tuesta, impatiently.

"It was a sunny night there in Three Crosses, in the heights of Pisacq-Pawkartampu. The Inka Manko Kalli came out from behind the sun, dressed in a long poncho we call a *cushma*. The Inka was covered by a yellow cushma, the costume of the sun, and the sun was ten times larger and ten times redder. The Inka Manko Kalli held a sculpted wooden grail against his chest, one of those vases known to the ancients as a *q'ero*. The q'ero that Manko Kalli held was full of the sun's saliva. Manko Kalli slowly walked toward me. I was Don Javier, and he told me to go and hunt condors. I was very old, and I told him, 'I can't; I'm very old and in any case was never good at hunting anything.' Manko Kalli ordered me to look at my arms, and my arms grew, crisscrossed by scars and weird tattoos. 'Look at yourself carefully,' said the Inka. 'Only the condor hunters have arms like those. You have always been a condor hunter; go and bring me the biggest one in the earth and in the air.' By that time, I was no longer Don Javier—or rather I still was, but I was another person as well, not César Calvo or César Soriano, but another someone I've never seen before."

"And that other person you were, that stranger, did he have scars in his arms?"

"Identical to those of Don Javier, and one of them less obvious in the coppery brown, almost black face, and another one in the right cheek, sliding off toward the neck, and another one in the forearm on the same side. I climbed, therefore, to the highest part of Three Crosses and there excavated two wells: one large, one small, connected with an appropriate tunnel. I covered the larger pit with a grill made of thick branches, tied together with gold and silver ropes, and in the grill I placed a fawn, still hornless, looking skyward with its forehead destroyed by shotgun pellets. Bait, to attract the condor! I entered the smaller well and crawled through the tunnel covered by *paka* reeds, being scratched in passing by its thorns, curved like the beaks of newly born condors. I dragged myself until I was seated at the bottom of the large well with the leafy grill over me, under the fawn bleeding the sun's blood, his hornless head traversed by *tohé* darts. There I remained motionless for seven days. Eventually the condor came, beating corrugated *lupuna* wings, both black and white, an animal vaster than the hill where I waited for him. It came near and descended on the deer. It struggled, trying to pry it loose from the grill. I took advantage, poked my hands through the branches, and grabbed one leg, panting, then the other, in a strong contest. Father condor picked at my arms full of scars but not wounds—the tears he caused in the flesh were born already scarred. The Inka Manko Kalli then reappeared and told me, 'You have delivered. I, Son of the midday Sun,' he said, 'husband of Mamántziki, I name you my *ayumpari.*' And with his smooth and olive hands, as if they were gloved

25

with a child's skin, Manko Kalli set the condor loose. It turned yellow and doc-ilely went, trembling, with the Son of the Sun. It was perched in the chest of the Son of the Sun, less than a butterfly on his heart."

"Was that all you saw in your dream?"

"No, godfather," I say to Don Juan Tuesta. I again saw myself as Don Javier, and simultaneously as my cousin César Calvo. We were in the heights of Pisacq, next to the Inkaic cemetery, above the Temple of the Sun. I saw that I, Don Javier, disinterred a ceremonial Inka vase, a wooden q'ero, from the old tombs and silently gave it as a gift to my cousin César Calvo. And I also saw that I, César Calvo, was myself, who received the wooden q'ero given to me by Don Javier—the wooden vase that I was giving myself with the hands of Don Javier. I stretched toward myself my own scarred arms. And in my visions, Don Javier began to play his instrument, closing his eyes as if gathering from the air harmonies and cadences, which flowed visibly, palpably, from his rhymed fingers. Suddenly he stood up, raised his hands to heaven, and put them in the well of the blood of the sun. And I saw his arms return without scars as he placed them before my face, darker, intact, unscarred."

"It was not I who told you that dream," muses Don Juan Tuesta. "It is just that things are not as they are, but as what they are. Now you are still too young to know that. Thirteen years are nothing. But some day, far away, you will real-ize this."

5

The Prophecies of the Flower of Tohé Are Fulfilled

"This rain is slightly insane, don't you think so, Uncle César?" asks Ruth-Ruth from her five years of age, the last daughter of Don Javier still here.

"Why?" I attempt to gaze off to one side, masking my surprise.

"Because dinnnn! it falls suddenly, and dinnnn! it goes away again, the same as our little Lord, this rain."

And her sister Selva, letting her eyes roam over the dining room table, goes to the window, beyond which the height of the afternoon suddenly flashes.

"Our little Lord must also be in bad shape: half-crazy, no? because he is the same as the rain: dinnnn! he appears, and dinnnn! he disappears."

"How do you know? Have you ever seen our little Lord?"

And Javico, the oldest of the three children: "Only they can see themselves, our little Lord, and those who have died."

Ruth Cárdenas saves me; she reappears and we continue yesterday's conversation. The downpour has stopped again, and in the front part of the room the wooden Christ carved by Agustin Rivas spreads its wings. I recover in the silence coming from the street. I wait until Don Javier's wife sits down, and then ask her:

"Don Juan Tuesta told me you have taken tohé. How is it? Do you feel it the same way as you do ayawaskha?"

"You do not hallucinate. It is different. With tohé you see everything very naturally, very real, as things are, only it is in another class."

"How so?"

27

"With tohé, you see another reality, another class of the natural. If you take tohé in this house, you will no longer see this house but other places, other people. Your eyes may be open, but you do not see what your eyes look at, what is around you. You see things that are not here, and you see them just as they are. I mean to say that you see them clearly, truly, af if you were looking at things actually around you."

"When did you take tohé?"

"I knew tohé when I was seventeen, out of sheer curiosity. A theft had taken place at home: someone stole all of my mother's documents, leaving her without proof of identity. A little old lady who lived above the town advised me to ingest tohé, saying that the tohé would reveal to me who was it that had stolen my mother's papers. 'When you take tohé, you see everything,' she said, 'what has happened, and what will happen. Nothing escapes it.' I accepted. During Father's absence on a trip, I went to the old lady's house and drank tohé. I didn't see anything related to the theft. I was under the effects of tohé for seven days and seven nights. With a little of the juice I was intoxicated for a week. I saw many things, many places. I spoke with many people, but nothing about the theft."

"How is the juice extracted? From the flower?"

"The tohé flower commands, but what you actually drink comes from the stem. The old lady—Rosa Urquía was her name—cut a tohé branch, which in virakocha land produces a smaller flower, not as white, and weaker. In the jungle it is bigger and has thicker stems, and the flower itself is more of a flower. It is double, one inside the other. Rosa Urquía cut a branch and split it with a vertical stroke, downward, and then scraped the heart of the wood, which looks like an apple, until juice began to flow. She let it drip, drop by drop, into a small cup; measured the amount by dipping her finger in it until the liquid covered half of her thumbnail; and gave it to me to drink. The first thing I saw was my dad. I saw him coming, naturally, and even though I knew he was away, I spoke with him. I spoke with him, knowing that it wasn't him, that it was the tohé, but he responded. The tohé responded. With tohé you can see people and talk to them, and people will respond naturally. Everything is natural—more natural than in this reality. Later on, I saw that I was hospitalized, with two nurses in white looking over me. The shorter one held a baby in her arms. 'It's a boy, madam,' she said. Years later I actually saw the same thing but without tohé. I was really in the same hospital, with the same nurses I had seen in my vision, and the baby was Javico, my first-born son, then and there, the same. That time with the tohé I also saw my husband. A young man wearing a flowery shirt and dark green pants was knocking at the door of my house in Contamana. I saw him through the window, and my first thought was not to let him in. He knocked louder, with more assertiveness. Nothing. He knocked again. 'Who is it?' I dared to ask, with fear (perhaps it wasn't fear). 'It is happiness!' the young man answered, laughing; 'it is happiness knocking at your door!' And I, as if it weren't me, also laughing, against my will, opened the door. Years later and without tohé, I again witnessed the same scene as in my original vision. I remember the same young man, but older, stouter, and bearded, accompanied by other persons I did not yet know then. You were among them. They pointed to the bearded man and told me, 'Look, it is your husband, the father of your children.' I laughed. In the middle of being inebriated, I laughed because I was conscious that I had never seen that man before. I was unmarried and without the intention of getting married. I didn't even know him."

"And when you finally met Don Javier, did you recognize him? Did you recognize him as the man you had seen in the tohé vision?"

"No, when I met Don Javier, I didn't think about that. Much later, I remembered when the tohé had introduced us for the first time, fifteen years earlier."

"That Don Javier of the tohé, was he the same Don Javier of today?"

"The same voice, the same laugh, the same features, identical."

"Did everything you see in those seven days with the tohé come about? Has it happened in your later life?"

"During my life here?"

"Yes."

"Almost everything. There is just one thing I saw with tohé that hasn't happened yet. I saw myself walking in a large city, with very strange buildings— gray, huge, with iron balconies and flower pots, things that I had never seen before. At that time I hadn't even been in Iquitos. I couldn't imagine such a large town, and I still can't. I didn't know buildings like that existed. I remember I was afraid to experience myself inside that city as if I were crushed between the buildings, walking, walking."

The evening grows darker. Lightning flashes more often. Little Ruth-Ruth returns to interrupt us: "What is the size of the souls of the dead, Uncle? If I die when I am still a little girl, will my soul also be little?" And without giving me time: "What are the faces of souls like?"

Javico intervenes: "Their faces come from afar, from afar. The souls live far away, seated on wood. That is why you have to run away. If the soul sees you, it rises and comes to you, and doesn't stop talking to you."

"What does it talk about?" I surprise myself asking.

"About everything. Because when a soul dies, it does so knowing everything."

His sister Selva contributes: "Our little Lord speaks through the soul. We found that out in Pucallpa. We saw a soul coming out of an envelope. It was the soul of Mrs. Chabela's dad. The envelope had a letter from her father. The soul emerged, shining and brilliant, 'I, in my life, have not done all I have done, only these things,' said the soul, 'because in my life I have as yet not begun to be.' We heard him say that. The three of us saw him, and heard him, isn't it true, Javico?"

Ruth Cárdenas asks them to go to the patio to play. The rainstorm has started again. The wooden carving of Christ on the wall shows its open wings facing the blue *renaco* tree painted by Yando Riós.

"During the seven days with tohé, did you have to fast?"

"Rosa Urquía gave me a piece of plantain each day, baked over a wood fire. And if I was thirsty, I could drink only some sips of the juice of the same bunch of plantains. No one was to see me, or touch me, or talk to me. Only Rosa Urquía, the little old lady. Tohé is dangerous, and if someone interferes it is very dangerous. There are cases of persons who never returned from their visions, people who have remained within the tohé, looking forever at the things one sees with tohé."

"And could you sleep?"

"Perfectly. I dreamed every night. But the dreams were also different, as in vigils. Even asleep, I continued seeing a strange reality. My dreams belonged to another reality. I slept little, for sure. Then I was very lean, but in my visions I saw myself as very heavy, as you see me now. I asked Rosa Urquía, the little old lady, 'Why is it that I see myself so fat?' and Rosa Urquía informed me that I would look like that as I became an adult, after I delivered my first child."

"How did the effects of tohé diminish?"

"The duration of the intoxication is seven days and seven nights as a rule, sometimes less. Once that time has elapsed, they cure you so you can return."

"To return?"

"Yes, so you can return to this reality."

"And how do they cure you?"

"They just put two small drops of cane juice in your eyes, in each side of your eyes, and all of the effects vanish as if by magic—nothing more."

30

6

I Saw a Joyful Christ Who Opened His Wings and Flew Away

The distance from the house of Don Javier far up in Napo Street to the house of Don Daniel Guzmán Cepeda in July 28 Plaza in Iquitos couldn't be more than ten blocks. But the dark sky, the burning air, make it ten blocks of sun. I arrive panting.

This is the house where I spent several of my school vacations twenty years ago, thanks to a note from my uncle, César Calvo de Araújo, the Painter of the Jungle. The wind hasn't stopped. There are the same wooden windows, painted many times over, shutters my uncle knew how to pry apart with turpentine and tobacco fingers and brushes, as he scanned July 28 Plaza, like a wise spatula gathering colors and memories, transposing everything to another waiting window made of stretched white canvas on a tripod. There is the same roof erected against the perversities of summer, the same wide and affectionate rooms like souls, the same stubborn singing youthfulness of Julio Meza Penahera, founder of the village in Muyuy Island, where Don Juan Tuesta distributes miracles. Hasn't the wind passed through here? Inside the dwelling new subdivisions, and thin walls and furniture that doesn't creak: steel rocking chairs, record players with dance music, sofas with cloud-like backs. Outside, the house has a new number: 59 Aguirre Way has now increased to 861. The dust of that time lies beneath the asphalt of the street. The dull rumble of the motorcycles fills the once peaceful air. An educated breeze slips under the unexpected downpour, shaking lean temptations, bell-

bottomed skirts and pants on the cement outside that now frightens away the old tiles of the ancient square. Something like a belated claim in the air announces that the mango trees, among others, have been decapitated, that Don Daniel Guzmán Cepeda is not at home, that he has gone out. He went out following the painter Calvo de Araújo without telling us. They both went, stepping on tender branches, already becoming the sole enigma they would never reveal to anyone.

The second child of Don Daniel Guzmán Cepeda, short in name and languid in height, whose name was Roosevelt, makes space for another bed in his room—almost in vain, because I can't sleep. I spend hours and hours walking in my memory around Muyuy Island, revisiting in the distance the last night of ayawaskha in the house of Don Juan Tuesta, tying my affections and nostalgias to the blue branches and to the orange hand of the Amazon in the sounds of the hallucinated night, remembering the gift of a story the sorcerer told me about my cousin and about an inconceivable yellow butterfly. I endure hours of insomnia, remembering the conversation with Ruth Cárdenas about the chullachaki and the tohé, hearing the breathing of Roosevelt in the bed next to mine under the great mosquito net. Through my own net I review walls of polished wood, the thick door secured by two excessive latches. I saw some tigerish lizards fleeing among the seven beams of the ceiling, There are no windows anywhere in the room, just a slice of horizon to let air in, an elongated space next to the ceiling. Even that was barred by the willful metallic screen, a fringe of inaccessible hairnet. The roosters chop up my memory—it must be already five o'clock in the morning. The incipient sky of Iquitos sparkles, lightless, from the orchard, outlining silhouettes in the boards of the ceiling. I finally scratch some sleep. I dream that Roosevelt is sinking in a huge lake covered with eels and calls me voicelessly. I see him; he calls me with flailing arms, attempting to reach the shore of the implacable lake, which sinks with him, more and more, among red trees. My dream is very short. I open my eyes and hear that Roosevelt is not calling me; he is just moaning on the bed to my left. I tell myself, still foggy in the clouds of reawakening, that it is just a nightmare, and I lift the edges of the mosquito net that shades my insomniac bed. I go toward Roosevelt and call to him in a whisper. Nothing, it is just the aches of a sleeper. I switch on the fluorescent light oscillating in the middle of the ceiling. "Roosevelt!" I insist, with a less than considerate voice. I awaken him.

*Pallid from sweat and tremors, Roosevelt Guzmán opens eyes that
try to leave. He holds his ankle in his right hand, bending his leg and
showing me the purplish flesh around a black dart. "Someone has shot
me!" he says. "Bring me a kitchen knife, quietly—help me to extract the
poison!" I do not understand. I'm afraid. I unlock the door, return to the
room. Roosevelt has pulled out the poisonous dart and makes a deep cut.
Sweating even more and trembling, he asks me to carefully suck out his
wound and then spit it out so I myself won't be poisoned as well. Then,
less breathlessly, he notices my horror and informs me that the dart is a
virote, that sorcerers have the power to shoot darts from a distance. There
is no wall that can stop any agent of the Evil One from wounding an
enemy. Between those who practice black magic and those like Roosevelt
who have affiliated themselves with the gentle darknesses that César calls
Green Magic, the war is eternal. Thus I learn that Roosevelt, godson of
Don Juan Tuesta, has also been his disciple for many years.*

*"Ever since he cured my lameness," says Roosevelt. "Do you
remember I hurt my right foot, slipping while I was repairing the roof, and
fell on a board with exposed nails and broke my heel bone? Later while I
was hunting in the middle of Muyuy Island, a snake bit me on the same
spot. Do you remember how I limped with this foot the doctors in Lima
gave up as hopeless? My godfather Juan Tuesta healed it, fasting in the
forest."*

*Only then do I recollect that yesterday, while opening the door to
lead me to my room, Roosevelt walked normally without a limp. And now
he asks me to go rent a fast boat at one of the Belén docks, go to Muyuy
Island, and explain to his godfather what has happened and beg him to
come to Iquitos. Roosevelt will pretend he has a cold to avoid alarming
his parents. I go to find the boat, still not believing.*

*"The guillotine is not in the hands of the executioner," says Don Juan
Tuesta, looking over that huge ankle, slightly less purple, lying on the
blood that stains the sheet. "It is in the neck of the victim, that is where the
guillotine is," adds the Muyuy Island sorcerer. I continue to disbelieve. I
prefer not to think of anything.*

"I also saw a celebration," I tell Don Juan Tuesta, who is sitting on the
espintana tree facing Rumania Plaza. "I saw a revelry that I've never seen before, a blood feast, yawar fiesta.

"*Raymiyáwar,* that's the name in Keshwa," he says.

"I dreamed about a round city," I interrupt him, "a town whose people had skin of hard clay, old people, children, girls who laughed on the lawns, taking off some colored robes."

"*Lliqllas* is their name," says Don Juan Tuesta.

"And all danced to exhaustion, happy under a full moon twice the size of the sun. I saw peasants, shouting sweet and intoxicating things, in pursuit of a giant black bull. They cornered it laughing and tied it down to a tree that is at the same time *pisonay* and *pomarrosa,* of red flowers. Two lines of shouting men came down from the heights of the mountain surrounding the town. Leading them was Don Javier, under a yellow poncho with black stars. He had a condor with wings of unreachable span perched on his arm like a sparrow. Tempestuously, near the flowering pisonay, Don Javier smiled and said something to the ear of the condor. The condor parted from the scratched arm tattooed with noisy scars. It seemed to be flying away to the summits—but no, it returned and landed on the back of the bull, which struggled under the stone condor, spewing blood and bellowing in blood. I saw how Don Javier, always smiling, encrusted the condor's claws into the back of the bull's neck and sewed them with ayawaskha ropes. He bent down to the ears of the bull-condor, which had shrunk to become smaller than a little bird with shell horns. The bull-condor, hearing the voice of the sorcerer, grew in size. It grew overflowing the town square, extending its wings from mountain to mountain, yearning horns from sun to moon. Over time it expanded from yesterday to tonight. That is what I have seen in my visions." I tell Don Juan Tuesta.

And I saw Don Javier, taking off his yellow *cushma,* holding it in front of him like a red bullfighter's cape, and edging toward the two-headed beast that was pawing the grass and flying forward. Several times Don Javier dodged him with the cape, mocking it. Several times the bull-condor, in despair, dug in its claws, its hooves, its horns, its wings. Later on, Don Javier, who by now had the face of Don Hildebrando, handed his cushma to each of the males of the town, one by one. They were all tall, double our size. I watched everything from one of the pisonay flowers, from within the trunk of the pomarrosa. At each parry of the man, the condor beak dug into the flesh of the neck of the bull to which it was tied. The males drank from a carved wooden vase, a q'ero of the Inkas, the black blood of the bull until the animal was spilled on the torn grass. I get confused with that corner of the vision: the face of Don Hildebrando left the body of Don Javier, and Don Javier unleashed the condor from the top of the prostrate bleeding bull. No, that wasn't what I saw. Don Javier took the condor perched on his right arm—no, climbed up on it, floated away in that blue-orange winged butterfly. No, Don Javier searched for the condor only to leave it—no; better but worse: he searched for it only to free it. I saw the condor rise toward the singing sun, toward the Inti, sounding like a well dammed with rainbows. The condor rose in the air and managed to seal the mouth of the well of the sun; it advanced the night. Night descended over the town with folded wings, and the evening light was golden, invincible and golden. That's all I could see.

But I kept on watching. I opened my eyes in the face of my visions, and I saw another fiesta I had never seen before. I rode on horseback into a small place with a name I don't know, Yauriski, with thousands of praying men and women. While it was still night, heavily laden with I don't know what, I joined the others and headed for a rocky hill, then to another one, more frozen and towering, then to another one still, until we finally arrived during the last night at the foothills of an impossible mountain dressed in eternal snow. "Qoylluriti!" they shouted. "Star of the Snow!" they called. Along the road from the village of Yauriski to the snowy peak named Qoylluriti, all of us were gathering small, luminous, colored stones, the most beautiful or difficult pebbles of the climbing path. "One stone for each sin!" they shouted. And I kept gathering. "One stone for each sin committed during the year!" I collected and collected. Some reached the base of Qoylluriti bent under a cargo of stones, while others arrived light, slight, as hypocrites, with their bags flapping in the frozen wind, barely engorged by one or another falsity, fear, tame theft, or perhaps injustice. I saw how at the foot of that snowy mountain, ascending, unending, we constructed little fortresses with our sins—little houses, little stone churches in homage to the mountain, to the Star of the Snow, in promise of repentance and most of all in promise of joy. Because after that ceremony, we danced and drank cane liquor and corn chicha, well fermented, and we fornicated and went to all extremes until dawn, there in the folds of the white summit. Then I dreamed that you came forth out of the belly of the snowy mountain. Qoylluriti split like a tree and from its inside, you, Don Juan Tuesta, came out very small, purple from the wind that took you in its arms. And you were already an adult. You shouted, "Visions, begin!" And all of us peasants that had undertaken the pilgrimage to this place (because in my vision I was a Quechua field worker, man of the Andes, *chori*)—all of the peasants (no, only the young ones) sliced huge blocks of ice and tied them to our shoulders. And with the weight of the ice on us, we started to climb the Star of the Snow, the inaccessible Qoylluriti, tumbling, panting, freezing, laughing incessantly, loudly mocking each other and threatening each other. I was the first to reach the summit. At the top of the conquered mountain, a cave of iridescent ice opened up to me. Inside, at the end of it, on top of an altar made of colored stones, smiled a crucified Christ. I saw that the face of that joyful Christ was the face of Don Hildebrando—no, it was again the face of Don Javier. I saw it very clearly, as clearly as I am seeing you now. And Don Javier, nailed to that cross of red stone, in that cross of bloodwood snow, said, "Being the first to arrive, you have earned the right to ask me for three wishes, all of which will then come true." Thus spoke the Christ of Qoylluriti, smiling, and I told him, "I want to be free."

He set his hands free and gestured a pardon, and I suddenly saw myself transformed into an invisible being. I looked: I was no longer there. No one was in my place. Next to me soldiers came and went, rubber workers, men I had never seen, tracking rubber trails in the forest next to me. They were cocking huge Winchesters and looking for me in the jungle. I laughed at them, silently deriding them in my vision. I laughed at their bullets pursuing me in vain through the air, in the earth, in the rivers. Thus I survived.

"What is your second wish?" said the Christ.

"I want to be free," I said.

Instantly I saw myself nailed to the stone cross, with bleeding open arms, smiling in front of Don Javier, who entered the mouth of the cave and was very absorbed watching me on the cross. With my hands, Don Javier untied the block of yellow ice on his shoulders, which I had tied on mine in the lower part of Qoylluriti. At the door of the cave he again asked,

"And your third wish?"

"I want to be free."

My words were still resonating in my mouth when I saw my arms becoming free from the bloodwood cross, turning into wings. I saw myself leave the cave flying, transformed into a condor, which cleaved the air day and night, gliding over a round city I had never seen, and landing his claws—my claws— in the shoulders of an interminable black bull. I saw myself sinking my beak into the back of the bull's neck, digging into it and drinking its blood. And the blood of the bull sang sweetly. It was too sweet, too late. That is what I dreamed.

"Condors were born in the jungle," rumbles Don Juan Tuesta in the dark of my visions. "In ancient times, very long ago, when the great otorongo fell upon the Campa and dispersed them, the condors fled. They came out of the bottom of a sacred wooden vase and escaped to the summits. They became used to living simultaneously under the sun and under the night, in the fierce hail of the Andes, and in the warm pasture. Since that time, and until today, condors continue to live there. The only thing they haven't learned is to tolerate the winds that travel over the sea, to resign themselves to live on the sandy coastal shores."

"I feel them returning, I am dreaming them this instant, I see how the condors fly toward the jungle," I barely hear myself reply, far away, struggling from within the ayawaskha.

"But you are not dreaming," murmurs Don Juan Tuesta. And I see his mouth say something else. Other words come out, dazzling. The hand of the Amazon— I see it now grayish and more rugged—erases the voice of the sorcerer against the golden air behind me.

7

I Saw Another Town
I Had Never Seen Before

Don Juan Tuesta rises from the espintana log and invites me to follow him
into the woods. Dizzy still, I cross Rumania Plaza, heading to the jungle in
the center of the island, which is framed by the roaring Amazon. After less
than an hour's march, a certain repose emanates from the eyes of Don
Juan Tuesta. Before us flows a river of air, a dry basin marked by a fallen
tree in the manner of a bridge. Don Juan Tuesta steps aside; I move past
him and stop again in the middle of the trunk. To my right, from the deep
of the landscape—a tunnel more than a landscape, with a roof of flexible
vines like thin and spiny canes—I note that in each node of the canes lie
two treacherous spines, like hooks. "Paka is its name," says Don Juan
Tuesta. From the bottom of the tunnel surges a butterfly with yellow velvet
wings spotted with black. It flies over me in silence and glues itself to a
dead branch in the invisible river. Beyond those wings I recognize the
view, but I've never been here before. I've seen it in a painting: the exact
site, the precise colors, the same light singing among the spines of the
maze of paka. There is no doubt the painter Calvo de Araújo sketched
that oil painting here, his memory seated on this tree; I saw him paint it
years ago in Lima. An untamable desire to express gratitude overwhelms
me—to talk to the landscape, to brush the silken butterfly.

    "You can just touch her," says Don Juan Tuesta. "She won't fly away
if you touch her."

I slowly approach, ever more slowly, and extend my hand toward the yellow gauze. The butterfly, insubstantial, motionless, lets itself be caressed, confusing me perhaps with the air that flows instead of the water, I think. I remain so, marveling, I don't know how long, and finally rise, breathing again. The butterfly again begins to tremble in silence, gyrates around me in more than silence, enters and leaves the frame of my view, makes up its mind, heads to my chest, and seats itself, quieting down, below my left shoulder. I dare not move for fear of scaring it, and the sorcerer again confides in me:

"You may start walking; it will not fly away."

In that manner I cross the bridge, the butterfly quiet over my heart. I continue one hour more, two hours, in the path that goes deeper and finally ends in a dark, watery kocha. *The heat drives me. A bath would feel good. The butterfly abandons my wet shirt. It flies off over the waters, which are covered with a slow, yellow slime, and crosses in silence, that way, in dreams, over to the island, which lies greenly in the center of the turbid lagoon.*

"It is not a butterfly," whispers Don Juan Tuesta. "It is the soul of your relative, the soul of my friend Calvo de Araújo."

In plenitude then, powerful and in plenitude, soaked with sun and contentment, I take off my shirt, my pants.

"Don't enter the lagoon!" screams a little old lady at my back. "It is full of electric eels!" she says in terror.

Don Juan Tuesta, immutable, says to her, "Rosa Urquía! Fear nothing, Rosa Urquía"; and to me, "Go on in. Nothing, nothing will cause you harm."

"Just yesterday, my calf fell in and the eels returned it to me black, burnt, dead!" insists Rosa Urquía.

I edge along the shore of the kocha *and spot the butterfly flickering ahead, on the island, a piece of jewelry in the bushes. I plunge into the waters, increasingly dark, warm, clear. I flee the sun, which is toasting the quiet air, and in the burning afternoon I swim to the refreshing island. The butterfly returns to Don Juan Tuesta, next to the silent old lady, who averts her gaze. I dive again into the dense freshness. I remember—I don't know why—a carnivorous bird called a* wapapa. *I swim underwater toward the shore. Something I can't see touches my belly under the waters: the sticky rough skin of one or an infinite number of electric eels—but it can't be. My breast shakes, my legs. Rosa Urquía is relieved to see me come out of the small lake, can't believe her own eyes, and departs with a concerned forehead. While still wet I put on my shirt and my pants in front of the sorcerer, who shows a tired and satisfied smile.*

"There were no eels," I say as we walk back to the village of Muyuy.

Don Juan Tuesta is silent for a long time. As we enter the village his voice returns:

"There were eels in that kocha," he says. "That kocha is full of deadly electric eels." Another stretch of silence. The first lamps appear there, ever nearer, from the nestled cabins, in sepia, before my eyes, which were long ago diminished by ayawaskha, though not completely.

"Before you entered the lake, I separated your soul from your body. The eels electrified you, discharged in your belly. Did you not feel them? But they touched only your body. Your soul never knew. That is why you are still alive," says Don Juan Tuesta, walking next to me, crossing Rumania Plaza already erased by the darkness of night.

After walking for entire days, worse than weeks with their nights, from the city of Pawkartampu, I saw another town I had never seen before. I was alone; I saw myself. I climbed the slopes of Challabamba and was lost on the way to the Cusco jungle, near Qosnipata. I remember a sign I saw there, high up on a pole, which said *Carbón River*. I don't know why I disobeyed it and went to the left, facing snowy peaks shining blue-orange and sometimes sepia. Laughing, I climbed those mountains, came down upon other, slower ones, less cold, crossing a village called Patria, some broken cabins in the middle of a shady clearing in those woods, and returned to climb and climb hills and hills. Suddenly, from behind a huge knot of garabatokasha vines entwined around the trunk of a pomarrosa tree, I looked upon the town.

I'm looking at it now, I tell Don Juan Tuesta; I'm looking at it, limpid, perfect: a small square of tamped earth, bordered with seven houses made of grayish, rugged stones, seven houses roofed with yellow and brown, blue and brown fronds, defying the sun. And I'm almost afraid to enter that square; I feel it. In front of me, the elders of the town, crouched in a semicircle, are chewing coca leaves, chewing them mixed with chamáiro, the sweet little vine used by Andeans, instead of the lime used by the jungle people. I also notice that they shape their coca bolus using capirona ashes, as the jungle people do. To their backs, behind the silent semicircle, hangs a huge *kosho* of *masato* in the shadow. A kosho is a container made of a hollowed-out log in the shape of a small boat, an un-reachable canoe overflowing with cassava juice and saliva. And I am even more displaced, more surprised within my own visions. Am I really in Cusco? I ask myself, in a cold sweat caused by the black ayawaskha, because I know per-fectly well, behind the hallucinations, that the type of Keshua language mur-mured by these elders is not spoken in Cusco.

"We are exchanging knowledge," says one of the old men, smiling with-out a smile, hardly speaking, telling me with only the climate of his voice, not his real voice.

"We are trading knowledge," says another, "but doing it in the ancient way, doing it astrally."

"Traveling without our bodies—that is how we exchange knowledge," says yet another, much older. And as if I were at the core of a child's game—that is the precise sensation: as if I were in a child's game—I notice another old man approaching me:

"We have fasted for months in order to come here, to exchange knowl-edge, wisdom of other epochs, of other worlds that exist in the air."

The most imposing one in the group (I've seen that face before) rises and interrupts the others, leaning slowly and with difficulty, with rage like a con-valescent, on a silver cane. It is the *varayoq,* I tell myself, the leader; he's the highest authority of the community, of all the inhabitants of that zone. And this village's name is Q'ero, I tell myself: named after the sacred wooden vase used by the ancients. Q'ero. No one has ever reached it, not even the Spanish conquerors or the later conquerors, we Peruvians, just as with the uninvaded territory of the Campa Indians, the Great Pajonal. Suddenly the varayoq shows a tense face: grayish, undefinable, blushed, rugged, rocky in the temples and chin, implacable in cheekbones, recent in eyes, remote in looks. I recognize that face! Do I recognize it? The memory's eyes! Memory already eyeless! The face of my grandfather Victor, devoured by the soil more than fifteen years ago, yet younger every day. Thus the ruins of the varayoq's face harbor the joyful features of Isidro Kondori, a young Quechua poet I met in Cusco, singing atop Sacsahuayman Fortress during the Sun God's ceremonies. A farmer, like all proud men, and like all proud men a solitary, Isidro Kondori sometimes condescended to speak Spanish, but when he sang he always did so in Keshwa, in *runasimi,* the language of man. "I am a commoner without community," he sang. "When I had a plow, I had no oxen. When I had oxen, I had no rain. When I had rain, I had no land," sang Isidro Kondori. "When I had land, I had no love." Judges and bosses took away Isidro Kondori's meager heritage of land. Hunger and fortitude later forced him to recover what had been stolen from him. In other words: Isidro Kondori became adept in the art of enticing cows and convincing horses. *Abigeato* is what our laws call the stealing of cattle. Even to this day, Isidro Kondori calls himself by the risky and honest title of *abigeo*. "But never do I flirt with cattle belonging to my fellow peasants. I only recover what belongs to us, the cows that feed in our ancestral lands."

His thin golden voice now flows harshly from the mouth of the old varayoq. Isidro Kondori is singing the "Dance of the Cattle Thief" from the lips of the Inka Manko Kalli! In that song of free males, exclusive hymn of heretical robber Indians, untamable and docile, loyal and womanizing and just and drunk—in that song I again see him, as the true life of the poet Isidro Kondori reflected by a leather sun, while the music of the "Wywa Suaq Tusuynin" brilliantly overflows. The boasts of that song composed by Isidro Kondori in the night of one of his prisons, maybe only to protect us, give truth to our weaknesses far away, there in the dungeons of the Cusco jail. Now, as I did then, I see that Isidro Kondori is singing:

Wywa Suaq Tusuynin

Kamaq qelqa maskawashan
sua kaskay rayku
nispa,
kamaq qellqallataq niwachun
imaraykun kawsani
mijuspa.

Juchuy allpa, sumaq allpa
paytan noqa yumarani
tarpuspa,
werasapa acendarutaq
charanq'arata ruwarasunki
suwaspa.

Koyway kamakoq weraqocha
noqapaq kasqanta
muchuyrispa
manaraq hatun llakita tarpushaqti
yawamuywan
nispa.

The rugged and grayish varayoq of the Q'eros pushes back within him-

self the features of Isidro Kondori, relegates them, and recovers his own millenary face, but his voice insists on rebirthing. I am not misled. I listen—it is the
voice of Luis Nieto, a poet from Cusco. In the voice of Luis Nieto I'm seeing the
"Dance of the Cattle Thief" emerging in light from the mouth of the elder mayor
of the Q'eros:

If the laws seek me
because I steal,
saying,
let the laws tell me
how to survive,
eating.

Small land, beautiful,
which I impregnated
planting:
the great landowner
made you a whore,
stealing.

Give me, Mr. Government,
what is mine,
suffering,
before I plant your undoing
with my blood,
saying.

The varayoq continues to pound the earth with his harnessed silver staff.
The soil rises like a condor, with audible colors. I see myself coming toward
him as he smiles. He is happy, with the face of Don Javier nailed to the ice cross.
I feel I should kneel before him and honor him. But no—I bow my head to him.
My forehead bows before the old Christ, and a black and yellow butterfly, in
yellow mourning, is born from my forehead and crosses the earthen square,
perches on the breast of the old man, who has now seated himself again, motionless in that semicircle of silences and shadows formed by the other elders
of the town. And the plaza is no longer a plaza in my vision but the atrium of
the Temple of the Puma God, the *Q'enqo* atrium, as this sacred place of the
ancient Quechuas, the ancient Inkas, is called. Next to me, out of my own body,
the altar of the Puma God has grown, a giant phallus of rugged and grayish
stone, penetrating the clouds in the heights of Cusco.

And I am to be judged. I am standing in the middle of the giant priapic
granite emerging from my groin. The members of the solar tribunal, the priests,

the sun-people, look at me with closed eyes, in a semicircle. The High Priest, the *Willaq Umu,* rises and points:

"You are not Manko Kalli," thus the old varayoq confronts me. And pounding the soil with his silver cane:

"Why do you use the face of Manko Kalli if you are not Manko Kalli?"

And bending down, consulting silence, toward the flickering shadow on his right:

"Manko Kalli is not a chori, not a virakocha. He is not a man of the Andes, nor a white man. Manko Kalli is beyond the far away, a direct descendant of the first children of Kaametza and Narowé, of the first human beings, who were thus called: Kaametza and Narowé, female and male.

"He is the legitimate direct grandfather of Juan Santos Atao Wallpa, the first rebel against the virakocha conquerors," the silence tells him, the shadow seated to the right side of the old varayoq exchanges with him.

"From him, from Manko Kalli, from the grandfather of Juan Santos Atao Wallpa, comes the blood we perhaps had," replies the varayoq to the seated shadow, to that sepia silence.

And extracting from the neck of his yellow cushma a sacred wooden vase, a scratched container, too remote:

"He left his blood in this q'ero, to us Q'eros he left it, so that our lives would circulate in that blood. In this vase carved from bloodwood, he directed our existence through time. From afar, he sent us existence, his blood, through the *Urus.*"

In that almost white alley known as the Street of the Bell Stones to those familiar with the Saqsawma Fortress, Julio Cortázar stands covered by a poncho interwoven with allpaka yarn. He places his ears on the highest stone in the Inka wall, adheres his person to it, and listens. Julio Cortázar's companion, Ugne Karvelis, attentively crouches down and touches her right cheek to the skin of a lighter and less gray stone. High up, on this side of the alley, a Quechua boy, red-faced like those Antapampa apples, picks a slow pebble with his hands and drops it repeatedly on the rocks crowning the bleached wall. At each blow from the boy, Ugne and Julio pull away their ears with enjoyment. The whole alleyway resonates with the sound of clear water, all of the Saqsawma Fortress resonates, all of the Cusco air resonates in the afternoon.

Before then, that noon, we walked to the Tampu Mach'ay, the Water Temple. Later we arrived at the outskirts of Q'enqo, the Temple of the Puma God, the Temple of the God of Fertility. There I searched for Aníbal Tupayashi, son of the caretaker of the Q'enqo ruins, whose friendship was a gift from the poet Luis Nieto.

"This gentleman is also a minstrel, a *haraweq*," I said to little Aníbal Tupayashi as I pointed to Julio Cortázar. "He is our brother," I told him. "He is our *wauqechay;* he has come from the other side of the ocean only to learn, in order to find out, so that you can show him the Temple of the Puma God, the Temple of the God of Fertility."

Aníbal Tupayashi took Julio Cortázar by his hand and led him, smiling, around those rocky wastes, ending at the foot of the place where the altar of the Puma God was erected, an impossible stone phallus splitting the Cusco skies. Dazzled by the stories Aníbal Tupayashi was telling him, Cortázar passed by the semicircle of seats carved from the stone where the Inka priests, the sun people, sat in ancient times. Ugne Karvelis remained at my side, both of us looking with the same eyes at the tender image of the Quechua child leading that clear giant under the black poncho as if he were his smaller, fragile brother. Later we saw them appear on top of the round boulder, in the summit of the Temple. The profiles of Aníbal and Julio were bronze outlines conjured by the peace of the sun.

"Those two little stone columns you see there," said the Quechua boy to Julio Cortázar, "on the top of the boulder—these two little columns are called *Intiwatana* even though the virakocha mistake them for a solar clock. But what do they know—the columns are not a solar clock. I could have told them. In the language of our ancients, *Inti* means sun, and *watana* means to tie down. Here the Inkas tied down the Sun, with gold and silver cords, so that he wouldn't escape during the night, so that he wouldn't abandon us. The Sun was tied down like that all through the night." "And this *Intiwatana* had other uses as well," Aníbal Tupayashi might have told Julio Cortázar. "On top of these little columns they placed girls, one knee in each column, to watch them urinate. If their urine fell exactly here, in front of the little columns, wetting that crack, that meant that the virgin was still virgin and worthy of acceptance into the *Aqllawasi*, the House of the Nustas of the Inka, the House of the Virgins of the Sun."

The child and Cortázar soon appeared in the atrium of the Temple, next to the remains of the great stone phallus, in front of the nineteen carved spaces in the rocks that form the sacred plaza.

"Here the priests sat down, the Willaq Umu in the center, the High Priest of the Sun, in this stone semicircle. Here they sat to do their justice," Don Aníbal

45

might have said to Don Julio. "Here they judged those who violated our commandments: *ama sua, ama llulla, ama qella*: be not a thief, be not a liar, be not lazy."

Later we went to the Saqsawma Fortress. Its true name is not Sacsayhuaman, as the white virakocha insist on calling it. Its name is not Gray Falcon, Stone Falcon: *Sacsayhuaman*, but Gray Head, Speckled Head, Stone Head: *Saqsawma*, Aníbal Tupayashi informs us. That is because the city of Cusco had the shape of an otorongo, a tiger, in the exact outline of the Puma God. Also that is why it was venerated by our ancients as the God City it was, as the Sacred City. And Saqsawma Fortress, the head of the puma, the speckled head made of stone, congregated all of the memories, all of the thoughts and dreams and felonies of Cusco. The breast and the head of the city were connected, still are connected, by means of a street named Pumakurku, the Spine of the Puma. The tail of the city was watery. The tail of the Cusco-puma was the Watanay River, that canyon which still flows incessantly in reverberating currents toward the village of San Sebastian.

Ugne Karvelis and Julio Cortázar were wide-eyed and attentive in the Fortress of Saqsawma. They repeated the same incredulous question: "How on earth could they bring or even move those colossal stones?" Aníbal Tupayashi informed us that the Inkas extracted and brought them from a quarry near by. It can be shown that these masses traveled only forty leagues. "Very well, but how," again asked Cortázar, "how, if even today anyone would be hard put to move even the smallest of them, probably twenty tons, with cranes—how is it that anyone could then or now move them?"

"They did it singing," said Aníbal Tupayashi. "With songs, *taytachay*, sir, with songs our ancients moved them, with icaros, with magic songs. Singing, that is how our elders made these giant stones travel."

Now, in my nostalgia, the Quechua boy has dark brown hair, almost clear eyes, and rather absent, bleached skin, under the darkening of four centuries of living beneath the sun.

"From afar, from this vase of carved bloodwood, Manko Kalli directed our lives," the old Willaq Umu, the High Priest, tells me, needling the earth with his silver staff in my vision, which does not cease to amaze me, sinking that cane in the prodigal land. I'm not sure of what I know or what I see, the varayoq forcing Sister Mama Oqllo under Brother Manko Kapaq, sending them to Mount Wanakawre so that there, on its side, at the foot of the refulgent, umbrous Qoylluriti, the incestuous golden phallus may penetrate the Navel of the World,

46

finally displayed, fiery premonition, the outline of stone and silence of the city of Cusco. "That is what I'm seeing, what I've seen," I tell Don Juan Tuesta, to his voices which grow more distant, with velour steps, claws, and canines of an otorongo, a puma. And the Amazon River falls out of his wise man's forehead. I see myself in the Plaza of the Q'eros, earthen rectangle, bloodwood carved by the nails of the Sun. I see myself traveling with the best Q'ero dancers, coming down to Challabamba, coming in to Pawkartampu, amid songs, flutes, and drums of the Bora Indians.

"I dreamed that I walked with the Q'eros," I tell Don Juan Tuesta in the village of Muyuy Island. "I walked, we walked, we the Q'ero dancers. After four hundred years we agreed to return to Cusco. Our 'no' has lasted four centuries. We refused everything for four centuries. In our town no one speaks Spanish, or dresses in Spanish, or lives in Spanish, the same as in the land of the Ashanínka, the Campa. We exist as we did before, as we always will—without police stations, schools, or parishes of the virakocha. We dress barely, like this, with a short poncho and long hair for the males and with mourning tresses for our females, just like the women in the city of Tinta."

"You should know that the women from Tinta," says Don Juan Tuesta, says the old Willaq Umu, says the smiling Christ of the Snow Star, "you should know that these women, ever since the invaders assassinated their countryman Tupac Amaru, the Shining Serpent, these women carry a mourning *lliqlla,* a blanket that painfully covers their shoulders. The women of Tinta keep the longest mourning period in our history: two hundred years of pain. Since the Serpent-God, the rebel Tupac Amaru, was executed in the central plaza of Cusco (the square that was then called Place-Where-One-Prays), a change in only one letter of its Keshwa name changed its profession and moved its solitude. It was then renamed *Waqaypata,* Place-Where-One-Weeps. Since then the women of Tinta have been stained with pain."

I see myself absolved by the Q'eros' tribunal, besieging the summits that surround Cusco, conquering with them the top of Mount Wanakawre. The old Willaq Umu orders us to halt. The dancers uncover their foreheads and weep. Below and far away, one hears the lights of the City of the Puma, the sacred city of the Inkas. Four hundred years later we return to contemplate Cusco. At a gesture from the High Priest, we go wild with dancing, playing flutes. We punish drums made with the skin of traitors, moving to the breast of the stone puma. We enter in a triumph of dances, our heads adorned with stuffed heads of herons and wapapas, with black-brimmed hats marked by yellow dots, the necks of which extend down our backs. Our beaks are sealed in blood. Our trembling and victorious waists are still darting! The foreboding city darkens. The frightened virakochas see us come into the Cusco square, into the iridescent ice cave. In the middle of the Waqaypata, the Shining-Serpent-God awaits us smiling from the bloodwood cross. Tupac Amaru receives us.

"Why are you late?" I'm recriminated by the painter Calvo de Araújo, from the dock of his plantation *shapshico*. I see him in my visions, seated behind the smoke from a large, tight cigarette made out of wild tobacco leaves.

"I thought you would arrive by sunset," he says. "I've waited four hundred years for you."

Instead of listening to him, I open the black condor wings adorning my head. Together with the Q'eros I hasten to a squalid track, a trail through the middle of the forest, overtake the others, and advance with them. With abandoned steps we move to the breast of Cusco.

"Why do you laugh like this, so intensely?" asks Don Juan Tuesta, frightened.

"Because when I cry I cry the same way, with the sorrow of centuries," I hear myself respond.

"Perhaps you have been unhinged by the ayawaskha?" says the sorcerer of Muyuy Island, even more alarmed. But I don't quite see his words: the hand of the Amazon erases them against the golden air behind me. And in the midst of the terror of the notables of the city of Cusco, shopkeepers trembling behind their scales and money registers, *tukuyrikuy*, executioners, *allqorunas*, all piling up remorses and late guilts in a single fear, in a tremor of jails, hotels, mansions, and the invaders' houses of prostitution, after four centuries we return, we are returning. We sing as we take over the square, we move it singing, we return Cusco to the jungles, stone by stone, silence by silence, singing. With songs we transport it, dancing, with icaros, with magical songs, with *bubinzanas* we move it, thinking.

8

Females Who Cannot Bear Children Deliver Rainbows

I also saw a rock as big as a house, all covered with moss and vines that skirted it along its base: an earth horizon coupled to earth. The entrance to the rock was a curtain of water. The water covered the mouth of the rock as a gagged waterfall, falling from the earth to the sky! And I was seated there, watching. Standing on the rock, I saw several men conversing in silence, in the shadow, their voices and eyes stopped by the vanishing sun. They had long hair, one or two smoky tresses, and wore a short poncho as pants, tied to the knees. They spoke a kind of Keshwa I shall never learn.

"This is the Temple of the Rainbow," said a face in my visions from the top of the rock, a face I remembered although I had never seen it before, directing its eyes toward the bleeding sun.

"Females who can't, come here. They cross that watery door, shoeless. They come in almost at nightfall, but while it is still day, the sky lies. The females leave the following morning after spending the night inside the rock, after having known solitude without color and without warmth, the true solitude of the rainbow. And they leave enabled. Any female who comes here unable to, leaves able to."

And the face turning toward the night that came rolling down from the Palace of the Inka Sinchi Roka, here in the town called Chincheros, one afternoon away from the city of Cusco, looking toward the night headed for the Wilkanota River, the Sacred River, which flows nearby, still adolescent, not yet with its true name, Urubamba:

49

"Yes, the females who can't, leave here able to. And the children they later engender, the pleasures they engender, are known as Children of the Rainbow."

I saw that from the top of that meadow, because the rock lies on the top of the meadow that leads from the Inka's Palace to the Wilkanota River. I saw appear an old man, very old, leaning on a colored bamboo cane, which needled the earth. He slowly descended with a pair of partridges, of the type they call panguanas. He carried the partridges with arms marked with gashes. Already near me, he didn't see me. He looked through me at the curtain of water. He shouted, "Visions, begin!" The conjuring of his harsh voice made me see the female panguana enter the rock, passing under the waters raining from the earth heavenward, lost in the humid, mossy shadows of the ice cave. "Qoylluriti!" shouted the old man. And I saw that we were already in the following day. The previous afternoon had joined this dawn, skipping over the night, ignoring it, lost forever in a timeless time. But no: the night had gone down river to the Wilkanota, farther on down to the Wilkamayu, and still farther down to the Urubamba, on the way to the jungles. The female partridge came out of the rock and laid five eggs in the place I occupied, in the site of my invisible body, on the earth that the earth did not know I was standing on, without seeing me. And the male panguana flew from the arms of the old man and sat on the eggs. And I saw that I was the nesting panguana.

"It is the male that does the incubating," said the old man.

"Why can't you see me, Maestro?"

"It is the male that does the hatching," he said again, alone, without hearing or seeing me.

And I, the place that was I, stubbornly and weeping: "Why can't you see me? I have become invisible only so that you can see me."

And he, gathering up the panguanas and the eggs, beginning to go up the meadow: "Maybe because you have lost your powers. Someone may have taken them away from you."

"You can sing icaros to me, magnetize me, protect me!" I claimed. "You can undo the damage."

"Everything depends on worthiness," I heard myself say through the sorcerer, who was moving away, panting, leaning on his silver-harnessed cane, which impregnated the earth. It was night again. And it was daytime again. Night again. They confused me: it was night and day at the same time. My visions were confusing me. I saw a black man coughing or crying blood under the sea, and the sea rang out like a cajón. I saw that it was not a cajón and that it was not the sea. It was a white *manguaré* made of lupuna, of moon, and it rang out in the bottom of the Amazon River. The black man's name was Narowé, and he had the face, the voice, and the hands of Don Javier. He entered his cajón with swimming strokes like someone entering the ocean, or death, or a bottomless dream, diving next to a wapapa, one of those carnivorous birds which ate without fear, and without paying him any attention.

"It has been four centuries since I last touched this cajón!" he shouted, "and I will never play it again!" He beat the moon with a bloodwood branch. I also saw the distant sound of two young cajónes that were wounding themselves instead of sounding. I saw the male cajón dissolving in the mouth of a creek, while the female cajón wept, cursed, and surrendered to the consolations of a bonfire in the night. Because by then it was again night. And my visions contradicted me. It was early morning. I saw two sweet drops, luminous as the tears of sugar cane, fall off from the curtain of water covering the rock and come flying, landing on my right eye. Two other drops, ever sweeter, came forth and submerged themselves in my left eye with a flutter of fins.

And I saw no more. I woke up.

II

THE
JOURNEY

I

Those Trees Are Not Called Bloodwood in Vain

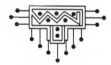

The twin-engined plane left us in Atalaya in the dying light. We had flown for two hours since leaving Pucallpa, besieged in the heights by gusts and threatening rain. Down below, in a spacious avenue staining the woods, full of obstacles of yellow pastures and dusty clumps of bushes, two strings of oil lamps outlined the precarious landing strip. It became completely dark as we descended from the plane. Only the reddish light from the lamps allowed us to see the trail to the village, profiling silhouettes of passengers and trees. We traveled two kilometers, carrying our baggage to the center of the place. Its population was five thousand, including crestfallen fishermen, government functionaries, pallid children, lumbermen in disgrace, obese merchants, and hostile cattlemen. The streets and alleys were full of dried mud.

"Winchesters against arrows—imagine! Repetitive firearms against wooden spears!" says the Spanish cattleman Andrés Rúa in Atalaya, exalted, remembering.

If the trip is made by canoe, it takes seven hours from the village. One rows without opposing the Ucayali River. A deep creek enters the great river unexpectedly from the left shore, flanked by two rows of trees placid with shade. Their steely bark is shinier and more stubborn than steel, lodes of the prized bloodwood, the skin of which shatters the blades of lumber saws even if they are diamond-plated. That lively channel which cuts through the red forest is the Unine River. *The bark of the bloodwood tree is a rusty green-gray, somewhat more than ten meters of trunk, thinned out and cleared of branches.* The Unine River begins up above, beyond those leafy summits, at the center of a great prairie known as the Great Pajonal: one hundred thousand square kilometers of jungled plateau. Today it is still inviolate, and there live the invincible, hospitable, ferocious, and dispersed families of the Ashanínka, known to strangers as the Campa. From the Great Pajonal, by way of this same Unine River, descended the bearded, tired guerrillas led by Luis de La Puente around 1965, carrying suspicious firearms and dress and colors of skin, eyes, and hair, going toward the mountains of the Sierra Pelada in Cusco. They were confident that the Ashanínka, without a doubt the most able and rebellious in the Peruvian jungle, would follow them in their campaign.

"No one would follow them," says Don Andrés Rúa.

Those few who did, thinking that they were descending to warmer lands from the forested plains of the Great Pajonal, descended really to their own deaths. *Bloodwood trees leaf only, and not excessively, at the top, exposing a great quantity of vain and lustrous leaves.* They also inform me that a long time ago there was a merciless conflict between the Ashanínka and the Amawaka nation of the great sorcerer Ino Moxo. Ino Moxo, by then the imminent heir of the Amawaka chief, Ximu, kidnapped one of the thirty wives of a chief called Inganiteri.

"The Ashanínka, the Campa, only know face-to-face combat," says the lumberman, Carlos Maldonado. "They never pounce with guns or conflicts from the shadows, disguised by the night or the astonished bushes. And they are inimitable in tensing the dark bows made of hard layers of ripe *pona*. In the air of their frank battles, they mock their opponents, capturing the enemy's arrows with their hands, or avoiding them with an imperceptible twist of their body, entangling them in the folds of their *cushmas*. Their females, those disquieting and tiny and silent females, with fearful eyes in their copper skin, have waists that appear to be oiled, undulating under the painted skirt. Those same women, who make love to whomever they please when they are ten or nine or twelve years old, become desperately loyal once they are married. The married Ashanínka woman never looks again at the eyes of anyone other than her husband. She can only be possessed by another man by force. And when that happens, usually in a soldiers' post gone out of control, the violated Ashanínka woman usually commits suicide."

Only the Campa sorcerers, the katziboréri, and with greater right the experts in tobacco smoking, the shirimpiáre, know the venom used by those warriors on the tips of their arrows and the darts of their long blowguns.

"It is a poison that kills without pain and very quickly," says Don Andrés Rúa. "It doesn't come from curare or from any other substance extracted from the poison of vipers." Apparently the Ashanínka sorcerers resort to a preparation made from tohé, the bell-shaped flower, like marble, whose essence produces an invulnerable and sweet dream and congeals the blood.

Deceived by the Amawaka Ino Moxo, the Ashanínka Inganiteri called together his principals from all over the Great Pajonal. In an infinite number of canoes, their cheeks painted with *wito*, with *achiote*, with *karawiro*, and with blood, hundreds of warriors came out of the mouth of the Unine. They descended by the bloodwood trails, all of them and their women letting out shrill war cries. They entered the Ucayali with great laughter, threatening and singing. They penetrated the Urubamba River, toward the Inuya; reached the Mapuya; crossed the forest to the Mishawa; and almost attained what the white invaders never could complete: the annihilation of the Amawaka nation. *The bark of the bloodwood tree has a rusty green-gray color, somewhat more than ten meters of thinned trunk cleared of branches: it leafs only, and not excessively, at the top, opening up a mass of vain and lustrous leaves. But these bloodwoods from the Unine, incomprehensibly widowed of bark, expose to the eyes that red insolence from which they take their name.* After weeks of incessant warring, when the Amawaka had been reduced to three hundred males, Ino Moxo, forced by his chief, Ximu, returned the thirtieth wife to Inganiteri. It is said that obediently, before returning to the Great Pajonal, the land of her elders, the denigrated wife killed herself by nailing a dart of tohé in her abdomen. *It is said that these bloodwoods from the Unine, incomprehensibly widowed of bark, expose to the eyes that red insolence from which they take their name.* Others insist that the story is false—that it was not the Ashanínka but the white rubber collectors who unceasingly massacred the natives, with the deceitful pretext of combatting cannibalism.

"Winchesters against arrows, you can imagine! Repetitive firearms against wooden spears—and only to deprive the Indians of their lands full of rubber trees!"

And they tell me more things about the Campa. That they have always been nomads, since before the whites existed, ever since an unmeasurable black otorongo fell from the heights of the Great Pajonal and dispersed them. That at most, every two years they change their living space, their life. They burn everything: their planted farms, the trails opened with machetes, the two cabins erected by sheer force: the *kaápa* destined for guests, the first one built, and the *tantoótzi* later, to be occupied by the family. In that way they return

57

what they for a time had borrowed from the forest, reestablishing peace with the landscape and their own harmony with nature. Then they march to another site in the Great Pajonal and begin all over again: they burn the impenetrable forest and open space for new plantings and dwellings.

"And they don't do this capriciously," says Carlos Maldonado. "They don't do it in ignorance, as we civilized people thought."

"It is only very recently that those scholars I believe are called ecologists," says Don Andrés Rúa, "have discovered what the Ashanínka have always known: that this is the adequate and wisest way to fertilize the soil of this land, because it is soft. Weak is the soil of these our places, and it will not support uninterrupted pregnancies. It needs rest, fertilizer and rest. The ashes produced by the Ashanínka in leaving do not bear death but new life. It is for the same reason that they bury their dead in shallow graves, enveloped in a double layer of lime, so that they too fertilize and continue and never die. And they tell me that neither the Inkas, nor the Spanish conquerors, nor the missionaries, nor the scholars, nor the armies of the present have ever been able to subjugate the Campa. That around 1742, one of their chiefs called Juan Santos Atao Wallpa rebelled against the Spanish Empire, proclaiming himself "King of All of the Indians of Peru," and that the Campa today, centuries after the disappearance of Santos Atao Wallpa, continue awaiting him."

"Every year, when the rainy season resonates, the Ashanínka chiefs meet in some nook of the Great Pajonal, possibly in the vicinity of Salt Mountain," says Stéfano Varese. "Near the city of Satipo, they unearth the sword they were given by Juan Santos Atao Wallpa, and they await him for days and days and sleepless nights. Finally, when they see him crossing the sky wielding lightning in his right hand, resigned, the Campa principals promise to meet again the following year, when the first rains begin to thunder, to continue to wait for him.

"Because they affirm," says Carlos Maldonado, "that when Juan Santos Atao Wallpa returns, the Ashanínka will again rise under his leadership, *and they will overcome the conquerors and give back liberty and lands to all of the Indians of the Kingdom of Peru.*"

All of that and more, more than the rape and subsequent suicide of the thirtieth wife of Inganiteri, more than the imminence of Santos Atao Wallpa, I gathered in the vicinity of Atalaya, thanks to the acquaintances of my uncle, the painter Calvo de Araújo. They were people who had shared everything with him, all of the Great Pajonal. Now, with the impetus for adventure abolished by need and by age, they were getting fatter, like cows over the pastures opened by the Campa with fire and machetes on both sides of the Unine, behind the flaming bloodwood forests.

"They went to war over a female, but they did not follow the guerrillas!" says Carlos Maldonado.

We had no time to go up the waters of the Unine River into the interior of Ashanínka country. Our goal lay in the opposite direction, among the survivors of the no less fabulous Amawaka nation.

We went on for two kilometers carrying our baggage to the center of Atalaya. In the only bathroom of the Grand Hotel de Souza, we showered in the dark, stung by mosquitoes and stepping on vermin. At dawn we left our lodging with the intention of heading to the port, but because of the friends of my cousin, César Calvo, and their unending hospitalities, we tumbled onto the dock overflowing with San Juan beer under the afternoon sun. A furor of rain welcomed us to the agonizing docks of wooden planks leaning on the left bank of the Ucayali River. There, among acquaintances huddled under leafy mango trees and palms ripe with fruit, César was reunited with his brother Iván, the silent, dark one. He showed an Indian heritage in skin and gesture, which I later learned came to him from his mother. It brimmed over in his eyes in a sort of unfriendly stalk. Iván Calvo brought to the expedition the benefit of the experience of a friend named Félix Insapillo, a local fisherman even more silent and brooding.

Fortunately, or unfortunately, it was because of Félix Insapillo that we were able to rent that very afternoon a canoe with an outboard motor, a suspicious and vacillating log, which almost sank outside the port just after we had embarked, when a wave pushed us against hidden boulders in the middle of the river. Half sunk in mud, kicked by the round boulders, and almost carrying our boat on our shoulders, César, Iván, Insapillo, and I opposed the current for a long time. We saw an animal struggling in vain pass by, carried away by the Ucayali. We persisted, with the canoe on top of us. We carried it to the protection of a nearby islet and collapsed under the setting sun, soaked and exhausted. After a minimal rest, we replaced the motor's propeller, its deformed bronze shattered by those camouflaged boulders, and proceeded against the current toward the Urubamba River, which roared in the distance, imposing its flow between colossal islands. We barely advanced. The sparse moon and the sizable logs that tended to float under the surface, those black screws capable of overturning larger craft than ours, forced us to camp out in a narrow beach, speckled with sand that shone like snow, by the junction of the Ucayali and the Urubamba Rivers. We set up stakes: a sturdy one to secure the canoe, the others to hold the strings of our mosquito nets. Insapillo offered to mount guard. In that way, we spent a sleepless night until dawn came to worry us. Insapillo mentioned that the face of the sky told him it would rain. It was June 27, 1977. We pulled up our minimal camp; wrapped the rifle, the shotguns, and the machetes in pieces of oilskin; and boarded the trembling canoe on the shore.

The days that followed would prove Carlos Maldonado right, because in order to reach Ino Moxo and the Amawaka lands, one has to elude contradictory waters and poisonous clouds that suddenly turn white. One has to stumble across cadavers of gigantic fish and sharp spikes, wragraponas, muwenas, masarandubas, and cedars pulled out by the anger of rivers and chained to the latest flood. One has to learn to listen to Iván and to Insapillo, whose voices make real the fables of the jungle night—the ghosts, the disappeared, the animals of dark tales, maidens grieving under the river, violated by a pink dolphin. And one has to learn to sleep, eyes open and shotgun ready, alert to the most innocent footstep, after having flayed an enormous monkey and having cooked and eaten it as pink as we ourselves are, while hearing a few yards away the bellowing of the slow lizards in the muddy waters, like logs floating next to logs eaten away by that blue-green-gold moss, while the *túnchi* flies by whistling, announcing that someone has just died or will die today. You hear the footsteps of *majaces* in the flats—hundreds of families of majaces, those fat gray rodents spotted in white and black, colorless in the shadows.

Night falls with a strange sound like that of a gigantic carbonized tree. I have already learned to distinguish, behind the rumors of the forest and the river, that immense, scratched silence—the night. But I see clearly: something that is not the wind gently insists again and again, as if someone were rubbing a sheet of cellophane against the gauze of the mosquito nets. I sit up with apprehension, scan the shadows, search around my feet, touch my gun with relief. Insapillo, next to me, doesn't move. I tense my whole body, alert between that shadow and that unnamed rubbing.

"Don't worry, they're just vampires," I hear Iván saying.

"What?" says my cousin César with consternation.

"Yes, this is an area of large vampires. You simply have to sleep squarely in the center of the area covered by your mosquito net. If you touch the net itself, they will bleed you for sure."

And he was suddenly silent. I heard him snore all night. I heard the stormy breath of Félix Insapillo, lying next to me and that obsessive flapping of wings, stalking the nets.

"We are near, it is another day," says Félix Insapillo. After a sleepless night we comfort ourselves in the foggy light that is gradually allowed in by the widening tops of the *yaku shapanas*, the thickets of the *canela-muwenas* and other proud trees, and the persistent brown embankments besieged by the waters. They are besieged and abandoned like broken landscapes, flanks of a millenary animal, showing a network of roots pointing anxiously skyward. We paid no attention to Félix Insapillo, who was exerting himself to affirm that those footprints sprouting among the bushes and accentuated in the sand, tracks that made no sense heading into the water, were not those of a majaz, still less an añaz, that almost jungle fox, nor the steps of the ronsoco, that other giant rodent and disdained relative of the wild pigs, but nothing less than the diabolic tracks of the chullachaki.

"Chullachaki!" warned Insapillo. "Chullachaki!" In the Keshwa language *chullachaki* means "only-one-foot," "single foot." According to our guide, the chullachaki, the devil of the forest, had been stalking us, seeking to ambush us. Perhaps the cursed soul, the lonely soul, had entered our dreams. Maybe it had walked on us with its equivocal steps, disguised as a human being but unable ever to hide its right foot, the one that leaves impossible prints, deformed as a tiger's claw or the hoof of an evil deer. César agreed, nodding, to Insapillo's stories. I didn't give them any importance, concentrating on Iván's return from a walk in the woods that had started while it was still dark. He had taken only one cartridge in his hunting rifle and was petulant, affirming that he needed no more to provide us with a full breakfast.

César had advised me about some of Iván's traits. He walked barefoot in silence in the most difficult jungle, over spines and dried vines. He knew how to smell the passing of wild boars on fallen leaves, and their direction and distance. He never missed a shot or an arrow or a blowgun dart. He sensed prey or danger with the same sharpness as that of a young tiger. In spite of his youth he was an experienced woodsman (they called him Cacique), and he had survived many risks, many unmentionable adventures.

The painter Calvo de Araújo disdained cities and lived in intricate jungles, as far as possible from civilization. He was living then in a tiny cabin facing the Utuquinia River, two days' journey away from Pucallpa. He was unexpectedly visited by César.

"You are late," he told him at dusk on the dock, seated behind the smoke of a long, slow cigarette made from wild tobacco. "I expected you before dark."

"'I had to stop to eat something," César excused himself, intrigued, since he had told no one about his intended visit.

"I dreamed about you last night. I dreamed you arrived by sunset; didn't I tell you?" he asked the woman who was his companion during those months.

"You certainly did," she confirmed. She was small, with a dark, tough skin and a fugitive look. "Your old man awoke me last night," she said to César. "He awoke me saying, 'tomorrow César is coming. He will come before dusk.'"

The painter Calvo de Araújo at that time lived with two of his younger sons; Angel and Iván. César faced unsurmountable hostility from both. Days later he reached an understanding with them. By then already painted by the sun of the Utuquinia River, toasted by the reflection of the sun in the lakes, he was fishing half naked on the shore when a shadow approached him. Iván placed his dark arm next to the already tanned body of César, compared colors, and smiled.

"Now you are truly my brother!" And rising suddenly, possessed by unbounded joys, he invited him to hunt.

They took two lances, an old gun, and half a dozen cartridges. That, together with their bodies, filled a narrow, short canoe. Iván was up front, sinking the paddle sideways into the water and taking it out the same way without even showing the drops that would come off the wood when it left the imperturbable current behind. In silence they surged ahead on the lean Utuquinia, muted by the vision of the shady vegetation that topped the white water trail. A few hours later, they had to step out of the canoe and carry it on their shoulders, climbing that staircase of irised stones through which the river disgorges itself in harmless waterfalls. Having passed that stretch, they entered again, riding the Utuquinia into a heavily wooded section. Always in silence, Iván pulled the oar out of the water. Eyes facing front, focused on a point of the forest tunnel that scarcely allowed the intromission of the sun, he snuffed on both sides of the shade and finally extended his right hand in the direction of César without turning his head. César continued motionless at the other end of the canoe, with the gun resting on his thighs, struggling to guess what he had seen—no, what his younger brother had smelled in that thicket. Half resigned and half alarmed, he handed over the gun. Iván, even more alert to the heights of the shady forest, slowly picked up the gun. Even more slowly, he rested it on his shoulder and took aim. César looked, less than blindly, at the spot where the gun was aimed. Nothing. Almost with the thunder of the discharge, from the knot of vines and branches, the body of a tiger, a black otorongo two meters long, fell pawing into the creek. Paddling with his hand, Iván advanced the canoe to the enormous feline, which floated without moving. César stretched out to grab it. Iván stopped him.

"It is not dead," he mused, glancing at the apparent quietness of the animal, and he touched his oar to the forehead stained with death. The beast, without opening its eyelids, which were veiled by blood flowing from its forehead, struck out with his powerful paw, shattering the oar. It was playing dead, only pretending. Iván recovered the gun and fired another shot at the otorongo. Hours of silence passed.

Within sight of the small dock at Shapshico (or "Little Devil," the name of the property of the painter, unlike the surrounding places, which were all given the sentimental names of pious women or Catholic saints), César asked his brother what would have happened had he not spotted the presence of the tiger.

"How could I not smell a tiger?" exclaimed Iván, incredulous, offended by the question. Since it was repeated, and after insisting, several times, "How could I not smell him?" he concluded by accepting the all-but-impossible possibility of a slipup, turned to César, and without altering his voice, said, "If I had not smelled him, he would have certainly killed us. We would not be conversing now."

"I don't know whether you know," César tells me, "that Iván is the godson of the Sorcerer of Sorcerers, Ino Moxo's protégé. My father requested and was granted that privilege from the Amawaka chief."

"How could that be?" I exclaimed. "Didn't you tell us that Ino Moxo hasn't spoken with anyone, with any Westerner, for many years?"

"Of course," he quieted me very naturally. "The thing is that my father requested from him mentally, from the Utuquinia River, that he be godfather to Iván. In the same way, mentally, he received the consent of Ino Moxo. Since that day, Iván can enter peril without fear: Ino Moxo protects him."

Nevertheless, that morning I awaited the return of Iván with more hunger than confidence, with more impatience than hunger, and with increasing astonishment. I was trying to find an explanation of what had happened to me weeks before in Pucallpa, while we were waiting for that disabled twin-engined plane to decide to function again and take us to the city of Atalaya. I was trying to fix in my memory what Don Hildebrando, Great Magus of that zone, had told me about Ino Moxo and his life.

63

2

It Took One Thousand Years
for the Holy Grail of the Cusco Inkas
to Arrive in Pucallpa

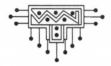

"Here, colors are fundamental," says César, "indispensable doors to intuition, to understanding. *Pucallpa,* for example: Quechua language *puka,* red; *allpa,* land. Pucallpa is a red land."

I believed him; I disbelieved him. Yando Riós, firstborn child of Don Hildebrando, transmitted to César his passion for magic. I believed him. Both went often to visit the Pucallpa sorcerer for several months, more out of curiosity than as disciples. I disbelieved him. That is how César came to find out, as I later did myself, that a rigorously respected hierarchy exists among jungle sorcerers. That the highest grade is granted to the Great Magician of certain areas. That the boundaries of those areas are determined more by stellar influences and by commands from the air than by demographics or by geographic imperatives. That some wizards officiate in spells, a certain magic whose origin and objectives boil in submission to the Evil One, and are merciless enemies of anyone who alludes to the diverse ministries of the magic of love. He also found out about sects that add profane practices to their rituals, inherited from a time without memory, with ceremonial invocations neatly impregnated with Catholicism and Protestantism. (The very same day we arrived in Pucallpa, the newspapers mentioned the finding of a girl's head, severed with a knife, cheeks painted with *wito* and *achiote,* inside a basket abandoned in the Federico Basadre Road.) According to César, the Amazon sorcerers cannot be classified into white or black magic. On certain occasions they use spells to do good, and one would have to then refer to a green magic, exclusive to the jungle sorcerers, within which complex guilds extend. It is a sort of medical-magic religion, and Don Hildebrando would be the Great Green Wizard of the Pucallpa zone.

We remained four days in the red land, and four nights we were present in Don Hildebrando's hut and witnessed his sessions of meditations and appeals. Four nights we left the Hotel Tariri, walking through winter-wet alleyways, crossing the grate supported by sharp stakes and negotiating a sinuous and narrow path. We entered his house and squeezed ourselves in among the sick and the believers who crowded his schedule of evening visitors.

"The spirit of an Inka protects you," confirmed Don Hildebrando to César." "Every time you come with Yando, he appears. I see him behind you as a great radiance, covered to his feet with a yellow cushma, that closed poncho, sewn along its sides, painted with lines, the color of red earth."

And offering to César a small dose of ayawaskha in a rusty cup:

"Every time you come, he accompanies you. It is the spirit of the Inka Manko Kalli. He appears behind you with a wooden vase in his hands,· a very old vase, engraved with the same design that appears in his cushma."

"I know that vase," César hears himself say after the last bitterness of the ayawaskha. "I have seen it. It is a q'ero, the sacred grail used by the Inkas in their ceremonies. Drinking only a sip from that vase and spilling the remaining contents on troughs carved in the stones of their temples, the Inkas complemented their meetings of adoration of the Sun, Father Inti, and the Moon, Mother Killa."

"Have you also seen it?" asked Don Hildebrando with doubt, sitting down on the striped wooden stool, and again standing. He crossed to one side of the room while making the floor of his cabin, located in the outskirts of Pucallpa, creak. He bent over something resembling a chest, opened its cover fringed with chambera ropes, extracted an old notebook and a pencil, and passed them to César.

"Draw that vase for me," he ordered, in a voice that became lighter as if asking a favor. César drew, and the sorcerer's eyes gleamed in the

dimness. "It is exactly that way. Manko Kalli always holds it close to his chest," he said. "When did you see it? Did you see it here in my house, or did you dream it?"

"I have never seen Manko Kalli," César corrected him, "but I have certainly seen that vase."

And after a brief silence, besieged already by the first visions brought about by the juice of ayawaskha, the vine of the dead, he remembered.

"I lived in Cusco until a few years ago. One afternoon, walking along the top of the Inka citadel of Pisacq, overlooking the Sacred Valley, I saw the Urubamba River flowing below me, silvery, still young, before it gets lost in the jungle. The Quechuas don't refer to it as the Urubamba. For them it is still the Wilkamayu, meaning the 'God River,' the 'Sacred River.' Higher up on the mountain range, near the origin of the Urubamba, they call it the Wilkanota and say that a long time ago, before the coming of the Spanish conquerors, the Wilkanota was a powerful river, impossible to cross. It walked standing up, rising over its two waters. When the invaders assassinated Manko Inka, the last king of the Quechuas, the sacred river turned red, worse than the blood of the innocent, they say. From that day onward, the waters became tame, divided, as the time without time of the first men, of the Campa. The waters gradually recovered their original color, but they continued to flow on their knees in sorrow."

Don Hildebrando looked even more intensely at César, his clay head tensed forward. More than expectant, his silence overflowed with another demand. César obeyed:

"I was contemplating the Wilkamayu, the Urubamba, from the heights of Pisacq that afternoon, in the afternoon of the city of Cusco. I wandered about, around the edge of the old cemetery, the city-of-the-dead of our forefathers, and just before nightfall, I found an old peasant dressed in rags. I was impressed by his beard tinged with white. He was excavating near the caves where his closest grandfathers are buried. He held in his hands this recently excavated Q'ero. The old man heard me murmur a greeting in his language, and he sadly smiled, holding out the ceremonial vase toward me, giving it to me without reason, while mumbling a word that I have not forgotten.

"'Ayúmpari,' he said.

"That is what he said: 'ayúmpari.' Later on, I returned to Lima, taking the q'ero with me. I still have it well secured in my house."

66

And leaning backward, as if scaring away a strange vision:

"I don't know why, now that you spoke of Manko Kalli and of the wooden vase, I knew that it could not be any other vase than this one."

"It is a vase that has been empowered by an icaro," said Don Hildebrando, pushing aside the wall of blue and orange bamboos that had filled the middle of his house from the saliva of the ayawaskha. To empower with an icaro is to return power to objects that do not naturally have it in this life. To empower with an icaro is to magnetize them with powers that those objects never learned, that they don't know.

The words of the sorcerer were lost in César's mind. Behind the colored bamboos, two dangerous, sulphurous eyes appeared: the vision of an old Campa dressed up in full battle gear.

"My name was Hohuaté!" he screamed inside César's memory and hallucinations. "But now my name is Andrés Avelino! Andrés Avelino Cáceres y Ruiz: that is my name!"

And the vision suddenly dispersed, its voice filtering down between the cracks in the floor of creaking boards.

Months later, I brought the ceremonial vase to Pucallpa, the vase that César told me was carved from a single piece of dark wood. I believed him; I doubted him. But when I met Don Hildebrando, Manko Kalli's q'ero occupied the center of his house. Four nights we gathered together to meditate around that q'ero, remaining silent to invoke "the powers that inhabit air," to put them at the service of "our brothers who suffer," as Don Hildebrando said. In the center of the main room, three triangular bases of polished wood stood out, superimposed with the intention of an altar, and the Sacred Vase of the Cusco Inkas was placed over the last platform, next to a small container made out of a gourd. A tiny black stone, round, flat, and shiny, trembled at the bottom of the vase, which was filled each and every night with the Water of Serenity. Before the start of each session, the participants drank from it. Then we took our places sitting on the floor, surrounding the triangles. We took off all objects made of metal, coins, buckles, and rings to avoid interfering with the coming of the spirits of the air. Without anyone asking for it, we remained with closed eyes during the entire session. We could feel the forces that were possessing us, the emanations (but they were not emanations), which seemed to descend to our deepest inner selves, coming from the deep of the air of the jungle.

*"I know who killed me!" shouted the vision of Hohuaté, the Campa
old man.*

*"I heard him clearly with my eyes, looking at his shout," César told
me in the plane going to Pucallpa. I believed him; I disbelieved him.*

*"But they haven't killed Hohuaté! They've killed my other self!
They've killed Andrés Avelino Cáceres y Ruiz!" the vision screamed
before dissolving into the cracks in the floor.*

At the end of each meeting, after returning to the Hotel Tariri, I remarked to
my cousin César that it was possible to feel how the space in the hut began to fill
with powers, and that those powers passed on to us an invincible and serene
anxiety, an indescribable omnipotence, which penetrated into us through our bare
feet and through our temples like very thin rivulets of air that found their way
into our pores, enlarging our chests and our existence. It was possible to see the
sorcerer in front of us without having to crack our eyes open.

"I did not see colored bamboos afterward but a grayish river and many
dead bodies," César is telling me while on the airplane, "a multitude of corpses
riddled with bullets, floating down river, and the river turned red and shone
like a red knife in the greenery, contaminating the afternoon sky. And later I
saw more things, which I cannot tell, which I have never seen before," says
César, while in the air, flying to Pucallpa. I believed; I disbelieved him—until I
met Don Hildebrando. The second night I went to visit him, there was so much
tension inside his hut, the accumulation of powers I perceived, that the whole
house began to tremble and make a noise. The flimsy wooden walls trembled
more each time. Everything vibrated as if for the last time, as if we were in the
epicenter of an earthquake.

*"I know who killed me!" moaned the Campa Hohuaté. "I know who
has thrown a poisoned dart to chief Andrés Avelino Cáceres y Ruiz!"*

I remained seated during this, refusing to hear the unspeakable cataclysm.
I listened only to the silent orders of Don Hildebrando, making me whole with
their serenity, abandoned over the reverberating wooden planks. I ignored the
great mosquitoes that were piercing my brow, my ears, my hands, my exposed
ankles, until gradually the trembling was attenuated and diminished, mingling with
the wandering of the wind and the rumors of the forest, and then disappeared.

"They have been overcome," sounded the voice of Don Hildebrando in the darkness. "Evil spirits have been trying to enter, but they have been overcome."

That night I happened to find out that the sorcerer had previously cured the black stone that slept in the bottom of the q'ero. He had put a spell on it with powerful prayers, with invoking chants. For seven days he fasted in the depths of the adjoining woods until he succeeded in impregnating it with the powers of the air and of the earth, so that the stone would breathe its strength, its serenity, into the water deposited in the ceremonial vase.

The Amazon sorcerers are able to cure any object. To do so, they go deep into the jungle and meditate for weeks, nourishing themselves by drinking water from ravines. They allow themselves to eat only a slice of plantain cooked outdoors, depending on the amount of powers that they wish to charge the object with. A seed necklace, for example, or a bracelet of snakeskin, or a wristlet made from the labia of the vagina of a red dolphin, or the most inoffensive ring, or a lock of hair, or a handkerchief—they can all be cured by a sorcerer according to the intensity and intention of the charge, to grant life, love, youth, forgetfulness, sexual plenitude, evil spells, or death. The same object, once cured, is capable of resuscitating, healing, making sick, or killing, according to the length of the fast and the direction of the charge .

Don Hildebrando cured the small black stone, charging it with repose. Such serenity was transmitted to us by means of the water held in the sacred vase. After drinking it, as soon as we returned from the meditation to this reality, Don Hildebrando, already invested by the benign spirits, took care of an endless number of patients. His assistant was a squalid half-breed with a sweet face, fifteen years old. Her hips had been widowed of any cadence, her feet of any steps, because of congenital poliomyelitis. The girl had been treated by Pucallpa's magician. I saw her walking normally, coming and going without rest, handing Don Hildebrando the ointments, the potions, the "stone or wooden vegetables" required for each complaint. In the most intense moment of a session, when the sorcerer resorted to strange chants, she accompanied him with her cracked voice, contributing to the healing of the patients.

Ira Ira Iraká
Kura Kura Kuraká
Nai Nai Nai
Epirí Ririritú
Yamaré
Yamaré Yamarerémo

Screeching, more than singing, the former polio patient reinforced the icaro of Don Hildebrando.

"It is just that each Green Magician," says my cousin César, "repeats or improvises his own icaros—untransferable magical songs—according to the nature of the meetings. There are icaros for calling, for protection, for learning, for exchanging knowledge, for healing with ayawaskha, for healing without ayawaskha. Some call a bubinzana the icaro that controls ritual sessions or initiation meetings. Others, like Don Hildebrando, demonstrate a more complex repertory in the case of healing sessions: they singsong specific icaros, generally impossible to repeat—a different one for each disease, even a different one for each patient."

"And that is nothing new," says Iván later in Atalaya. "The Inkas centuries ago used music as part of medical treatments. It is said that they had charged melodies, concretely directed toward a specific objective. They had a music to cure tuberculosis (which I believe they called yanawayra, meaning "black wind" in Keshwa) and another music for another disease. They even had a unique melody that was only used in making love, to return sexual vigor to elders."

But some cases do not require an icaro. I was a witness: the wife of an engineer who was a friend of mine, a manager in the San Juan Beer Brewery in Pucallpa, was the victim of an unbreakable phobia. The mere vision of any snake or any viper led her irremediably to fainting. It only sufficed that she contemplate a snake, even a stuffed one or a photograph of one, according to her own confession, for her to be possessed by an invincible vertigo and for her to fall backward, with open legs. Psychologists from Lima and Buenos Aires, some of them infallible, had no success with her. I was in Don Hildebrando's house when the lady went to seek his counsel.

"I know what you have," said Don Hildebrando, with a certainty that was more authoritarian than solemn. "You are not to worry," he reiterated, with his eyes fixed upon the lady. "I know why you have come to see me. I am going to cure you."

I saw how the words of the sorcerer immediately pacified the young woman.

"There is a stone which grows only in certain bends of these rivers, and which is helpful in containing the confidence, in maintaining the clarity of soul which you need." And while looking at her, fixing his eyes upon her with increasing intensity, he remarked, "I am going to prepare that stone for you. I cured it long ago, but now I am going to direct it toward you, toward the harm that torments you. I will give it to you tomorrow."

In barely two sessions, Don Hildebrando eliminated the phobia of the hysterical lady. César considered, or so he told me, that the sorcerer had taken advantage of his unfathomable power of suggestion and the exhausted helplessness of the patient. I myself would not dare to explain it in that way. The truth is that the phobic woman healed, and when I visited her on the eve of the journey to Atalaya, she was already fully recovered. The only thing she did was drink now and then from a glass jar that had a flat, small, black stone glittering in the bottom, the Water of Serenity.

At the end of the third night (or was it the last one?) the Great Green Magician of the Red Land remembered Ino Moxo.

"The times when I saw him, he was not yet called Ino Moxo. He had another name. *Ino Moxo* means 'Black Panther' in the Amawaka language. I remember he had skin like day, chestnut hair, eyes of a half-breed. I never asked him, and he never told me, but I knew his father had come from Arequipa searching his fortune and that the Amawaka had captured his son under the orders of the great chief Ximu. Ximu was the shirimpiáre then, the chieftain-sorcerer of the Amawaka inhabiting the Mishawa River. I never knew precisely why they captured him in particular, or why they took him into the forest and up the Urubamba by the jungles of the Mapuya, or why they prepared him as a child to become the successor of Ximu. Because for many years, the great maestro Ximu educated him to be chief. Why they selected him especially, kidnapped him, and taught him everything—that is what I don't know."

"Don Hildebrando himself— you have seen him in Pucallpa—" says Iván, "knows an icaro that can charge a drink with sexual youthfulness. I asked him for it once for a relative who is almost seventy years old. I have seen how his wife looks at him now, and his wife is barely twenty years old."

Don Hildebrando also told me about Ino Moxo's powers, about the speed with which the kidnapped child expanded the teachings of Ximu, and about how he became unreachable, not only in the fearful kindnesses of magic but also in the more redoubtable ones of love, and in the less tricky ones of war.

"Wisdom, strength, and love," he said. "Knowledge of power, and the power of knowledge. Water is a secret. Rivers can exist without water but not without riverbanks. And those are Ino Moxo's riverbanks: wisdom, power, and love. The life of a sorcerer worthy of the Amawaka could not transpire without these."

I recorded everything that we talked about during those three nights, without Don Hildebrando knowing about it. More because of my insecurity than his timidity, I assumed he would not agree to record his voice on magnetic tape. I would slyly turn my recorder on, assuring him that it was a radio, while I pointed it at the stool where he usually sat. After the end of his talk, we would return to the Hotel Tariri. Once in our room, with only César present, I would rewind the tape and we would listen to it. We heard everything: the sounds of the night, the complaints of the unpolished wooden planks of the floor, my voice, my cousin's questions, even Yando's scratching when he lit a cigarette. One heard everything, everything—but not one word of Don Hildebrando. Not one word of his, at any time, in any part of the recorded tape. The first time it happened, we attributed it to some defect of the built-in microphone. Perhaps it was poorly oriented or too distant. The second time, we wanted to believe in some insufficiency of the volume adjustment during recording. The third night, we could find no excuses, and on the fourth one we preferred to question the matter no longer.

Now, submerged in the jungle, besieged by the fears of Félix Insapillo regarding the chullachaki, I stubbornly refused to accept the unexplainable as another truth. I was trying to fix in my memory the gift about life that Don Hildebrando had given me during those four nights.

I scanned the high bush behind me.

Iván was nowhere to be seen.

3

Our Guide Gets Lost

I scan the high bush behind me.

Not one sign of Iván.

His lateness should concern me, I know, but it is inevitable: after Don Hildebrando, my memory returns to Don Javier. It was in La Baguette restaurant in Pucallpa, less than one hundred meters away from the Hotel Tariri, where I met that jovial sorcerer, owner of nineteen children of his own, in four legitimately established homes.

"You are very home-loving, Don Javier," I smiled at him.

"That's what they say," he responded, flattered, "and some also say that I am forty years old and that I have sixty million *soles*. You know that the reverse is true, my friend Soriano, because I have forty soles and am sixty million years old." Again, he smiled. He was passing by, as usual, and as usual was polishing off a glass of San Juan beer, which he interspersed with shots of brandy made with hiporúru, clavowaskha, or chuchuwasha.

"The Campa that followed Inganiteri by the thousands refused to join the guerrillas. The rebel Luis de La Puente should have told them that he himself was going to fight for a woman." And, darkening his quiet smile, "He should have told them that he was going to rescue a female, that female who some still call . . . I believe some still call liberty."

"How was it then that the Campa did go to war with Santos Atao Wallpa? Was it because they were other men, from another time?"

73

"The Campa of today are different and they are the same. With time. This time is identical. Luis de La Puente was the same: he was white and he was a virakocha, but in his heart he became an Ashanínka. Within his soul he relived Santos Atao Wallpa—but Santos Atao Wallpa did not come to the Great Pajonal; he came from it. Maybe that's what it was."

"Don Javier is my godfather," boasted Félix Insapillo while we were navigating toward the Inuya River. "He protects me," he said.

Stepping off the plane in Atalaya, we came across some German doctors, a couple returning to Pucallpa. He climbed the steps toward the twin-engined plane arm in arm with his wife, with his eyes lost and white. We were told without asking that the young stranger had gone deep into the surrounding area, getting lost in the maze of narrow trails used by the Campa. He spent a whole night not daring to do anything, wounded by the rain and the darkness, exposed to the sightings of vipers, vampires, and fear. The following afternoon they found him seated leaning against a leafy shiwawako, covered with ants, insane, and numbed by panic. His wife sobbed while holding his arm, speaking to him and hurrying him into the airplane.

"This is a cursed jungle," someone said the next day, intruding into the anxious group formed by Iván, Insapillo, César, and me. Addressing our shining guide in a taunting voice, he said; "Is it not true, young Félix? Our jungle is beautiful but very cursed—full of apparitions, of snakes, of lizards, of otorongos. You know that better than anyone else, no?"

Then we found out that some years back, Félix Insapillo had become lost in that area. He wandered about for several days alone, without a compass, firearms, or anything. Innumerable expeditions searched for him in vain. He had already been given up as dead when he suddenly reappeared, a wreck, in the path that goes from the cemetery to the town. It was two in the morning. Taking advantage of his habitual insomnia, I questioned Félix Insapillo about it on the night we made camp after nearly sinking the canoe. But before transcribing what the guide told me, I must say something else about Don Javier.

Five kilometers down river from the mouth of the Unine, on the same bank where the the forests of bloodwood shine, lies the property of an affable Spaniard named Andrés Rúa. Don Andrés Rúa is fiftyish but looks like his own son. He is massive, although veined with a wrinkle here and there, especially on the hands. The tops of his hands are full of white hairs, as is his copious mane. His moustache is stained by tobacco, or by a stubborn, probably blond adolescence. His face has uncertain cheekbones tending toward evening reds. Ten years ago he was given up by the specialists in the Lima Hospital of Neoplastic Diseases. Made mute by throat cancer, Don Andrés Rúa refused to have his larynx removed—"I will leave this world with everything I brought with me"—and he returned to the jungle resigned to die. Back on his property, he came across Don Javier. With no hope at all about his cancer, he limited himself to consulting Don Javier about a circulatory difficulty that painfully affected his joints. In exchange for boarding with him for a few days, he was prescribed an infusion of garabatokasha, a spiny vine abundant in the trees of that region. Drinking daily from that golden water, Don Andrés Rúa healed not only his circulatory afflictions. To the amazement of the cancer specialists who incredulously examined him, the garabatokasha had stopped the death gnawing at his throat. When I was introduced to Don Andrés Rúa in the bar of the Grand Hotel de Souza, in front of the Central Square of Atalaya, he could already drink cold beer and smoke fearlessly, and he laughed and spoke with a voice only distantly scratchy.

And now, let's hear Félix Insapillo's story, from the strapping, coppery, proud godson of Don Javier:

"That afternoon, I was traveling to Pucallpa. I had my seat in the airplane already reserved. I was flying for the first time. My godfather, Don Javier, wanted to give me that experience out of affection. Since it was early, to kill time and to say goodbye to this jungle, as I thought I was leaving it forever, I decided to take a stroll. The previous night I had dreamed about Juan González. Juan González told me not to travel; he told me that in the dream. But I did. I took a stroll as you see me now, without boots or machete. I got lost because of my pride in thinking I knew everything. I followed a wide path for a long time, looking here and there to the better-looking branches, saying goodbye to them. I considered returning, and did turn around to go back when the sun was burning bright in the middle of the sky, directly above me. I looked upon a madhouse: an infinity of identical trails spread before me, crossing each other. Partly guessing, I picked one. Praying that it would be mine, I walked and walked. Worse. Then I heard the noise of my arriving airplane. I went faster. I became tired, without avail. I kept going. Nothing. Before I realized it, suddenly it was dusk, and I told myself: Félix, you are lost, now more than ever you must be Insapillo. You must be the son of your father and your mother; you must remain calm. Because you should know that even the smallest animals can smell fear. If you let fear take you over, you are a dead man. The tigers will hunt you. The rattlesnakes and even the bees will hunt you. And I sat to one side of the trail to breathe deeply, to calm myself down. Slowly I became calmer. I searched for a tree to sleep in before it became dark, away from the reach of wild animals. The snakes already began to be heard, invisible among the dry leaves on the ground. Their rattles murmured. I selected a tree, a medium-sized young charicuelo. I climbed it. There I spent the night, tied to the highest branch with a rope I used as a belt. I hardly slept. I came down with the first light. Again I walked and walked, but this time I began to eliminate trails as the Campa do, the Ashanínka, cracking small branches to the right as I went, in the direction of my travel. In that way, when the trails appeared to confuse me again, I could tell, thanks to the broken branches, which trails I had already traversed and which I had not. I discarded trails until sunset. Again I selected another tree. Because the night came so suddenly, it gave me no time. I had to climb the nearest one, a medium thick one rising next to a tzangapilla. Have you ever seen a tzangapilla? It is a beautiful plant. It is a bush that produces only one flower, a single one, and that flower is enormous, with an orange color and a delightful perfume. And it is a hot flower. The skin of the tzangapilla petals is warm, just as you're hearing it. That flower is very hot. It appears to be more an animal than a flower. When you cut it, it begins to cool very slowly, gradually losing its perfume as well. As they lose their heat, they lose their aroma—or vice versa, it is the same. Once cut, once plucked from its stem, the tzangapilla flower doesn't live more than seven days. That happened to me. A week after I was lost, my soul began to get colder. I started losing my courage. I lost all hope. I had to hurry. Drawing strength from I know not where, I climbed the nearest tree, just to one side of the tzangapilla. Darkness prevented identification, but judging by the wrinkles of its bark, I believe it was a tortuga-kaspi. The cursed tree was thick. At least it was crisscrossed by ropes, its trunk covered by chaotic hairy vines. Holding on to them, I began to climb. I barely reached the top with a little breath left, sweating and cursing. It was then I lost my belt, a rope newer than this one I'm carrying now. It was so high that perhaps it was not a tortuga-kaspi. Could it have been a machimango? Perhaps. Because I was received by a pleasant odor when I reached the height, as high as possible. I leaned against one of its branches, half dead from sleeplessness and hunger and close to suffocation. I could not sleep that night either. A tremendous itch invaded my shoulders, the back of my legs, my neck, and my waist. I almost jumped in desperation. It was so dark I could not distinguish anything. I swept my right hand over my back, scratching myself madly in the full darkness, and smelled my fingers. They smelled of pure, stinking acid. That tree was the home of ants, a nauseating nest of ishinshímis, great ants that make up for their lack of venom with a fetid and painful sting! I wished that I were a bullet and the trunk was greased, so I could come down faster! I grasped a vine and I started to slide down, cursing. I don't know how in hell the vine broke as I was still grabbing it with my hands. And I fell all the way to the ground. It was night. I could not see. I could not judge the distance to the ground. That is why I crashed standing up, without bending my knees, like a poor ass, stiffer than a spear. I wanted to be a bullet, but it is so funny: instead of a bullet, I came down like a spear. That is where I damaged my spine. I doubled over with a pain that I don't want to remember. With my face lying on the soil I heard the snakes—ssssss! ssssss!—very near, surely disporting themselves on the wet grass, dry and wetted by the drizzle. And I could not even stand up!

"I could not stand up for several hours. To this day, I don't know why the snakes did not bite me. Finally, when I could stand the pain, I rose halfway and thought, the only way out was to keep on walking. I had no strength left to climb trees. I walked and walked in the darkness, feeling my way with my foot to avoid straying from the path and going deeper into the woods. I searched for hard soil, for the hardness of the compressed soil in the path, shunning the softness of the grass, which would lead me nowhere. Walking in this way covered my face with cobwebs. Several hours later, sleepy against my will, I leaned on a pomegranate, which had a strong, nice smell. There I was bitten by a vampire in this arm. It was lucky that I woke up, because these vampires are noiseless. They are not betrayed by their wings or their bite. Their saliva first numbs you, and they need not suck your blood. With their saliva they also put an anticoagulant in the bite and your blood oozes out while you feel nothing. I was lucky to wake up, thanks to the fact that again I had a dream about Juan González that night. I dreamed I was floating in midair, floating just before falling down, with the ground far below me, when Juan González peered out from behind the sun and said, 'You have to walk.' I told him, 'How could I, with no path below my feet?' He shouted, 'You have to keep on walking!' and pushed me with his right hand, which was very warm—and his hand was a tzangapilla flower. It was the smell of his hand that woke me, frightened and not comprehending. I started walking again, holding my wet sleeve, my shirt warmed by the blood. Somewhat farther on, I came across a clearing in the darkness, a black space full of small fixed lights like eyes that were watching me. Fireflies, ayañawis, eyes-of-the-dead, they could not be: they did not twinkle. Neither could they be tiger's pupils, so close together. I panicked. I was frightened and at the same time controlled my fright. If they smell my fear, they will kill me, I thought. I reached out to the closest little lights; they did not move. I touched them; they were branches. I breathed deeply and felt relieved. It was moss that accumulated on the cavities of dead trees, moss that is nothing during the day and goes unnoticed, but at night shines better than one hundred little lamps. I went back to walking with confidence, always feeling my way with my foot in the darkness. I came across a creek, drank like a madman, and lay down in the grass. Then I remembered: if I follow the course of the creek, sooner or later I will reach a bigger river. And if I reach that, I am saved. Some traveler or some fisherman will rescue me. I waded into the water laughing, and went walking over the stones in the middle of the creek. I was so confused that in order to know which way the creek was flowing, instead of using a leaf I tore off a piece of my shirt and put it on the water. I could not see. Touching the strip of cloth that was moving, looking through my fingers, I could determine which way the creek was flowing. I walked with water up to my chest, sometimes over my head. I walked and walked, until I could hear, very near in front of me, the roar of the Ucayali. I was about to hurry when I noticed that the creek ended. The accursed creek ended some miles before entering the river—it dispersed into a gigantic swamp! It was impossible to continue. I remembered that swamps are full of snakes. And I also remembered that all the creeks, all of the ravines, and also the smallest rivulets in that area are inhabited by the small, black, deadly venomous viper called naka-naka—and by another, even more ferocious one, called the yaku-jergón! Trying to cover up my fear, I began to backtrack along the creek. I went for hours, fighting against the current, thinking I would be killed at any instant by a snake. Finally I arrived at a clearing, left the creek, and collapsed in the grass, in surrender. I give up, I said. But no. I am confused. What I am telling you now happened days later, on the seventh night. Let the critters eat me, and I fell, unconscious.

"Some time later, I thought of my godfather, Don Javier. I very clearly remembered that one time he told me, 'Godson, when you are in trouble, call me, fix your thought on me, and call me with confidence and I will help you.' I closed my eyes and began to call him. I remained that way for a long time, with closed eyes, lying on the grass, calling him. I felt nothing; I heard nothing. I opened my eyes and saw nothing. I raised my head. Then I saw!

"Then I saw through the ceiling of branches ahead of me a multitude of yellowish lights, like oil or kerosene lamps, over the huge trees. 'They must be my friends,' I said to myself to give myself courage. 'They must have hung their lanterns in the crown of the highest lupuna to orient me!' And I started walking in the direction of the lamps.

"Later, entering another clearing in the forest, I could have a better look. They were not lamps. It was the moon, shattered, very high, behind the branches! 'Accursed moon!' I yelled, knowing well that it was not the real moon I had seen but only its reflection in my soul, the reflection of the lamps—what my hope wished to see. I collapsed, this time forever, on the grass. But right then, immediately, I thought that Don Javier had made me believe that they were lanterns, that they were signal lamps, so that I could return to him. In that way, driven by an idiotic illusion, I kept walking toward the moon. It was not, however, an idiotic illusion. It was the moon of my godfather that was lighting my way and dictating my path. I did not walk in vain. Farther on, I was stopped by laughter. The laughter came from the left, and one could hear it clearly. It was the laughter of Don Javier! I deviated from the path that led in the direction of the moon. It was a full moon. I shall never know why it shone so in that sky, because it was not its time. Neither shall I know why I could never see it in the previous nights or those that followed. I followed a very narrow trail to the left. 'At this hour of night!' I wondered, 'at this hour of night my godfather is living it up. Surely he must be with a young woman,' I thought then, forgetting that my godfather could not be anywhere around because he was waiting for me in Pucallpa. And in spite of days without food or sleep, seven days of fasting like a sorcerer, feeding myself only with a piece of plantain and with ravine water, I moved resolutely toward the laughter, forcing my way between the branches and pushing away vines and bushes I could not see.

"I could hear the the laughter more clearly every time I became discouraged. When I heard it I recovered my determination. I went after it with renewed persistence, and I heard the laughter ever closer, sharper, clearer.

"That was the way in which I returned, safe and sound, when everyone had given me up for dead."

4

Iván Returns,
Bringing Us a Deer and a Child

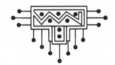

This is the Urubamba, insatiable and unsociable, the red Wilkamayu of the Inkas!

The Inuya ravine, prostrate, facing downward as if drinking from the Sacred River, pretends to be napping under the sun. Our canoe interrupts it; penetrating it with five meters of screw-wood, splitting in two the warm current, scaring away macaws and herons upward and eels, fish, turtles toward the bottom. In the prow of the boat, César jokes, pointing out all the dangers: malevolent trunks, sudden shoals, the hypocrisy of stone banks lurking under the water in the straits of the Inuya River. To the rear, near the rudder, Iván guesses at the most propitious course, domesticating our evil-tempered ship. In the center of the boat, seated between the two brothers, above the pervasiveness of the jungle and the motor, I lean over to a sign from Félix Insapillo:

"Three nights upriver, we will arrive at the mouth of the Mapuya. The Amawaka will have seen us by then, long before then. Someone may give us an indication about their chief." And turning toward the greenery growing to our right, as if he were no longer addressing me: "But if he doesn't want to see you, if he doesn't want to receive us, surely nobody will tell us anything."

"Every male will know, if he is an Amawaka," Iván had informed me. "That is why all males are chiefs. They already know that we are coming to see them, and they also know why. They can smell souls from afar."

"That is quite the way it is," insists Félix Insapillo. And always alert to crumbling riverbanks, to gigantic sliding trunks, to forested shores rising and rising as our canoe advances, and always talking to no one, he consoles me:

"But he will like you, I believe. The chief will like the depths of your soul."

We sleep at the edges of the Inuya for another three nights, inside crumpled mosquito nets in the sand, in small elevations, abutments of perfumed earth. Four nights we cut the current. More than once, in order to get through the rapids of the river, we have to step out of the boat and pull it with ropes from the shore over a carpet of marooned trunks. Trunks are immersed in the mud banks, with branches sticking out like waiting lances! Threatening trunks from above, unexpected columns like gallows! Fallen trunks with water to their necks were worse than collapsed bridges! Kilometers of trunks! Almost the whole of the Inuya is a fearful cemetery of trunks! And when we think the worst is over, we approach the rapids, the difficult traverses, the rock piles on both sides, which annoy the waters, provoking their wrath into swells, infinite boiling spots, and quiet whirlpools beneath the deceiving calmness.

In spite of everything, we surge ahead and ahead. Each time more narrow and opaque, the river canyon suddenly opens up, exposing itself in a rendezvous of convoluted waters. It is the Mapuya, of tricky currents, penetrating to the Inuya, moving like a pendulum! And the canyon of the Inuya rings out in the afternoon, resists, then rings out louder again!

"Hold on tight!" orders Iván. "One has to know how to enter the Mapuya! Insapillo, you lead us now!" And he reconnects his whole tense body to the board that serves as the pilot's seat. César leaves his seat in the prow to Félix Insapillo, and the canoe motor suffers, surrenders to one bank, and almost parts with the Inuya, searching in the waters for a long time for the entrance to the Mapuya River, disguised by deep vortexes with a slow, yellowish slime. Finally we enter the Mapuya and leave the swaying behind us. Something like thunder passes under the boat, something stuck as if in ancient shells: molluscs turned into stone, seashells millions of years old. The perforated song of the Mapuya, the last defensive frontier of Amawaka country!

Félix Insapillo unexpectedly points with his hand to a landing. Our canoe becomes encrusted on one bank of the Mapuya, in the middle of reddish mud. We step out and are stained up to our thighs. Hounded by the voracity of swarms of flies and by the mantablanca humming in our ears, impatient and with naked arms, we climb up a stretch of riverbank. We build a hearth of leaves and dead branches and make a fire for whatever coffee we have left.

Iván disappears into the woods, petulant, with only one cartridge in his hunting gun. The rest of us collapse over the sparse grass. How much time went by? I slumbered, I believe, half aware of the afternoon as an inert barrage of colors in the bloody wind, when I sensed a creaking behind me.

I scanned the tall bushes.

It was Iván reappearing, pushing aside vines, tangles of leaves, and spiny tendrils to make room for the body of a deer. He dragged it by the hornless head, too young, blasted by the shotgun pellets. He approached, panting, throwing the body of the fawn in front of us as he opened his eyes to make a sign I did not understand. He went back to the bushes, partly opened again the curtain of vines, scratched himself again, opened up more vines, and said something with a distant voice. Someone replied from the shadows. An instant went by. An eternity went by. A small native came out of the bushes.

Iván brought him to us and again opened his eyes in a sign. This time we understood: he was asking us to remain silent. Flustered, we concentrated on the task of slaughtering the fawn. Iván did not allow it; he did it himself, immediately. We cooked it in silence, and we ate in silence. I tear a piece of meat with my hands, and look at the boy on the sly. He hasn't stopped observing us for even one moment. When we have finished eating and don't know what else to do, or what else to say, or even where to look, he abandons his reserve, comes near the dying campfire, tears a piece of burned meat and takes it to his mouth, looking around him, and chews it, smiling now and then.

I distribute cigarettes. We smoke in silence.

The boy's cheeks—is he eleven, nine, thirteen years old?—the cheeks are painted for either celebration or war. They are striped with karawiro and appear before us in full regalia, plowed by the achiote with red, disquieting scars. The native boy finishes eating, stands up, and wrinkles his eyes above a big smile. There is no doubt that his face is an invitation, echoed by his hands. And we do not need to have Félix Insapillo or Iván Calvo translate his quick and rasping words, because his whole presence speaks to us. He is welcoming us with his eyes, with his high and tattooed cheekbones. We forget our last doubts in the shore, in the campfire that Insapillo disorders and puts out with a stick, and in the boat mired next to the guns, which I rapidly unload and hide away inside the rolled mosquito nets.

The figure of the boy already becomes indistinguishable in the background of the forest, high above the riverbank, walking away silently. We hurriedly follow him. César and Insapillo go in front, wielding machetes to widen the trail. I turn toward Iván, who is straggling behind, contained. I verify in his eyes that the boy is a messenger from the Sorcerer of Sorcerers. And unable to believe, I finally believe it: the inaccessible, legendary Ino Moxo, Black Panther of the Amawaka, has extended us his welcome.

5

A Dead Tree Forbids Our Moving On

"Can you hear the river rising?" The voice of Iván sounds in front of me.

The trail chosen by the Amawaka boy seemed to head deep into the woods—but no, two hundred meters after crossing a sort of portico made of branches, the trail turned parallel to the riverbank, peeking over the greenish black waters of the Mapuya through the cracks in the vegetation. Obeying the snaking path, after we had gone one hour or two, I began to think that it would have been better to go that stretch in our motor canoe, to save our poor bodies more stress. Soon I was to be grateful for the boy's decision. The noise of the river was becoming a din as we walked along, and the riverbanks were becoming ominous, rising in walls of black, moist, shiny clay. I almost felt a certain nostalgia for the fear I had when I discovered the thunder of the Urubamba, because the Sacred River, whose muddy bottom attenuates its stubborn waters, imposed a type of music of wider riverbanks but more honest and languid. The song of the Mapuya, however, seeming to get narrower, truthfully developed an edge over a bed of fossils, scandalous stones, and whirlpools, malicious gravel from time immemorial. The gullies, until recently timid, became insolent cliffs. The current became a maelstrom covered with trunks—with crocodiles pretending to be trunks, inert and mired in the clayey bends, or taking the sun lying on the sand of white beaches. Our craft could not have overcome those obstacles, so tricky was the Mapuya.

"Can you hear the river rise and rise? If we had continued in the canoe, we would have gone under at this point. Do you hear?"

Paying more attention to the puddles and roots barring my way, I followed Iván in silence. Did I mention that I was the last in the file? Before him, barefoot, Félix Insapillo tracked César, hurrying, jumping, and stumbling, trying not to lose sight of the Amawaka messenger.

An aroma of pomarrosas hit us, and we stole some of the fruit at random without stopping. Somewhat farther on, we had to feel our way like blind men. The forest provoked a brief night when it suddenly became mercilessly dense under the thick ceiling of vines and leafy crowns. We glimpsed moist noises, stagnating perfumes, invisible fruits and flapping of wings, which turned the path into a disquieting, undescribable tunnel that we traversed on all fours, afraid and in wonder.

The voice of Iván oriented me in the darkness:

"The narrows of the Mapuya are guarded by immense snakes, huge boas forty or fifty meters long, called the yakumamas. In Keshwa, *yakumama* means the Mother of the Waters. Do you understand? There is no reason why such a lean river would produce such a din, such a thunder of terrible currents. It is the yakumamas that produce it."

Insapillo's voice, which I had not thought was so near, interrupted him in the shadows:

"I have seen yakumamas in the lakes, but never in the rivers and never so far up on the Mapuya. In the lakes, the yakumama will give birth without warning to whirlpools, to muyunas, tempests that overturn boats as large as houses. I have seen them swallow fishermen as if they were fruits."

"Might you be mistaken?" Iván's jeering voice provoked him. "Maybe it wasn't a yacumama that you saw but a koto-machácuy, the two-headed serpent. Because the koto-machácuy lives only in the lakes, very deep in the lakes. Don't you know that?"

Insapillo was about to reply but couldn't. Only his snort cut through the end of the darkness in the tunnel. Just at the exit of the part of the jungle condemned forever to darkness, where the path again became a path, widening and becoming reconciled with the burning sky, we faced a new impediment: the incredible enormity of a fallen shiwawako tree, covered with moss, roots, leaden spiders, and mold, rising in front of us and barring the way like a greenish melancholic wall. Only a few bayucas—stinging green, white, pink, yellow, and red caterpillars—ventured their phlegmatic, poisonous, imprudent slowness over the surface of the shiwawako. The extremities of the fallen tree were lost on both sides of the trail under two confusions of spiny bushes and ferns:

lace made prestigious here and there by one or another orchid as if in the ruins of a conflagration that happened long ago. The Amawaka climbed the dead tree in an instant. Iván followed him, then Insapillo, cleaving the bark with hands and feet as if with hooks carving steps. We followed slowly, climbing one over the other, chaining up toward the top of the wrecked wooden wall and clumsily falling on the other side. We regained our trail, upholstered with loose vines and with dry leaves rustling wet. It had not even drizzled, but the enormous trunk was moist. Fat drops fell from a sky broken by a fearful sun. I looked up: the drops didn't come from the sky. Rain from another time, accumulated in the crowns of the trees, now uselessly fulfilled its duty, flowing intermittently and senselessly, sliding in vain like the tears of the dead.

"The first man was not a man; he was a woman." Don Javier unexpectedly continues his story.

6

Don Hildebrando Reads from the Air a Book by Stéfano Varese

Don Hildebrando mistreated the package of black cigarettes, took out the least damaged one, and lighted it.

"That is what Inganiteri told me the last time I stayed at his house, a handsome house next to the beginning of the Unine, the largest house he ever had in the Great Pajonal."

"In the Great Pajonal?" I happily asked. "A friend of mine lived there for a long time."

"I know," Don Javier interrupted me.

"Did you know him? Do you know Stéfano Varese?"

"No, I've never seen him."

"Some months ago, he published a book."

"I know," Don Javier again intercepted. "It is a study dealing with the Campa, with the life and customs of the Ashanínka."

His looks gleamed behind the smoke and the voices coming from the tavern facing the Ucayali River, there in Pucallpa, toward the surrounding forest washed or smudged by the moon.

"I've never seen that book, but I know it—I know it very well."

I turned my face toward the window, repainted in yellow, in black: the shore in front was tinged with blue like an underwater landscape, with no convictions of wood, or of the breathing of anyone, or of earth. Don Javier returned his gaze to our table, combed his lean beard with his fingers, and hastily drank his third glass of brandy.

"The thoughts of well-meaning people live in the air. They inhabit the air as we do our houses. Before they are placed in books, and only by thinking them, and even if they are never written, they already live in the air. Maestro Ino Moxo revealed to me that ideas are recorded better in the air than they are in notebooks." And, pointing to my tape recorder, "And they keep better than in those gadgets. Even before we are born, every-thing is recorded as in a tape—a silent tape. It is magic that puts sound in the lives of men, that is the way it is. As I was telling you, they keep much better than in those machines and they last much longer: an eternal beginning. Because the air belongs to everyone. Perhaps it is the only thing that nowadays belongs to everyone. The sound of life. And without our knowing it, without our understanding it in our heads, the ideas and souls of ideas that inhabit the air nourish us and encourage us. Maestro Ino Moxo taught me how to read the air, to distinguish and select the thoughts that live in the air. We must now be very clear, my friend Soriano. I have never seen that book by your friend Varese you told me about. Nevertheless, I have read it several times. For example, it doesn't matter if one day they were to burn all of the copies of that book, because the thoughts, the doubts, the certainties of the person who wrote it, like generous, great truthful spirits, live in the air, and they belong to us."

"What Don Javier told you is true," confirmed Don Hildebrando with his head lowered, slouched on a bench that blocked the way. Like all other dwellings in that area, Don Hildebrando's house was raised one-half meter above the ground and supported by stout huacapú beams. Thus it was protected from snakes, far above the floods unleashed by sudden rains or by the senseless damming-up of rivers. Just by climbing three steps, one gained safety. To the left of the shadowy room, in front of the altar of polished wooden triangles, it was impossible to avoid bumping into the bench with the waiting sorcerer. In order to come in, you had to go around it. Certain participants, especially the foreigners, always arriving late and incredulous, sometimes brushed by him while he remained immutable. Were it not for the mends in his lead-colored shirt and his pants of uneven drill, and seated as he was with his short legs crossed in an X and the toes of his broad, muddy feet wriggling, any careless newcomer would have taken him for an oriental clay statue or a funerary package, mummy of an Inka recently embalmed. He appeared to me more as the shadow of no *one, sitting there silent and painfully motionless—eternal almost—next to the frame of the door, in his pitiful hut, which sounded and smelled like a forest in the night of Pucallpa.*

"It is true. The house of air is the house of life. Nothing dies once it enters the air. The souls of all times, the knowledge and the feeling of all times, including the ones that germinated before our first ancestor appeared, the souls of always noble and dangerous ones, high and low, are better than planted in the air. There they may grow or stop, but they never die. At this very moment they are there, within reach of people who prepare themselves and are able, who merit it. It is all there, intact: everything that has been thought, even before human beings had thought. Everything that has been written is there. All of the books are there, in the air. What Don Javier told you is the truth."

For an instant, the face of Don Hildebrando ceased resisting our eyes, and he rose, gentle and resigned, but his words were blunt and reminded me of the Inka Manko Kalli's q'ero.

"The same thing happens to me sometimes. That book you discussed with Don Javier, for example, I myself know too. In the same way, I have never seen it and no one has told me about it, but I know it. As a great emanation, as the breath of hidden flowers of tzangapilla, the thoughts of your friend Stéfano Varese have entered my blood—not only what he says, but also what he never pronounced, what he could not yet give form to in the air, his pure thought."

Don Hildebrando closed his eyes forcefully, with even more force, and became lost in his peroration. He spoke strangely, as if he were reciting a text from memory or reading it. I began to think that the sorcerer was repeating word by word what somebody was dictating to him from God knows where. His voice was not his voice, and neither was his face. As he spoke he gleamed with the pallor of a dead man. Someone who was not him but yet was him and occupied his body, overflowing it without control, came out of his sleepwalker's mouth, saying:

"The Ashanínka, the Campa man, exists only as a transient on the surface of the earth, and no more. Death will end this transit and open the new way. But there are different deaths in the life of an Ashanínka, various states that allow him access to the mysterious worlds, to the sacred spaces. The dreams of sleep, the visions gifted by the ayawaskha, can open entry to these worlds of the beyond. In the jungle itself, the small

*lagoons, a pomegranate hugged by vines of garabatokasha, the stone trail
that covers the bottom of a ravine, a dead shiwawako, the sound of
laughter in the woods, the skin of rivers which peels off like a mosquito
net cover, a thousand lamps in the night which are not lamps, over the top
of a lupuna which is not a lupuna, the rocks, the caves of the jungle, the
clearings in the bush—all are just so many doors that open up to those
worlds, those worlds untouchable by the hands of a material body. The
virakocha—the whites—do not understand those doors. For the space of
four hundred years they have known only how to mislead themselves,
clouding their vision in so many things, confusing us with their thoughts.
The virakocha don't see; they have no eyes for seeing. They do not touch
the religion of the Ashanínka because they don't know how to touch their
own memory, not even their own past and future memory. An example:
the Campa, the Ashanínka, religiously await the return of Juan Santos
Atao Wallpa, their leader who rose against the Spanish conquerors around
the year 1742. The Campa have religiously awaited him for several
centuries, but the virakocha do not see that religion. Another example: an
Ashanínka exchanges presents, gifts, with another Ashanínka, establishing
a timeless relationship, a sacred commerce. They become ayúmpari—that
is the name they use to call those who enter in sacred commerce with one
another, ayúmpari—but the virakocha do not see that religion either.*

> *I have my hens at home*
> *I give them away when asked*
> *Because we never must be stingy*

"So goes an old Ashanínka song.

> *Rest at dawn*
> *sleep late into the morning*
> *do not separate your hands*
> *they will always open the window*

"So goes a song by Raul Vásquez, the Minstrel of the Jungle.
*"Because a Campa who does not generously give to others, like the
shore to the river, is set apart from the course of his nation. Not respecting
guests, not giving them gifts, not richly interchanging things with them,
means that the fluid uniting man with man will be cut. Because he who
receives gets an essence of the one who gives, and that would be danger-*

ous if there were no correspondence. Ayúmpari: *that is the word that defines the man with whom one engages in sacred commerce."*

Don Hildebrando stops. I scan the darkness trying to find him, not recognizing the moment candles give out. I can barely hear him breathing with the anxiety of the suffocated. A strange tension returns to lay siege to the house. It sways the capirona beams, the floor planks, the fragile, splintery walls. It must be the wind.

"That afternoon I was contemplating the Willkamayu, the Urubamba, from the heights of the Inka citadel of Pisacq, when I came across an old man excavating near the caves where our Inka grandfathers lay buried. I saw that the old man had a recently unearthed q'ero in his hands. He heard me murmur a greeting in his language and he sadly smiled, gifting the ceremonial vase to me with a word I have not forgotten."

"'Ayúmpari,' he said," my cousin César tells me. "That is what he said: 'Ayúmpari.'"

It must be the wind, I tell myself, while my eyes become accustomed to the dark. The moon unravels through the yarina branches that form the roof of the hut. I can make out the sorcerer sitting on the bench, a wooden pedestal, which miraculously supports all of his motionless body. His body, in opaque silence, is chiseled in the edges of warm light. Don Hildebrando leans forward, retreats, and lifts his forehead. His head turns as if it were screwing slowly around the imperturbable neck, very slowly. In that way, very slowly, as the sorcerer returns to his quietude, the house gradually ceases to tremble. A voice that is not Don Hildebrando's again opens his mouth:

"The world, coming from the hand of the god Pachamakáite, is impregnated with divinity. Nature is not natural—it is the creation of gods, it is divine. Everything that is in the world shares that condition, everything shares the powers, the great spirits that rule existence from the air. It is the same with words. Whoever pronounces words puts powers in motion. That is why the Ashanínka is forced to live in harmony with the powers of the world, of these worlds. The Ashanínka harmonizes himself with those powers in order to be able to hold within a single body both his material and spiritual bodies."

We, on the other hand, slowly climbed over each other, forming a chain up to the top of the dead tree that barred our way until we could finally go over it, triumphant and bruised, only to let ourselves clumsily slide on the moist bark, only to fall on the other side of the mossy trunk, on the same path! Even though we were in bad shape, we continued walking. I raised my eyes. The drops were not falling from the sky, parched by a fearful sun. Rain from another time, accumulated in the heights, now overflowed the tree crowns, sliding down in vain like the tears of dead men. Then we started to run on the trail, seeking to overtake the envoy from Ino Moxo. For several hours we could not find him. When we had almost given up, thinking we were lost, the Amawaka appeared behind us. A certain reproach flowed from his eyes. I now understand he felt sorry for us, because when we advanced pell-mell, zigzagging, avoiding branches, going faster, skipping over fetid puddles—truly we were not advancing. We were escaping. We were fleeing from ourselves, from the primal fear, from that useless rain.

> *Don Hildebrando observed the roof of his hut, which had ceased trembling, and lowered his face. As if he were surprised to see us there, he moved back while looking at us.*
>
> *"That is the way it is," he said to me with his own voice. "In the same way you see an island from afar—one of those islands that look like floating forests, and you know it is an island and you are familiar with it, and deep inside you know it is a forest full of trees and you know they are trees, although in the distance you cannot distinguish one tree from the other—in that same way I have seen the book of your friend Varese. I have known it in that way. I have seen his ideas as forests, even though sometimes I may not have picked up exactly each and every one of his words."*
>
> *Don Hildebrando turns his head again, breathes air that is dense, immense, and warm, wafting the fragrance of hidden tzangapilla flowers, and rears himself up on the stained bench.*
>
> *"That is the way it is. Whoever pronounces words puts powers in motion, unchains other powers and other words in the air, never to know their end—infinite powers. Words are not just words. In the same way the world, this earth—all the real things we see or dream—are more, much more than what our eyes can reach whether we look within or without. In the same way, I would like you to receive what I have told you in these four days. It was more than just words; it was a good gift that I owed your cousin César. I have today been able to pay off that debt, thanks to you. When he gave me that sacred vase of the Cusco Inkas, he was really*

giving me a lot more. Since then I have been indebted to him. He became my ayúmpari. Now we are even."

And he apologized for having to leave. He said we could stay longer in his house but could not visit him the following night or the one after that because he would have to recover. His material body needed to sleep for several days; his spiritual body for several weeks. And he left dragging his feet, bent, with defeated arms, like a convalescent, very slowly.

The last night in Don Hildebrando's house in Pucallpa was not a fortunate one. In the midst of meditation, everyone seated around his altar of three triangles and long after we had strengthed ourselves with the Water of Serenity, one of the patients waiting to be cared for after the session ended, a pallid and paunchy half-breed no older than four years, began to cry in his mother's lap. Without opening his eyes, Don Hildebrando extended his right hand in the direction of the child and traced a design in the air. The child quieted down. The sorcerer's hut, shaken by dark gusts, had almost recovered its normal quietude, a contagious omnipotence, when the child's cry again rent the silence. Don Hildebrando's hand sliced through the air three times more, and each time the child became quiet. Finally, alternating between screams and laments, he gave in to unstoppable sorrow and fear.

"You will have to wait outside," the sorcerer gently addressed the mother without opening his eyes. And without moving his lips he began to sing one of his icaros, a magic song of calling.

> *"Ibáre pawane*
> *Ibáre pawane*
> *Warmikaro yamarerémo*
> *Yamaré Yamarerémo*

My memory became joyful as I thought of the first icaro I ever heard him sing: a magnetized healing song.

> *Ira Ira Iraká*
> *Kura Kura Kuraká*
> *Epirí Ririritú*
> *Yamaré, Yamarerémo*

Putting aside the cadenced syllabizing of the icaro, which became deeper in the mouth of the sorcerer, getting lost in rugged resonances, I thought I had found a clue. I tried to understand it as if it were Spanish.

92

"Kura Kura Kurakà" perhaps was nothing other than an appeal to a
certain spirit to fend off the disease: *"Heal Heal Heal here."* And *"Epirí
Riríritú Yamaré Yamarerémo"* could very well mean *"I will call, we will
call Spirit."* I am not aware of what alien powers touched me then. I left
my place and went toward the crying child. I felt powerful and dizzy, as if
several souls possessed me. Master and simultaneously slave of all of the
powers of the real, of a mystery without limits, and obeying I know not
whom or what, I caressed the child's hair and whispered:

"You will fall asleep now, little one, quietly. You will fall asleep now."
And I closed his eyelids without touching him, brushing with one finger the
air next to his face. The child fell asleep immediately, and I tiptoed back to
my place. He remained motionless in the arms of his mother until we
finished the session.

In parting, I requested the opportunity to talk further with Don
Hildebrando a few months after my return from Atalaya, after my hoped-
for interview with Ino Moxo. Possessed by an evident restlessness, as if he
were shooing away an evil thought, Don Hildebrando turned and gave me
a brusque "no." I headed for the door, more with damaged pride than
surprise. The sorcerer stopped me with a gesture that did not fully emerge
from his bent body.

"There is a certain order in the architecture of the air," he said,
annoyed. "A certain hierarchy exists, which cannot be altered. Not only
the benevolent spirits exist in the air. There are also great souls that
generate harm. And when someone interrupts that order, those evil spirits,
which are very powerful, take advantage and percolate through that
architecture, which has already cracked. They anticipate the pure souls,
and they fall as fire upon defenseless humans. In those cases, even though
no one else sees them, I can. And I have to make a great effort to contain
them, to prevent them from coming in. I have to rise against them, since
only I can sense their presence. After defeating them, because that is my
duty, I may remain without any strength to do anything for many days, as a
pile of debris, as an empty cushma."

Only then did Don Hildebrando's eyes meet mine:

"Tonight, and only because of irresponsible vanity, something which
I do not understand yet, ignorant and without any right, has violated the
hierarchy of the spirits that live in the air. Something has disordered the
architecture that must be perfect even in the midst of its imperfection. It

has cut the curve of the spheres. I don't know it well yet, but I have felt. During all of this session I have had to accumulate within me all of the strengths. I have had to resist the battering of the stained souls. From now on I will have to meditate more, concentrate more, because I have sensed the harmful spirits descending, going round and round outside. They are still there. To disband them completely, to send them back to where they came from, I will have to concentrate deeply. I will have to start at the beginning, before the beginning, as if time had not gone by. As if no time had gone by, over the earth or among men."

7

We Learn That the First Man Founded the Campa Nation and Furthermore That He Wasn't a Man

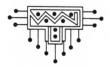

"The first man was not a man—he was a woman," Don Javier tells me, entangling himself in deep laughter.

Discrete in stature, already hesitating between strength and stoutness, when Don Javier doesn't speak he laughs with his whole body and even with his shirt, printed with insolent flowers, and with his bottle-green pants, which stretch and resist. He is seated at a table in a cane chair, in this dusty bar smelling of sugar cane and tobacco and urine and beer and cheap perfumes, facing the Ucayali River, here in the outskirts of the city of Pucallpa.

No one knows how many years are hidden by Don Javier's face. His olive hands are excessively soft, as if they were gloved by a child's skin. No one knows when he began to practice, or who was (or were) his teachers. But people in the villages receive him with fiestas. They overwhelm him with consultations for sicknesses, which he diagnoses and happily cures. The young woman looking for her husband, the child possessed by a spell, lovers with unrequited love, the fisherman bitten by a viper, and the old man who coughs too much—they all have confidence in the wisdom of the amiable eyes of Don Javier. His eyes are barely more brown than his face and less brown than his lips, which are always telling stories gathered from the old wizards of the Amazon nations. They say *that they place their confidence only in Don Javier—a risky confidence justifiably inaccessible to others.*

"Tales that I was to learn at random, by sheer luck," he tells me, "tales I learned when my soul was young and I knew how to lose myself among the tribes and I listened quietly to all that was said, and even more quietly to what was not said. . . ."

This wandering witch doctor, given to chasing women, lacks the resignation of Don Juan Tuesta, the haughty helplessness of Don Hildebrando, and the clear enigmas of Ino Moxo. He is rather closer to Juan González in thinking of diseases as being cured by joy and not by herbs.

"It was not a man—it was a woman," he is now telling me. "And that was told to me by my Campa friend, a healer who was very famous and whose name was Inganiteri. Inganiteri in the Ashanínka language means "It is raining." For ten years now, Inganiteri has no longer rained. He decided to die, and to return to the earth. But shortly before that, he could inform me about the way in which human beings were first born. It was not as you may think, as you shall see. My friend Inganiteri told me that thousands of moons ago, when even the moon was only a piece of a dead trunk, in that time everything was ashes. God was not even born then, and the earth was all ashes. And light, and the stars, and air—look, air itself— and the forests, the waterfalls, the rocks, the rivers, the scrublands, the rain, the small lakes and the endless ones, and health and time and animals that creep and those that fly or walk, and the rocky places, the beaches—everything that now exists in its own way, according to its condition, what we can see, and what we do not see, everything was nothing. And that nothing itself was ashes. There was no sea; the oceans were also empty places, full of ashes. That is how the world was when suddenly lightning came down upon a pomarrosa tree. And the pomarrosa tree was ashes; it was not yet a pomarrosa. Inganiteri told me that in that instant, from that tree, that burned pomarrosa tree, which was split by lightning, a beautiful animal sprang up. The trunk of the pomarrosa opened in two, like a flower, and from the inside came the first true being. It was an animal without feathers and without scales, which did not have a memory. And the first shirimpiáre, the first wizard chief, who was already alive at that time even though he did not have a body (he did not have anything but was dissolved in air), the first shirimpiáre

was very surprised and told himself, "It is not a bird, not a fish, not an animal. I don't know what it may be, but it certainly is the best work of Pachamakáite." As you know, Pachamakáite is the Father-God of the Campa. Pachamakáite is Páwa, husband of Mamántziki, son of the highest sun, the noon sun. The first shirimpiáre, then, thought for a long while and finally pronounced sentence: it must be human. That is what the number one shirimpiáre concluded after giving it thorough thought, and he decided to name that animal Kaametza. Kaametza in the Campa language means "She, the very beautiful." So we began with Kaametza, a female. As soon as she sprang from the pomarrosa tree, she began to search. She thought she was walking, and it was true she walked the jungle, crossing forests of cold ashes. But actually she wasn't walking; she was searching, though she did not yet know for what. Thus was Kaametza walking and searching for years and years, when one afternoon. . . . "

Don Javier pretends to look for the bottle of sugar cane brandy and refills the glass he has just emptied. I accept two sips from my glass while the sorcerer goes on talking:

"I told you 'one afternoon,' emphasizing it with the same intention that Inganiteri used with me only to be precise, so you can better see what I am remembering, because in those times there were no afternoons, no mornings or nights or noons. Time passed, but it was different from the one we know now. Time was also ashes and had no limits, like a river with three shores. Only much later did it become tame; it divided and did what the Urubamba, the sacred river of the Cusco Inkas, would do at a later time. In that era, time did not get tired and lie down to rest as people do. It wasn't as it is now, cut up in pieces. Today only some sorcerers, katziboréri, or smoking sorcerers, shirimpiáre, are able to make that time come back, but never for more than one night or perhaps two full nights. They make it descend from the air. They bring down those pieces of time that are passing, dispersed and orphaned. They join the pieces together during many nights of concentration, after fasting two or three weeks. During those days they eat only a plantain baked over charcoal and drink only creek water. They remember, repeat, or invent the strong prayers, the magical songs, the precise icaros, the most appropriate and powerful invocations. Then time returns as a loving cloud or silvery pollen and again occupies the House of the Called One. Maestro Ino Moxo is one the few shirimpiáre who have the gift of convincing time to return to its original state so that it can fulfill its first function. You should know that before, when Pachamakáite had not yet determined that Kaametza would be born, time did not serve to frame the cycle of the living. It was not its job to fix the passage of the living into the dying and the dead into what lives again in a different form, eternally. No. The first function of time was to manufacture happiness, to prevent harm in this life and in the other lives beyond. If something or someone was taken over by evil and filled up with it, time made that something or someone stop growing. It did not kill it, because death had no space in the conditions of that epoch. It just stopped it, which was worse. And simultaneously it enlarged the greatness of the great. It developed the spirits above. It gave a young spirit the experience of one thousand years. Don't forget that it had three shores—it could come and go at the same time and was quiet at the same time, fixed. The landscapes moved on both sides of it, returning and advancing toward the sea. That is why Maestro Ino Moxo, when he is under a cloud, once he has strung together those pieces of time and has made them descend, already insufflated by little silvery winds, then feeds his understanding with that ancient pollen. He multiplies the population of powers that live and work in his wisdom, fills his memory with the intelligence of thousands of lives, strengthens his power of seeing."

Only one table retaining any appearance of activity is left in the bar. There are three customers, obsessed less by the excesses of alcohol than by the disdain of that young woman with too much makeup and a dress with a low breast line, whose copious laughter presides over the ruins of this evening in front of the Ucayali River. Don Javier looks at them with mercy, with a scant disdainful curiosity that hesitates between the breasts of the woman, returns to the window, and observes nothing.

"One afternoon, then, in a creek that was also ashes, Kaametza went to see her reflection, or to drink, or to wash. She leaned over the still waters of the river coursing down these three shores, and from the heights of the jungle surged an awful panther, a black otorongo, bellowing. At first she remained motionless, though she was without fright. Did she know? Would she have known what fright was? what a furious otorongo was? Everything was eve and presage in the soul of Kaametza, a great dark and innocent afternoon in her understanding. Claws she could not distinguish or imagine. No words were formed in her mind, no names for anything. But thanks to that unknown knowing, the unconscious, which we still *possess even today, Kaametza understood enough and she eluded the otorongo. The otorongo again pounced upon her, its claws exposed and ready, like splinters of heated stone. And Kaametza again eluded it. Again and again the black otorongo tried to capture her, but its claws only grasped despair. And Kaametza discovered a giant fear inside of herself. She understood the closeness of death. Without thinking or attempting to do anything, she pulled a bone from her body. From in front, next to her waist—look, right here—she extracted a rib as if obeying someone, without pain or bleeding and without leaving any scar or open wound. Wielding her bone like a recently sharpened knife, she sliced through the neck of the otorongo. At this point, I remember well, my friend Inganiteri, who was telling me this story, closed his eyes and remained silent, motionless, listening. Something was coming from the depth of the woods, from the creeks that were sounding nearby, joining the waters of the Unine. We were seated at the entrance of his hut, to one side of the kaápa, the small hut he had assigned to me, on the little staircase of three thick timbers. We were looking at the forest moving in front of us, beyond a patch of cassava that marked the beginning of his property. The edge of the first sun of the afternoon was hitting the round, tamped-down patio, cleared of vegetation. But it wasn't because of the light in the patio that Inganiteri closed his eyes; it was because he spoke to me of the black panther, of that great otorongo. The face of the Campa healer aged from pure tension, increased by wrinkles on both sides of wide cheeks. After a moment he trembled. It seemed as if his soul were returning from far away, very far away, and his neck enlarged, filled with bursting veins.*

"And he said that Kaametza fell to her knees after killing the otorongo. Gratefully, she knelt in the sands of ash, at the edge of that river, on its third shore, and contemplated the knife that had saved her. With her hands she brought it to her mouth slowly, very slowly, telling it things, almost kissing it, perhaps . . .

"Forgive me, Don Javier," I dare, interrupting his reverie. "Forgive me, but there is something I would like to clarify: when did chief Inganiteri close his eyes?"

"His eye," interrupts Don Javier, as is his habit. "Because Inganiteri—I don't know whether I told you—had only one eye. The other one was lost because of a wife stolen from him by Maestro Ino Moxo. He was blinded by an arrow in the midst of a war started expressly to recover her."

And he squints his eyes in the fog of the bar, against the smoke of strong tobacco and the bitter perfume of the mangos, the pomarrosas, and the yarina palms, which in the darkness overflow the borders of the Ucayali in front of us. The young woman's laughter has already deserted the neighboring back table. Don Javier bestows a condescending attention upon the three defrauded drunks.

"I'm sure he did it to remain silent," he murmurs. "I'm sure my friend Inganiteri closed his eye to keep himself from telling me any more. There he was, without seeing—he was speechless. It must be that something difficult, dangerous, forbidden to retell, perhaps must always be there in ancient stories. Speechless, then, speaking like a blind man, Inganiteri told me that Kaametza caressed her bone, perhaps lifting it to kiss it or perhaps to tell it gentle things, and the knife drawn from her body did not retain any blood from either Kaametza or from the otorongo that had scratched her. Kaametza thanked it with her breath, with the love of her mouth, gasping, and the bone was lit. It trembled like lightning you see but don't hear, lightning that knows only how to produce light. (Have you seen it? When it rains in a nonrainy season you see lightning like that.) And she released it as if it were burning her hands, and Inganiteri told me that the bone began to turn around, growing in size like a drowned man gasping for air, occupying a form that was already in the air, that has always awaited it as a destiny in the air, and which gradually resembled Kaametza more and more. It momentarily became dull and returned to brilliance, becoming the shadow of a tree on fire, a shady pomarrosa tree, the stone of an animated tree, an old footprint on a large boulder. It imitated the eyes and the arms and the hair of Kaametza, as if the body of Kaametza had always had a mold there in the air waiting for it. Then it retreated and again advanced, shining, gasping, and searching—searching for differences in the air, differentiating itself from the correspondences in Kaametza, and finally quieting down and triumphantly stretching itself upon the beach of ashes, in the darkness, identical to and different from Kaametza."

Don Javier downs in one swallow the last of the brandy in his glass and remains another moment looking at nothing, my anxiety increasing.

"That is how the male appeared. That is how we appeared. And the first shirimpiáre, who by that time already lived lifelessly without a body, and who was observing everything from the air as a witness, was happy

and decided that man should live. He decided that it was good that man
accompany woman and that together they should reproduce and also
gave him a name. So that he could continue to exist, he gave him a name,
pronouncing it loudly from the air.

"'Narowé!'" he named him.

"And the first male, hearing the name that the god Pachamakáite
had approved, continued sleeping. He continued to sleep, but blood began
to move all over his body and air entered his blood, impregnating his
heart with the lights of generosity, spreading strength and courage over his
muscles. It gave him a soul and words so that he could open the doors of
the worlds, including those that cannot be seen with the eyes of the
material body, so that he could be thankful to the gods and to men and so
that he would know how to make war and to work and to make sons and
so embellish the earth.

"'Narowé!' he called him, which in the Campa language, in the
Ashanínka language, means 'I am' or 'I am who I am.'"

The three customers at the back table have returned to drinking
loudly, and they laugh and argue without noticing us. I invite Don Javier to
smoke a cigarette, slowly, underlining my gesture and encouraging him to
continue his story. His right hand sketches a refusal upon the palpable air
of the bar, but his lips separate, are about to speak, become discouraged,
and show an absent nostalgia, a half-smile. Suddenly I think I understand.
I think I finally understand.

I still remember his departing smile, the obstinacy of his tight lips.
Through the clouds of a strange drunkenness, however, I kept on hearing
his voice. Dizzy as never before, irremediably bound to a whirlpool of
hummings, heats, and shadows, I surrendered. I suspected that it was not
Don Javier but the air, the voice of Inganiteri himself, already deceased,
insisting in the air, who was telling me the story of Narowé and Kaametza.
I broke down upon the table, abandoning my forehead over my arms. The
last thing that my memory could retain from that night was the vision of
my own head bent over, collapsed next to several empty bottles of brandy,
as if I were to return through the arch of my crossed arms to the first
moment, to the time when time was not the passive computer of the
inevitable, not the builder of ruins and guide to death, but the fabricator of
beauty and happiness.

I sank into an unconscious sleep as in the waters of a known and *forbidden lake. The trembling of a net awakened me, dragging me back to the beach. It was not a lake; it was a river. I saw Kaametza on the third shore, luminous and naked, upon the black blood of the knifed tiger, in the presence of the sleeping Narowé. I tried to approach her, but the net again captured me and returned me to waters that were ever darker, warmer, clearer. With my last strength, nearly asphyxiated, I tried to free myself. The net enlarged, with tentacles secreting a whitish glue, and wove itself into invincible boas that surrounded me and forced me to the bottom of the waters of the river, which was now again a lake. My head came to the surface and I screamed. Nothing was heard in the air; my voice was empty. I verified that my body was also an open space, merely the location of a body. Finally sinking, with my eyes covered with salt water, I could see Kaametza on the shore, a statue absorbed before the repose of an awakening Narowé.*

The boas, the net's tentacles, loosened, lied, insisted. But it was not a net. It was a hand shaking me, two hands holding my shoulders. The bar manager was waking me up with apologies—everyone had left long ago, and it was almost dawn.

I stumbled up, paid for the brandy bottles, left into a morning that began to insinuate itself from the other side of the Ucayali—its third shore—behind a double file of bamboos or perhaps bloodwoods. I do not know how I could have walked so many blocks to reach the Hotel Tariri. I only remember that in the reception lobby, pretending to look over the board hung on the wall where the room keys were placed, I was welcomed by an unvanquished smile of complicity and two open arms: Don Javier.

8

How Light Was Created Above the World

With my face already under water, finally sinking in the lake, which had again become a river, I managed to open my eyes. I saw Kaametza on the third shore, watching over the awakening Narowé.

Kaametza was the first thing Narowé saw as he came from the void, she and the sun. But that happened inside his soul, before his first sensation, before his first knowledge, beyond his heart. Because outside, in the beach of ashes where they both were, over the forests and the sky of ashes, the world was in shadow. Pachamakáite, the Páwa, the Father-God of the Campa, had already created the moon and the stars but had not yet assigned them the function of light. Everything was the color of the dead night, of the skin of closed night. And time was a torrent without channel or direction, absolute and eternal.

Nevertheless, Narowé saw Kaametza and could distinguish her clearly. He rose and went to her, and she welcomed him, all-knowing. Opening, she let him come in. As the Inuya River penetrates the Urubamba River, in the same way Narowé entered with a great sound, all of the tempests of his body fused in a current full of ardor going backward, lying, returning, insisting, just as the Inuya would, if the Inuya had the hardness of a canoe. And Kaametza was sky. She became sky so that the sun born from her body, ascended and burning through her body between two noons, could return and fall again toward dusk, mixing its white light with the blood of the sky. Embracing, obeying themselves supremely, Kaametza and Narowé created life. They glued existence with gleaming, bleeding glue. Everything was clean. Without boundaries, their plenteous bodies were like tongues flicking over themselves in a single deep and salty honey.

Over the blood of the black otorongo, tumbling in the same slow vertigo, they knew love. On that still warm blood, there they made love. They discovered their bodies, the fire and the sadness of bodies, and the void (not the first ash, but the other one that offends after conflagrations), and silence, and the idea of the inevitable, of the death that inhabits everything living—they discovered it all.

At least that is the way in which Inganiteri told it to me. And he said that Kaametza and Narowé climaxed together, together. And in that climax, exactly in the moment they climaxed, light was created in the world.

"From that first climax in the first love, light was born, light was created over the earth," Don Javier tells me.

9

Don Javier States That He Is Only Sixty Million Years Old

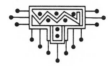

He asked me to please carry his drum very carefully. Have I told you that he prized himself as a musician above his innumerable mortal occupations? Did I tell you that he also was a percussionist, a cajón player better than most? Almost all of these players bang that sort of sonorous cube, that cedar drum, and draw out the cadence of vertigo by force, the channel for dances that lie sleeping under the face of the instrument. Not Don Javier. His fingers extract neither music nor rhythms from the instrument, but when he plays it almost appears as if his fingers were the music and the rhythms. Vacillating, I went after Don Javier to the bar and dining room of the Hotel Tariri, where in the midst of the inevitable traveling businessmen, stripteasers, military men disguised as farmers in their Saturday clothes, and other solicitors of drinks and smokes, leftovers from the night behind swarms of flies, we breakfasted on fried meats and onions and mashed plantains, restoring ourselves with great big cups blackened by a very sweet and bitter brew containing no coffee except in name.

"Kaametza and Narowé created light while making love, and it was thus they founded the Campa nation, our first humanity, the Campa people."

He put his drum aside, stood up, took out a bundle of folded papers from a pocket, and reviewed them with exasperating slowness. "Here it is." He handed me a piece of old newspaper.

"This article refers to a human footprint found on a crystalline rock in the Ascope region. They sent samples of this rock to determine its age, to determine the time when a remote man stepped on that rock before it was a rock, when it was soft and the foot could be imprinted on it and kept as such until our time. They sent samples to the University of California. In that newspaper clipping you will find the answer. Could you read it aloud?"

The rock samples from Ascope, sent by Dr. Juan Luis Alva for analysis, correspond to a hornblendic graneodorite, which probably has been extracted from the Longitudinal Andean Bartholite. The absolute age of this Bartholite has been determined by Professor D. Jack Evernden of the University of California, who has assigned it the age of about 60 million years.

"Do you see?" Don Javier was excited. "Is it that human beings already existed sixty million years ago and left their tracks here, stepping on a rock that was not yet a rock but only clay, witnessing clay?"
I pretended not to have heard and continued reading:

Research on blood groups by Dr. César Reynafarje, Director of the Institute of Andean Biology, confirms the thesis that man originated in the Americas, or at least that man also originated in the Americas. In Peru, there are fossils of primitive animals and vegetables, like the ammonites and algae, as well as a whole spectrum which includes fossils of developed animals and vegetables. Therefore there is no reason to doubt the autochthonous origin of American man. What remains to be discovered in Peru and the Americas is not one but several missing links. Dr. Reynafarje's research reinforces my opinion, since he has determined that the Campa and the Tzipíbo aborigines of the Peruvian jungle do not have antigens A and B, which are found in the blood of all the other races of the world.

"There, you see, my friend Soriano!" Again Don Javier became more excited. "Could it be that our forefathers were Campas? Don't they have the oldest blood in the world? Wasn't Kaametza our true Eve, and Narowé our true Adam? Could it be that the American Earthly Paradise is really located in the Great Pajonal?"
Finally he ordered me to please continue reading. The article by Dr.

Juan Luis Alva, published on page 7 of the Sunday Supplement of the
Lima newspaper El Comercio *on June 20, 1977, ended as follows:*

> Could it have been that American man originated in the Amazon re-
> gion and from there moved first to the mountains and then to the coast
> heading to both oceans?

"*And you must take into account that there are Campa populations*
not only in Peru. Campas live also in Venezuela, in the Guianas, facing the
Caribbean."

"*It is almost finished,*" *I tell him;* "*there are only a few lines left.*"

Because in the petroglyphs of Jequetepeque Valley, perhaps the oldest
anthropological records that exist in the north coast of Peru, monkeys
stand out as cultural elements of maximum importance.

"*Imagine: Amazon monkeys in petroglyphs found facing the ocean!*
And in the middle of the jungle, ten kilometers away from the the the central
plaza of Tarapoto, a friend of mine, the archaeologist Wilson Leon Bazan,
has discovered other petroglyphs where one can see not only figures of
prehistoric plants and animals but also very clear graphic symbols—
symbols of a type of writing which we are not yet worthy of deciphering. I
was in Tarapoto not long ago and saw those petroglyphs in the area called
Polish, scattered stones trying to say something, tattooed with profiles of
dinosaurs, snakes, gigantic birds, and signs, many signs within God only
knows what order, what secret system similar to the Inka killkas. They
have also found human fossils buried next to the Polish petroglyphs. I saw
a millenarian human skull, looking like that of a monkey but human. And
I have seen identical petroglyphs in San Tosillo and in Shapaja-Cerro San
Pablo, and in Jara, near Moyobamba, and also in Chazuta and in
Achinamiza, with the same drawings as those discovered on the coast,
where they found that human footprint in the rock, that track from tens of
millions of years . . ."

Don Javier quieted down and contemplated his cajón. He drummed
on it almost imperceptibly with his fingers and again raised his wide smile
to me:

"*You will see it for yourself. When you arrive at Atalaya you will see*
even more ancient testimonies. In order to visit Maestro Ino Moxo you will

*have to go through the Inuya River, and after that the Mapuya River, and
then the Mishawa River. The whole bed of the Mapuya River is littered
with petrified animals! With your own eyes you will see, and with your
own hands you will touch, those stone fish! Shells millions of years old,
gigantic medusas transmuted into stone, immemorial messages from a
time when this jungle was not a jungle but the bottom of the sea, when the
sea was over us and we did not exist, and the sea was ashes and everything was darkness, and Kaametza and Narowé were not born yet!"*

10

A Certain Bird Devours Entire Cities

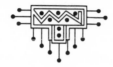

Hunger stopped us, rather than the approaching night. We camped there shortly after encountering the Amawaka youth again in the fretful space allowed by the maze of wild canes, which resemble the sugar cane in width and appearance but not in height: these could boast of no less than seven meters.

Ino Moxo's envoy spoke for a while with Iván, spurned the trail, and entered the bush, returning immediately with a pukuna—a long blowgun—which I assumed he had hidden there as a precaution when he came through that spot on his way to meet us. The length of the pukuna easily exceeded two meters. The Amawaka gazed at it with meticulous silence, letting his eyes and his fingers linger over the tubular, veined surface. He looked for a long while through that orifice, blowing through it repeatedly. He approved the horizontality and sharpness of the darts crowded together inside a container of colored bamboo; uncorked another shorter one, very thin and full of a thick black substance; dipped the tip of three darts in it; and covered it up again. Iván helped him crown the nonpoisoned end of the darts with pads of hairy, yellowish cotton, and after both of them had performed those preliminaries without looking at us and with ceremonial solemnity, they entered the grove behind the cane field to the left of the Mapuya, as if hypnotized by the unmistakable racket of a family of monkeys.

While waiting for our two hunters to return, and following last-minute instructions from Iván, we cut thick branches and hard staffs, the hardest and youngest we could find in the area, and as many canes as our arms would allow. Hours later, curled up at midnight, we understood why our refuge must be solid: the choshnas and the tuta-cuchillos, huge apes, spent the night dropping fruits and branches on us, imposing and invisible on the high trees, shouting and harassing us until daybreak. Had it not been for the hut under which we attempted to sleep, the cover of beams that Iván had us connect with vines (a precaution and demand I felt exaggerated), we would have succumbed buried under the cascade of sticks and brawlings of those owlish monkeys.

Iván and the Amawaka suddenly returned; looked at us panting, tired, and spent over the grass and collapsed among the machetes and the cut branches; and broke into uncontrollable laughter. Their derision finally subsided, and they showed us, with less pride than malevolence, the agonizing bundle that was to be our dinner.

Some time later Don Hildebrando advised us about the poison used by the Amawakas in hunting. I even had the occasion to test its effectiveness: it kills in less than a minute and apparently without pain. Only a medicine man was authorized to prepare it. The potion, absolutely harmless to a white man (which I also had occasion to verify), was extracted from a plant that grows abundantly at the bottom of wooded mountains traversed by the Mishawa. Maestro Hildebrando did not tell me the name of the plant. Nevertheless, I was able to see how he sectioned the bark and scraped its outside, leaving it whitish but later darkened by contact with air. Then he peeled it off in splinters into a pot of boiling water. As the contents evaporated Don Hildebrando replaced them with more water. He did this seven times. The last time, having already extracted the remains of the bark, he boiled the extract until it was reduced to a lazy, brown viscosity.

A single drop of that glue, accurately aimed by the Amawaka's pukuna, was enough to kill the stout monkey, the makisapa being flayed by Iván, which in its bare flesh seems to resemble one of us. We help speed up the quartering of the corpse, regardless, and we put some pieces in the fire. And eat them without regret.

Our refuge, without a doubt, had to be solid.

At daybreak, even though the choshnas and other nocturnal monkeys were still throwing sticks at our lodging, the Amawaka youth decided it was time to renew our march. Did I say that his face was tattooed with achiote, the sacred paint used by natives to protect themselves from enemies visible and invisible? Amawaka males cover their nakedness only with a string around their waist. They use one of the ends of the string to tie to their penis, which they carry upward, against their abdomen. And achiote stains not only their cheeks but also their chest, their arms, and their thighs. Ino Moxo's envoy, however, wore a cushma long enough to reach his ankles, attire allowed only to sorcerers. Even more surprisingly, it was a flaming cushma. The Amawakas as well as members of some other Amazonian nations, when some mission requires them to be in the woods for more than two or three days, abstain from bathing if they are naked or dress in special ancient cushmas, never washed, if they are following healing fasts. The cushmas blend into the stink and the colors of the deep jungle, so that the animals and souls aren't made restless by the smell of man. This Amawaka disconcerted me with his impeccable yellow tunic. Through Félix Insapillo, and assuming that we were going to go deeper into the forest, toward the mountains, and definitely away from the Mishawa, I negotiated a delay with the youth so I could return to the river.

The sharp whistling of a tiwakuru, fussing about nervously in the higher branches of a flowered wimbra, guided us to the river's edge. In the bend of the Mapuya, a medium-sized black bird, with a beak as yellow as the base of its open wings, was shaking a mass of feathers over the water.

"It is a wapapa," brooded Iván. "It is fishing."

"It is true," added Félix Insapillo. "That is what they do. That bird has three spikes in each of the wing joints. With those spikes, it penetrates through the bark of a tree called a katáwa, which has a poisonous sap."

"The wapapa moistens its wings in katáwa sap and then submerges them in the water," said Iván. "You will see. Pretty soon the fish will come up."

"Stunned by the poison, the fish will float."

The wapapa left the river, walked lazily a few meters, stood guard on an outcrop of disturbed land, intently observed a stretch of water that was already fatally turbid, and froze in position. It was a strange statue, waiting. One could say it was plumed with tranquil anxieties, and it was completely undisturbed by our proximity. Its victims appeared, many dying tails flapping in vain. The unlikely fisherman parsimoniously jumped from the red border, entered its water trap, lifted a fish in its beak, even more slowly returned to the shore, laid it on plain grass, reentered the river, and repeated the task. Without the slightest hurry it repeated the job until the water was cleared of fish. Only then, and always absorbed in a calmness that was beginning to rattle me, it began to devour them with a delicate meticulousness. Not even the din of our jumping and diving bodies next to it managed to disturb the wapapa. It continued to eat and eat while Insapillo, Iván, César, and I were bringing up from the bottom of the Mapuya the remote medusas, the great shells Don Javier had talked about, the gleaming gray oysters, the petrified sea horses.

"From a time when everything was ashes, and everything was dark, and Kaametza and Narowé were not yet born!" he repeated over the tables of the Hotel Tariri dining room, which had gradually emptied. He was speaking coarsely, with opaque words, which he pronounced as if underground, as if he were in the inside of a rock, masked by a sudden majesty.

"There in the Mapuya, you will be granted knowledge about how it was that sons devoured their fathers, how the virakocha exterminated the Indians. In what perverse way and with what a cold manner they still poison the oldest race on earth, our present and living ancestors! You will be granted knowledge about the real reason, not the pretext, that brings so-called civilization to our jungle. Because what represents progress to whites is regression to Indians. Rubber was gold to the white men of yesteryear, but to Indians it meant extermination. To the white man of today, petroleum is life, but for the Indians it is ruin, plague, and displacement. You will truly see who have been, and are in reality, barbarians, who are the cannibals, and who are the Christians! Listen to me clearly, Soriano: If you get sick and need blood, I donate mine and save your life. But if I give my blood to a Campa Indian, or to a Tzipíbo, I kill him. Because their blood is different. It is different, do you understand? What for us is existence means for them something worse than death. And it is the same with all creation; it is the same with rocks and plants and animals. Air, for example, is vital to birds, but to fish it is asphyxiation, the black swipe of the wing, the beak of death."

We piled up the fossils far from the river's edge to protect them from the slides provoked by floodwaters and rainstorms, trusting that we could recover them on our return. Again we headed toward Ino Moxo. Before entering the woods into which my companions had already gone, I stopped and turned my eyes to the prodigal Mapuya. I'm not sure what I perceived upon its waters: a certain bloody radiance, something like an unquenchable light staining the dauntless currents. The wapapa kept on eating on the shore, immune to the katáwa poison that had destroyed so many lives.

"To you will be granted knowledge of the truth, the lying face of truth, and the timeless truth. You will see the three shores. The glow and the shadow of the blood of time, the time which is one and all. What was true yesterday will not be true tomorrow. The same ancient time that brought us death brought us the life to come. Listen to me well: the air shall be water, and water shall be air. Everything, absolutely everything is in reverse. Everything is in reverse, always. And the water, which is the air of fish, shall drown the wings of the Evil One."

Don Javier is speaking to me with a strange voice, as if another person has inhabited him for a long time and is only now coming out through his closed mouth. I believe it might be the voice of Inganiteri—but no. As I later verified in Amawaka territory, on the night that Ino Moxo offered me ayawaskha, in the midst of visions I again heard that voice and recognized it without surprise or doubt, and I knew who was really speaking to me that morning in the Hotel Tariri. I knew who was speaking to me right now from the mortally still, gray lips of Don Javier.

"It is now time, and I can tell you the the rest of the story told to me by my Campa friend, Inganiteri. And now you are able to hear it. Let us return to Kaametza, where we left her. No. Even better, let us return in search of her husband, the first man, born from her body for the first time. More than anyone else, he needs hope and companionship. And I will. immediately tell you why. You will learn when and for what reasons he turned inconsolable, he who before then knew only happiness: Narowé."

I dove into the bushes where my companions had vanished. I advanced only a few meters, hesitated, made up my mind, and returned to the Mapuya. The wapapa kept on eating on the shore. I silently approached it, prepared my gun, and aimed at its head.

I hesitated.

I made up my mind.

I did not fire.

A limitless calm occupied my memory and lightened my body. I entered the woods almost flying. Three hundred meters into the woods I bumped into Iván, apparently returning. He hurriedly tried to explain something—I don't know what—with a seemingly guilty voice. And turning his head again to the trail, a little farther ahead of me, he said without stopping to walk in the direction of the others, "I heard your shot. Only I heard it. So I came back looking for you."

II

Don Javier Tells Us About Babalú, the Black Man, and of Others Buried in the Sea

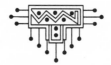

"I will tell you sometime of a fisherman friend I had in a small port called Eten, on the sands of the north coast, well to the north of Lima," says Don Javier, turning toward the door through which no one comes, the wasted light of noontime riding waves of dust. I don't know how many customers have come in and converse dimly in the back of the bar, behind the increasing airlessness besieging the Hotel Tariri from the street.

Pucallpa: thousands of wooden huts not so much disseminated as flattened, raising straw-covered fronts in the outskirts, over mounds of insects cut up by dusty alleys. And tens of two-story houses, painful mirages of mansions with overflowing gaudiness, behind which bake the mistresses of smugglers, wives and step-children of equivocal pioneers and rubber men, heirs of lumbermen and heirs to no one. And several buildings made of concrete and steel, more stupid than ovens stuck in an oven, disfigure by themselves the business center of the city. Stores and bars, stores and bazaars, hardware stores and radio stations and restaurants are strung along the baking avenues of dust. Foreign music, strident and sterile, jumps from the bars, from flea-infested movie theaters, from air-conditioned offices where big industrialists languish—those with black-ringed eyes who fabricate cocaine—and high officials from the armed forces, musty and stately bureaucrats. The music competes with the racket of the motorcycles and the broken-down taxis in the ups and downs of dusty routes that are not consoled by rain but are turned by it into muddy traps. But today there has been no rain. The fatal yellowish breath of midmorning enters through the windows of the Hotel Tariri. Don Javier rises from the chair and sits down on his melodious cedar cajón. His fingers caress the face of the wooden box as they slowly, slowly touch it, and the instrument sounds as if it remembered something with a hidden sadness.

"I will tell you sometime about Babalú, the black. That was his name: Babalú, the name of some African divinity."

Don Javier's hands fall off the cajón, but it continues resounding a few moments more, in debt to coarse echoes.

"Sometime I will tell you of the singer, dancer, cajón player, and guitar player by necessity and by blood, who died of tuberculosis, some believe. But I well know that he died of music. With the feet of music he reached death. Constant late nights, patriotic feasts, familiar or for no special occasion, finally made his body, unreachable in another time, fall prey to misery. His face was reduced to a single black circle around his eye. At least Amador Escajadillo, fleeing Lima because of the injustices attached to justice, sought refuge in Port Eten and took residence less than one hundred meters away from my friend Babalú. There, in Port Eten, Amador Escajadillo became in a short time cook, owner, provider, cashier, guardian, waiter, and often the only client of the Pregnant Sea Bass, the best restaurant there at that time. And if that were not enough, one day, in addition to naming himself notary of that location, Amador Escajadillo appointed himself as spiritual guide to my friend Babalú. It was good, because by falsifying seals, dates, signatures, the unexpected attorney concocted a last will and testament that the late Babalú's creditors, even the toughest ones, recognized as irrefutable. In that document it appears that three years before his death, Babalú legally favored or *had legally favored* his female companion as "sole universal heir." The owners of the bakery, the meat shop, and the three bars in town had to resign themselves to getting old without getting paid. My friend's widow refused to sell anything to pay the debts, so she not only inherited but retained all the assets. All of them: a hut with mud and straw walls mercilessly drilled by the wind, a guitar sans strings, three small fishing nets and one torn big one, an infinity of fish hooks that were smart enough to fish for themselves according to Babalú, a broken little dog called indistinctly "Waskar," "Admiral," or "Blueblood," a book of poems by Nicolás Guillén, which we all recited by memory, and the obsession of his hands and his whole life: a dilapidated and hoarse cajón.

"Unmistakably coughing up blood, toward the end of a spongy drunkenness, Babalú had tried to comfort his wife: 'If some day you don't hear from me, partner, then listen to me.'

"According to Notary Amador Escajadillo, it was not that but another confused promise my friend Babalú had made, and it was more than a promise—it was almost a demand: 'Listen to me only when you stop hearing me.'

"It might have been that way. Babalú was inclined to utter worse, strange mutterings in his later years, when too much bad drinking put him out of commission. It might be. Many different things are bandied about now. The only thing I'm sure about is the sadness.

"Unbearable days, slower than weeks, followed the affair that attempted to disguise his funeral. A sorrow without limits filled Carmela's existence—did I tell you his widow's name was Carmela? In vain she tried to numb herself by working to excess for others, cooking the anemic rations of night fishermen, sweeping the restaurant for Notary Escajadillo (which was only a short block away from Babalú's hut—did I tell you?—a little behind, also facing the sea). In vain my friend Carmela did everything, needlessly. She thought she could fool time that way: mending school uniforms, taking over the most untransferable difficulties of others, in the market, in the small square, during the scandalous hours in the port, on Sundays, when people came from Chiclayo looking for free fish and for cheap fresh seafood. Everyone lowered their voices when she dragged her feet over the tiles of the pier, as if their passage produced only sorrow and silence, as if the holiday mornings for her were nights of mourning or pure winter. But Carmela was stubborn. In vain did she get lost in coastal rocks, in vain did she return with baskets overflowing with crabs, in vain did she distribute them to the miserable hordes of children. In vain she washed and dirtied, and washed again and dirtied and washed and ironed the three shirts and the two pants of the dead Babalú. She could not prevail against sorrow. I remember very well the day, a Sunday night, when her eyes confused her soul as she faced the cajón belonging to my late friend.

"'Here he comes—he's coming! Do you hear him?' she cried.

"Truly, truly, I seemed to hear him coming.

"At first, I heard his footsteps, walking far, far away, then near. The steps of my friend were inside the cajón! Later I heard his hands, no longer in the cajón but in the sea! There, just as you hear it, my friend Soriano. The sound of the sea was different, with a precision and rhythm that could not be anyone else's but Babalú's. A musical Babalú was playing the cajón in the bottom of the sea! Am I losing my mind? I thought, and for the first time I noticed the cajón's color and I remembered Babalú's skin, darkly shining, and even those scratches on the board similar to his famous scars, one on his right cheek sliding toward his neck, and the other one on his forearm on the same side. 'Work accidents,' he boasted. Two bullies had decorated him in his youth, one night in two different taverns of the Port of Callao, for reasons that varied according to the audience. The last time I heard him speak about this, Babalú attributed the reason for both fights no longer to the honor of a girl from his town who was exerting herself in Ivonne's bordello, but to a disagreement in a game of dice. It couldn't have been. I pinched myself, and I remembered another set of three smaller scars, almost branches that insinuated a triangle on his chest. But the sound of Babalú playing the cajón was increasing outside, more and more clearly. Unmistakably it was coming from the sea. And in his cajón, inside the dilapidated hut where his widow and I sat in unified astonishment, we began to hear the waves. The sound of the waves began to clearly come out of his cajón! A melee of waves was issuing from the worn wood, favored by his miraculous hands!

"Sometime I will tell you how Carmela leaned toward the dirty cajón, which began to sound even louder, making the sound of a thousand waves together as if several seas were fighting between themselves inside. 'You will drown yourself, my friend!' I warned her. 'Don't go inside that cajón!' But what would she have thought—she would have told me that I was going insane, wouldn't she? That is why I remained silent. Later I regretted not having told her. I should have asked her; you yourself will agree with me. Well, then, I tried to stop her, but I didn't have time to. I didn't have time to? Perhaps I even shouted and she didn't hear me, couldn't hear me because of all that racket. On one side was the sea, so many seas bellowing in the cajón, and on the other side Babalú, the hands of Babalú playing the cajón nearby, ever closer, increasing under the sea.

"Carmela rose from the stool from which she had thinly pretended to endure my visit, opened a path between sobs, rejected the impossible, and lunged with wishful arms toward the cajón. Hallucinating, and wiping tears, she passed fingers over the wood, striking it with fear, then with disappointment, calling him: 'Babalú,' then with more fright, 'Babalú,' then with assertion. She fainted, calling him, 'Babalú,' calling him. I concluded that I should leave her alone. I emerged into the shadow of the beach. The sea no longer sounded—or rather, it did not sound like Babalú's cajón. You could barely hear it; again the sea sounded as it should. I turned my back, crossed the sandy area in search of Amador Escajadillo, and was going to tell him everything that happened. Had I gone mad? I was about to tell him everything when what was to happen happened.

"We both saw it. An inexcusably cold wind—it was February—pushed open the hut's door made out of hammered tin cans, dispersed the sands, and magnetized the woman in the direction of the beach. Notary Escajadillo and I were about to serve ourselves the brandies prior to the closing of the restaurant, as had become our habit, when something—a movement? a scream?—distracted us. It shone in front of us through the window, coming from Babalú's house: the red of a faded skirt, phosphorescent, heading to the water in the blackness. We saw her. We came out and ran in vain: the wife without a husband was already walking into the water. She was far in, and without hurrying, her arms extended in exactly the same gesture with which moments before she had come unhinged while advancing toward the cajón of her late husband. I saw her. I think I told her, but she didn't listen, 'Don't go inside that cajón!' How could I tell her such a tremendously absurd thing? But I should have told her, don't you think? And instead of warning her, I became afraid. She was playing the cajón in a strange way; from the door I saw her. She was not striking it— no, she was playing it softly, as if she were touching the head of a child (did I tell you she was childless?). In that way I left her, next to the cajón, playing it as if she were caressing a child that was dying right there, then, in that instant. I should leave her alone, I concluded, and I went out into the shadow.

"She went in. 'You should have warned her,' I thought Notary Amador Escajadillo was telling me, gasping, while we were running and running in vain. The husbandless wife, her hands already bound by the waves, kept going, motionless, toward the islands. She was barely a pink stain made of wool, an orange stain, blue and woolly, and she disappeared behind the mollusc-covered boulders."

Don Javier abandons his cajón and returns to the chair in front of me, opens his lips, hesitates, opens his uncertain hands over the table, delayed in the palpable and dusty air, and finally speaks:

"In that breakwater in Puerto Eten, every last Sunday in February, at the end of the night, not when the sea is arguing but later when it makes peace with the proud reefs, you can hear the sound of Babalú's cajón, clearly the same playing I heard that one time. But now it also includes sing-songs, reproaches, and joys, in a clear voice, the cajón of Babalú sounding louder than the moans of a woman in heat."

And again Don Javier briefly stops, considers a sigh, combs his thin beard, and looks at me without warning.

"This, which is still talked about among the old fishermen of Puerto Eten, and which perhaps I will be induced to tell you some day, is one of many stories that constitute your life, that give form to our life from the air. Even if we don't know it, and even if I were never to tell you about it, Babalú's life, from the air, also orders your life, from the memory that cannot be remembered. This is why it doesn't matter if you know it or forget it. Some day I will tell all of it to you. And if you wish, if you are worthy of it, you can verify it. If you go to Puerto Eten and you see dancing to the rhythm of a cajón, you can verify it. Because any time someone dances there, with violence and sweetness as the blacks dance, the waves begin to sound from the cajón. In any given moment the musician stops playing it, his hands as if dead, and yet the dancer continues dancing but now to the rhythm of the sea—the sea coming out of the cajón without anybody there. The cajón seems to want to burst open. If you ask anyone, they will tell you that it is Babalú, that Babalú asked to be buried in the sea. You will feel him returning through the foam of the cajón, and you will come out to the beach and in the shadow will feel him again, Babalú returning through the wooden cadences of the sea."

And suddenly raising his head, Don Javier changed his voice with incredible excitement. "You can verify it right now!" Again he stood up and leaned toward his cajón. "Look, I don't hit the wood hard either. Look at how very softly I do it. Do you understand?"

And coming out from behind a bitter smile, Don Javier began to sing:

> *Landó, Landó,*
> *black star and foam,*
> *landó, landó,*
> *black foam and sugar,*
> *landó, landó,*
> *black sugar and whiteness,*
> *landó, landó,*
> *black whiteness,*
> *landó.*
>
> *Be very careful, landó,*
> *remember where you came from,*
> *never allow, landó,*
> *your game to become tame,*
> *don't burn in vain, landó,*
> *dancing what seems right,*
> *always remember, landó,*

that you have only chains,
that you are not free, landó,
no matter how much you sway.

Give me the dance, landó,
give me your nipples and your belly,
give me your trust, landó,
stop the trembling of my pulse,
we will dance, landó,
the dances that are owed us,
in the open air, landó,
even if you scratch your forehead
with the stars, landó,
standing against the current.
Give me your hand, landó,
so that my machete won't tremble!

Landó, Landó,
black star and foam,
landó, landó,
black foam and sugar,
landó, landó,
black sugar and hurry,
landó, landó,
hurry, black, and bring light,
landó, landó,
landó.
Caramélame, Carmela,
Carmela, Carmelling!
Landó!

And giving himself up to pure rhythm, his torso reiterating circular distractions:

"I don't play the cajón, I navigate it!"

His hands drumming between spread knees, coming and falling, without coinciding and without contradicting themselves, as if they were the opposite of the same as well as the reverse, the two sides of an oar, rising, returning:

"I caress the face of death!"

And closing his eyes, gathering harmonies, balanced dissonances born at each turn of his shoulders, concordances that descended like snakes down his arms tattooed with oddities, scars, cadences ostensibly flowing from rhymed fingers:

"I embrace my friend Babalú!"

And suddenly quieting down, clouded:

"But I can no longer play the way he taught me. After he died, I began to play like this, silent, as you just heard, different."

And returning to seat himself facing me:

"Furthermore . . ."

And pointing to the cube of darkened cedar:

"This is Babalú's cajón."

Iván, with a distrustful aloofness suitable to those who live protecting some remembrance, looked at me in spite of himself, I would say with alarm, standing in the trail from the Mapuya. More than several persons and several lives seemed to inhabit him, as if the different parts of his body had divergent wills, which he harmonized into a single existence for the sight of others. Obeying his look, his face became resigned to flee. Then his shoulders turned toward the trail. Approving the movement of his shoulders, he then also turned his chest. Finally, like cats, his legs followed suit. After that, his feet, like a fighting couple, making up and fighting again but in silence, quietly crushed the grass, the branches almost disintegrating into soil. He talking to me:

"I heard your shot."

And without stopping his forward walk:

"That is why I returned to look for you."

I followed Iván, sweating, scratching myself full of mud and bruises, my back a bleeding mess, and the horde of insects harassing me. It was always my blood, never Iván's. He energetically went on ahead, and I saw the moon at noon, knowing that it was not the real moon but its reflection in my exhaustion. It was the laughter of Narowé, the first man, guiding me from the bottom of the river. I told myself, "You are already hallucinating— wake up." I told myself, "Wake up." Juan González said to me, "You have to walk," and I asked him. "How, since there is no trail under my feet?" because I was in the heights looking at a small earth, and Juan González insisted, "You have to keep on walking!" He was pushing me with his hand, which was warm and perfumed like the tzangapilla flower, and I woke up, and the hand of Juan González on my shoulder was not a flower but a vampire that was silently sucking my blood, and I told myself, "Wake up." A little distance ahead I saw what appeared to be Iván next to the tzangapilla, and I lunged toward him and abandoned my body over the squalid trail in the direction of that wall of bamboos and columns of smoke. Without strength to think, I thought that if I were to reach a large river I would be safe. But the river, I told myself, the river has to be the Urubamba, the Wilkamayu, the Sacred River of the Inkas, so that I may go up it to the mountains four hundred years up to before the arrival of the Spanish conquerors—the virakocha. And I understood then that Iván was infecting me with his personality made up of several lives, and I could distinguish the lives in my body—each person in my body—and I realized the same was happening with my memory, my memories, exactly as Don Hildebrando had forecasted in Pucallpa. I understood that the stretch of jungle was not merciless but rather a baptism that was demanded of me in order to reach Iván, to get to be, as he was to be—in I don't know what manner—one with the jungle: a single existence with the jungles and with the animals and with the stones, with all the peoples of the forests. And in that instant fatigue disappeared and my legs became lighter and the insects disappeared and I persevered in the journey but with joy. I no longer gasped for air. The woods were different and the sun lowered its voice, becoming slower, weaker than a lamp, when we reached the other members of the expedition.

Almost reclining on the earth, his back leaning against two rough roots of a lupuna tree, the Amawaka was biting a quiet smile. To his right, in the middle of the clearing created by the leafy lupuna tree, César was directing his attention to Félix Insapillo. The latter, standing, facing the sudden appearance of Iván and me, was speaking.

Iván, his shirt stained with insect bites, blood, cobwebs of trees and pieces of rain (I don't understand), stopped before them and turned his head toward me, or more accurately, to not see me. Don Hildebrando would state that it was not Iván who turned toward me but his soul, the eyes of his soul finally welcoming me back.

"But you are hardly listening to me, my friend Soriano. It seems to me you are somewhere else."

"No, that isn't true."

"You are surely thinking about Chief Inganiteri, about the story that Inganiteri told me."

"That isn't true, Don Javier," I lie again, and Don Javier looks at me closely.

"You are thinking about the Campa, the Ashanínka of a long time ago! Is that it?" And questioning me further with his gaze: "Yes, you are thinking about Juan Santos Atao Wallpa, in the rebellion of Santos Atao Wallpa against the Spanish conquerors!"

Someone who was not Don Javier, but who was Don Javier, was occupying his chair, seated in the chair at the Hotel Tariri bar, overflowing over him without control and coming out of his sleepwalker's mouth:

"For the Asharínka, who retain the fire of the great rebellion against the virakocha, Juan Santos Atao Wallpa never died. Only his body disappeared, spewing smoke; it dissolved in the heights of the forest in a yellow cushma, promising to return."

Don Javier spoke strangely, as if he were reciting a text from memory or as if he were reading. I even thought that he was repeating word by word what someone was dictating to him from who knows where.

"I am looking at the sun of my ancestors, this sealed well where one can still hear their invincible voices!"

"I don't understand, Don Javier," I wished to say, but his closed eyes frightened me, and his voice, which was not his voice, continued the peroration:

"Grandfathers with green skin who loved fiercely, and tenderly made war, and ate each other as fruit, and sorrowed in solitude hearing distant footsteps of animals! All of your luminous army of another time, today negated! Remains of your broken laughter now lie beneath the hooves of an iron horse! Beyond us, behind the twisted snows, a strange nation made of thirst and nothing collapses to the sky as gray alms, but from your shoulders rise forests and rain! The sun still shines, Juan Santos Atao Wallpa, since your youth! We are alive! Look! We are alive!"

Félix Insapillo, standing before the lupuna tree, was talking to César. "To drink ayawaskha," he was saying, "the first time I drank ayawaskha, it was seeing the face of the two persons closest to me, whose names I cannot mention and who were then very far away in Cusco. Only their faces, without deformation, with smiles that bring tears to your eyes. Huge faces, the size of my body, close to each other, laughing. And later, drinking ayawaskha, the first time for me was not seeing my godfather, Don Javier, who was seated right in front of me, but seeing only his spot, the spot where he sat, and behind him a pyre of ancient containers, blue and orange drugstore bottles, rough-surfaced and burning. Later, it was seeing myself rise and leave the house to vomit, while at the same time a

body that was my own body remained seated at my place, while I left and
vomited tzangapilla flowers, which elongated and became two-headed
snakes, koto-machácuys, which left my mouth and vanished on the way to
the forest, leaving a sad trail of sadness, a slow, yellowish slime. Drinking
ayawaskha was also looking at the functioning of my internal organs, my
heart, my stomach, to see how my lungs moved, my guts, to see how they
died. It was to walk in a huge room, in a wake for several dead, and to see
that the coffins were occupied by my friends, and all of my friends had
their eyes closed on the same face, which was my face. And it was finding
myself suddenly in a canoe, with only one oar which I did not know how
to use, in the middle of a gigantic lake, heading toward a group of lizards.
The lizards had eyes bigger than their bodies, and the sun was setting and
I never seemed to arrive. The first time I drank ayawaskha it was like
speaking and hearing my voice amplified, as if it were coming from those
speakers in the Indoor Coliseum of Iquitos when Raul Vásquez sings, and
hearing my voice outside, far from my throat. And it was seeing my whole
body prostrate, lying down on the floor. And it was seeing my godfather
again, but seeing him shining, shining, covered by a cushma made of
thousands of fireflies, and watching how he gradually turned gray, getting
darker, burning out as he spoke. If you are fighting a strong hex, my
godfather was telling me, what weakens you is fire. Your defenses will
weaken if there is fire nearby. This is why one shouldn't smoke much, or
light matches during an ayawaskha session. And it was seeing him
wrinkle up and sing like an old man. 'Visions, begin!' he sang, slowly
transforming himself into a woman with a child's voice, a newborn that
sang like an adult who had just been born in the voice of the icaro.
'Ayúmpari! Ayúmpari!' he sang. But more than anything else it was seeing
the Evil One, to see him three times in the same night, always dressed the
same way, arrogant. The Evil one had an admiral's stripes, the face of a
sick dog, and a blue-black coat with a penguin's tail. He had red pants and
an embroidered shirt with billowy cuffs, and a tremendous beard—a steel
beard like the armor of a Spanish conqueror. And it also was to see him,
at the same time, with long braided hair, and short poncho, the same as
the drawing of Atawallpa that appears in schoolbooks. Yes, the Evil One,
in my first ayawaskha vision, was Atawallpa, that bastard Inka who
helped the virakocha Spaniards against his brother the legitimate Inka
Huáscar. He had a very long sword, long and unsheathed, and he was

cutting off heads like flowers. The necks were warm like tzangapilla
stems. And the eyes of the Evil One, in the three times that I saw him
during my first vision, the black eyes of the Evil One were red and shone
in a cross, the same as a viper's eyes."

Don Javier, cracking his eyelids open with an endless gesture: "It is not
this that I want to tell you about, but rather about an old black man, Alfonso
Cartagena, now dead." He raised his eyes, and his head began to trace circles
in the air, gyrating as if screwing itself down on the imperturbable neck. And
as if he had just returned, Don Javier, this time with his own voice:

"I wouldn't be telling the truth if I told you that I personally knew Don
Alfonso Cartagena. Neither I nor anyone else could know him. I always saw
him from afar. As a child, I went with my grandfather on school vacations to a
place called Las Salinas, next to the town of Chilca, south of Lima. Old man
Cartagena lived beyond the bathhouse, beyond the third lagoon of thick, green
waters, in an immense cave opening toward the sea. His bed, an outcrop of
bluish porous stone, almost touched the roof of the cave on the back wall. Every
time the old man meandered along the beach, with a wire hook and a battered
cardboard box, and while he awaited the dubious fortune of a distracted fish,
we trespassers ventured inside the moist, mossy shadows of the cave. We were
never able to reach his bed. Below the bed, circled by three unlit candles, shone
a glass of water unevenly supported by three copper coins—old ones that you
can no longer find. We never dared steal them from that structure, which we
thought was a devilish altar. According to a mulatto witch doctor called
Baldomero, the only doctor in town, we found out that it was impossible to
know anything about old man Cartagena.

"'Trees are not fathers or sons' was all my insistence could wring out of
Baldomero. Nevertheless, because of someone's indiscretion (I don't remember whose), we found out about a certain visit that the old man had stealthily
paid Baldomero. In the wet shade of the sorcerer's hut, Alfonso Cartagena might
have unburdened himself of the reason for his troubles and his solitude to such
a degree that Baldomero could not but transfer some powers to him.

"'Make a cedar cajón, and another cedar cajón,' they say he told him. And
surely that is what happened. Because the day after the consultation, the old
man persisted almost desperately in a task. With love and fury he cut eight
cedar planks and caressed them by polishing them over and over until a mirror could envy them. With unsuspected obstinacy he overcame the distrust of

the abused planks, which finally accepted treatment inside a wine cask the old man had brought from Chincha, a land famous for its females and dancing athletes, sorcerers, and grape plantations. The last Sunday in March, right about midnight, he took four planks out of the red-black wine cask, washed them in the sea, and cured them, charging them with the strength of Yanachaska, which means "the Black Star of Dawn" in the Quechua language, and in Spanish refers to Venus. So that his first cajón would be worthy of the powers of the morning, and following the advice of the wizard, old man Alfonso Cartagena drew the following icaro upon the sand."

And on a paper napkin from the hotel's bar, Don Javier drew with a black felt pen:

"I saw it with my own eyes," he said. "The lines of the drawing, once impregnated though invisibly on the front side of the cajón, were later erased by the undertow. But Venus, the morning star, had already imprinted its character through the icaro upon the instrument, which was to become female because the first offspring of Alfonso Cartagena was to be female, named Rosaluz, and was charged by the impulse of Yanachaska, the Black Star of Dawn. The second one was male, its name was Benjamin, and it was charged by the rebuffs of the sea. That same night, inside the cave, the old man lit the three candles that protected the glass where the Lone Soul dwelt. Baldomero told me that the name of the Lone Soul is Elegguá, a divinity who accompanied the grandfathers of his slave grandfathers when they were brought over from Africa."

Don Javier stops in midsentence and takes in air as if he were breathing who knows what bitter memories.

"It appears that later on they brought no more slaves. Ostensibly, Baldomero told me, ostensibly Europe banned slavery, but its merchants increased the slave traffic. If a slave ship was surprised by a patrol in the high seas, the slave traffickers, to avoid being fined, dumped overboard their merchandise of moaning bodies and shackles. Baldomero told me that thousands and thousands of our ancestors cover the bottom of the Atlantic with their bones and their chains. And he told me that of course the slave business became less attractive. But with the sagacity that still characterizes our virakocha entrepreneurs, they discovered at least a surcease, if not a remedy, for their investments. They decided not to bring any more slaves but to manufacture them here, to avoid fines and losses. They brought only studs, sires, strong and efficient females and males. America was humbled by an infinity of slave factories. The fathers of the fathers of Alfonso Cartagena were born in what is Colombia today, on the shores of the Magdalena River, delivered in a stable for cows. Worse than cows, men. That is why old man Cartagena fished only from the shore, and never from a boat, and never entered the sea. But I was telling you that the old man lit three candles, with the smoke ritual united his children, with the smoke ritual over the captured water, upholstered with bones and chains where Elegguá lives.

He's going to sell me, he's going to sell me, so goes a song from that time. *He's going to sell me, what life will I lead?* And a shadowy echo of silences sunken in the sea echoes back: *The Virgin of Carmen will pull you through.* And that same night, Benjamin and Rosaluz became husband and wife. Their father begged them to try and be happy.

"*I was born in the shores of the Magdalena, under the shade of a payande. Since my mother was a black slave, I carried the mark as well, so goes the song. Alone at night, I raise my eyes and pray to God, but he listens only to the master, even if the color of the sky is my own.* And almost toward dawn, old man Cartagena came out to the beach. No one knows whether he went into the water or whether he disappeared in the trails. The truth is that we never saw him again. A young couple then occupied the cave next to Las Salinas. *Slavery was banned many, many years ago, but we continue being slaves.* So goes the song. *Today we weren't paid, he's going to sell me, the children of the masters no longer need boats.*"

Don Javier's eyes sharpen in the noon light. They dig other words in the air and under the sea:

"Many, many days went by like this. And each day had many nights, because there were eternal nights in the cave inside which the siblings consummated their love. More than once, imprudence made me approach the cave. Kneeling behind a boulder, I heard them but did not see them. One could hear

Benjamin and Rosaluz in the back of the cave. The child that I was tried to understand and became frightened. I assumed their voices to be agonizing, like the screams of the drowning, stories quartered by knives, and pirates, and dreadful cannibal crimes, there where nothing was happening but the events of love, where nothing was heard but that feverish silence, well damaged by innocent excesses, adulterated only by the music of naked bodies and that of the sea—until one morning when Rosaluz became a shadow. We never heard again from Benjamin. The sorcerer assured us that the stone bed broke and a spring surged from the cleavage, which we could verify, but the rest of the story he tried to foist upon us sounded more like pure invention on his part: that from that spring appeared the Lone Soul, Elegguá, who with feminine manners and harmonies had seduced Benjamin while Rosaluz slept. That the youth entered the spring, leaned into the mouth of the stone bed, and was lost among currents and delights. Rosaluz kept calling him through entire nights, first bitterly, sweetly, begging, and later with unlimited fury. The storms that besieged the village that summer were due, according to the healer, to the anger of the spurned sister-bride. The maiden disappeared shortly after that. Baldomero showed us the remains of a campfire in the cave, wanting us to believe that Rosaluz had incinerated herself."

Don Javier quiets down and deeply breathes again, more outwardly than inwardly.

"My grandfather's house stood facing the first lagoon, the biggest and happiest one in Las Salinas, several kilometers away from the cave. Yet I heard very near, in those daily nights of my childhood, the last protests of Rosaluz, howls and fights, the daily nightmare of her body burning."

And taking his eyes away from the door, from the air of dirty gold obsessed with turning everything to ashes there in the street, behind the windows of the Hotel Tariri:

"But you are barely hearing me, you are somewhere else. You are surely still thinking about Inganiteri! You're surely wondering what all of this has to do with the story of Kaametza and Narowé, which you want to hear!"

"It's not true, Don Javier," I lied again.

12

The Best Method of Shrinking Heads

"Many, many lies are told and have been told about the Tzipíbo, about the Ashanínka, and about all our nations. That the Amawaka cook and eat Christians. That the Machiguengas kill their children if they are born as twins. That the wife of a Shapra is at the same time the wife of all Shapras. That the Cashibo tear their prisoners apart in horrible feasts that last for weeks. That the Aguaruna sorcerers are godchildren of evil and transform themselves into vipers or tigers to exterminate rubber collectors, oil men, and soldiers. Even more calumnies are told about the Bora, the Kulina, the Piro, the Witoto. That the Jíbaro, among other atrocities, shrink human heads without rhyme or reason, out of pure savage pleasure, worse than the worst ferocious animals."

Félix Insapillo, while talking, has grown in height under the shade of the lupuna tree.

"Almost always, those who fill ears with those falsities do so out of ignorance, if not out of seeking gain. They speak from impotence, in rancor, since our nations never submitted to the virakocha nation, or to the virakocha religion, or to their habits of falseness, ambition, and plunder. It is they, descendants of the foreigners who did not know how to live for life, who existed only for lowest gold—that servant of the flesh—it is they, heirs of theft and of the slave trade, of fortunes like sad houses without feelings, raised not on the soil, but upon the bones of thousands of human beings: *they* are the legitimate barbarians, not the Jíbaro."

Félix Insapillo briefly enters and leaves the bottom of a small silence, and gathers his words with even more force within César's attention.

"Tell me, is it not true that not long ago the virakocha built ovens to burn human beings, murdered millions—children, women, males, old people—without mercy, millions in the most atrocious ways, in showers that spewed venom instead of water, not too long ago, like yesterday, perhaps? Is it not true that all of this happened in front of the false blindness, in front of the consent of judges, of authorities, of the virakocha priests, accomplices, worse than the murderers themselves? Tell me. And are they civilized, while our Jíbaro are barbarians?"

The next to last sun barely penetrates, frazzled, through the high netting that embroiders the top of the lupuna tree and the branches of the other trees that surround the clearing, lighting up in red and orange, in impossible glares like traces of a dark spatula, the faces of Iván and César. The image of the Amawaka child leans against the roots of the giant tree. Félix Insapillo lifts his eyes to the light and recovers his calmness.

"I have lived among the Jíbaro, and I have seen. It is true that they shrink heads, but only those of enemies in face-to-face battle, fallen in legal combat. A Jíbaro warrior has the right to shrink the head only of an opponent that he himself has killed in battle, that he himself could overcome fighting as an equal, without advantage or deceit, war duly being announced beforehand, and with identical weapons. And not all enemies killed in those skirmishes (I have witnessed several) are worthy of decapitation and shrinking. The chosen ones are the bravest ones, the strongest and most agile ones, full of virtues. Only they secure the approval of the Jíbaro witch doctor. I am a witness; I have seen them shrink heads from beginning to end, through a number of ceremonies. It is not just a simple matter, just like that. It is a complete religious act, sacred, with a lot of respect, and considerably dangerous to the one who performs it."

"Part of a magical cult," I suggest, more as a question than a footnote— but in vain. Félix Insapillo doesn't even ignore me.

"For them, the shrinking of heads is a sacred act, a gathering of war trophies, the last step in a ritual process that begins long before actual combat. The Jíbaro not only risk their lives in combat, they risk it two moons before and one after the battle. They risk it in preparation, protecting themselves from the curses of the their opponents' sorcerers. They risk it during several days of sincere fighting. They risk it capturing heads beneath a storm of arrows, poisoned darts, infallible spells, charged lances, and battle shouts. And not only do they risk their lives several times: each time they risk several lives. Because when two jungle nations face each other in war, besides the combatants, who can see each other and turn aside or impose their valor or their skill, their sorcerers and their accomplice souls fight even more ferociously from afar, from the air near by or far away. From two irreconcilable airs, the sorcerers surge forward with all their powers, knowing—as they know—that in each dead man, more will die than just a man. The soul of that dead man will be stolen by the opposing sorcerer, and that body's soul will never rest. Death itself, the restfulness of death, will be denied to it. He will not be able to visit past or future lives, or any of the houses of deaths that live on the air. That man's existence, inhabited by so many diverse existences, that man's world, which at the same time is all of the invisible worlds that coinhabit the visible world, will be stripped of the best memories, the best powers, the possibility of occupying another life, of enduring and perpetuating himself in something: a solitary tree, a small stone, a bird, the flight of any bird. And any return will also be barred to him. He will not exist in a child, or in the belly of a woman, or in the desire of the first being, of the first having been. That man, now widower to himself, his soul stolen, can never be even what he might have been."

Félix Insapillo takes a pause, which Iván and I use to seat ourselves next to the Amawaka youth under the whitish protection of the lupuna. I imagine I see another face lodged in the features of Insapillo, somebody that isn't him but yet was flowing out of his mouth. As if only César Calvo were present, our first guide, reduced to the status of storyteller, recovers his wooden gestures and the ever-grating sound in his throat and goes on without paying attention to us.

"They face the greatest perils at the moment when the heads are shrunk. That is the time when the vanquished sorcerers attack most fiercely. It is then that the great souls that protect the small souls of the beheaded seek their greatest revenge. Each Jíbaro warrior places his trophy facing up, and kneels on the ground in front of it, pressing downward with both of his hands. Warriors and heads form a semicircle of silence, of shadows, traversed by the Jíbaro shaman, jumping haphazardly while chewing tobacco and blowing the juice into the nostrils of the men. One by one, with tobacco juice and icaro chants, he immunizes them and makes them impenetrable to the spells of the opposing shaman, who at that same time is surely working and casting his powers to stop the shrinking, to prevent the Jíbaro from kidnapping the souls and the virtues of those decapitated, when their heads are shrunk. Once the head is shrunk, forever separated from its body, the spirit inhabiting the head is condemned to eternal separation from the spirit that lived in the body. The head will never be buried, perhaps far from the body but at least in the same soil that might reunite the two. If the enemy shaman succeeds in preventing the shrinking, and the heads are buried at their normal size, each one will inexorably advance underground until it finds and is reunited with its corresponding body, again welding itself to it. But if the enemy shaman fails and the heads are in fact shrunk, the Jíbaro then take possession of the best parts of the souls of those bodies, left upon the battlefield, as well as taking possession of the best elements of the souls of those heads which they brought back in triumph to their nation."

And only then, with distant eyes, Félix Insapillo looks at me.

"To shrink them, the first thing they do is to separate them from the skulls, to leave them as nothing but skin, hair, and flesh, without any bone. Each warrior takes his skull and makes a cut in it from the forehead back to the nape of the neck, with a bloodwood or bone knife. If bone, it must be very old, like those that have already been converted to stone."

"And Kaametza discovered a great fear within herself. She understood the nearness of death. And without thinking and without aim, she tore a bone from her body like a recently sharpened knife and sliced the throat of the otorongo," says Don Javier. "At this point, I remember well, my friend Inganiteri stopped his story, closed his eyes, and remained silent, motionless, listening to something coming from the deep woods, from the creeks splashing near by, joining their waters to those of the Unine."

"Then the Jíbaro perform several more cuts, very precisely, at the height of the nose, the eyes, the mouth, to help them come out easier. Then they slowly, very slowly, peel off the skin and muscles, leaving the clean bare skull. Human beings are very ugly that way, faceless, nothing but bleeding bone. They leave only the eyes and the tongue inside the skull: why, why? I'm sure you're asking yourself."

"Surely, Inganiteri closed his eyes so he could avoid telling me anything else, that's why. With his closed eyes he was silent. Perhaps something hard to tell, dangerous, prohibited, is always present in old stories," Don Javier tells me.

"Then the Jíbaro closes the back cut, closes all of the cuts that were necessary, sews the eye cavities, the empty eyelids, the lips—everything but the neck opening. The eyes are firmly sewn so that nothing seen by the dead man can escape, filter to the air, or return from the air to nature. So that everything he kept in his eyes, during all his existences, can be transported and deposited within the eyes of his killer. And especially the lips are resewn, closed with more fear than anger, so that no word may escape, not even a sigh.

"The Jíbaro know that the breath of words puts powers in motion," says Don Hildebrando. "The breath of words is the only invincible thing against any spell, the only thing that would liberate the soul-in-the-head and reunite it with the soul-of-his-body."

"Thus closed, if the lips are sloppily sewn, the opposite will take place: the silence of the head will attract the soul from the distant body and will join it with that other beheaded soul, but the uniting will take place on a small scale. By that I mean to say that the body, under orders, will come reduced to the size of the head and will unite to it in equilibrium. Only then is everything under the control of the Jíbaro sorcerer. No word will be able to unleash any force against him from the air. The only mouth they allow is the mouth of the neck, without tongue and without language. And then, lips and eyelids brutally pierced by wikungu spines, the heads are submerged in huge earthenware pots filled with river water and placed in the fire. The heads must be taken out in a short time, exactly when the water appears to begin to boil but does not quite boil. If anyone gets distracted and lets the water boil, the head is spoiled. It doesn't turn out; the eyelashes, hair, and eyebrows fall out, and the flesh softens. It's no good. The last time I witnessed this, only one head was spoiled, all the others were taken out at the right time. I remember that the spoiled head looked like the illustration in history books similar to that of the Inka Huáscar, that skull from which his very brother, the traitor Atawallpa, drank the chicha of victory, as if it were a q'ero, mistakenly. The Jíbaro, then, introduce handfuls of very hot sand through the mouth of the neck and make the sand substitute for the absent cranium. With flat hot stones, they iron and iron the face of the trophy, changing the hot sand several times and reheating the flat stones with which they give form to the face, remembering the dead man's features and shaping them gradually as if they were sculptors. With the heat of the sand and the stones, the face begins to sweat, to release fat and water from the enlarging pores. The head shrinks and shrinks, reaching the size of a closed fist, tight and frowning but identical to what it was when cut. The Jíbaro spends hours and hours in modeling the small face of his enemy. When the work is finished, it no longer has any importance to him. He has already extracted its soul and has expropriated its virtues. The soul-of-the-head can never rejoin the soul-of-the-body. The head without size and without body is nothing to the Jíbaro anymore. That is what I remember from the first time my godfather offered me ayawaskha to drink. That is what I saw."

"My father knew how to shrink heads," says Iván Calvo. "He did it more than once in the jungles of the Napo River, among the Jíbaro of Ecuador. It was there where he lived and learned and told me about it in detail. The earthenware pots you mentioned, Insapillo, are special pots. Only the sorcerer can touch them or even look at them. The sorcerer covers them inside with broad leaves known only to him, and he himself carries the pots to the site of the ceremony, one by one, walking practically through blind men. And the witch doctor has cured the pots beforehand, has fasted a long time to charge them with powers that not even he himself can completely control. The same thing applies to the water in the pots: the witch doctor prepares it with herbs and roots he must reveal to no one. Finally, what you said about the heads once shrunk having no value is both true and false. Each Jíbaro pays special attention to cutting the hair of the little head and keeps it as a precious possession, since they measure the courage of a male according to the number of hairpieces he displays tied to his waist in ceremonies, in wars, or in celebrations."

Dusk had come and gone, yet Félix Insapillo and Iván Calvo were still talking, this time about the feeding habits of the great vampires of the Marañón River. While they talked and I listened, we failed to notice the absence of the small Amawaka, the envoy, who now, I noticed with relief, was returning with exciting company, considering the hunger I had been feeling. He returned dragging a big, white, very tender lizard, less than two meters long, which we promptly slaughtered and prepared and baked and tasted, hardly believing. It was without doubt the most delicious meat I had ever eaten in my life. And later, to top it all, we did not need to sleep barricaded behind mosquito nets, for the first time since leaving Atalaya. Night arrived fresh, with a newly laundered wind, which blew away insects, fears, and vermin and brought us fragrant and amiable sounds, languages, and flappings of peaceful animals, music and footsteps, only good memories.

Seated on the clean earth, leaning on a tree trunk that smells of mint, of dew, of new notebook and new mechanical pencil of my youth, I breathe high confidence. I light a cigarette, the very last one, with the last match I have. The light of the match more than shows me an inconceivably beautiful landscape—

it regales me an evil beauty, the cruel innocence with which certain dreams are given to us, as are even certain loves when we know full well that they will never be repeated. Nevertheless, I look beyond the light of the match, which is about to burn my fingers. I look and look at the forest, at the night of the forest, as if it were the first and only night of my entire existence.

"What's happening to you? Your eyes are shining," says César, smiling and looking at me. I throw the match away, hearing it fall in the dark, there inside the landscape, which continues to be here, by and for us, even though we can no longer see it. Instead, I manage to see César's voice, which insists, lightening the darkness:

"That is the exact word: *shining*. Yes, your eyes were shining, they looked as if they were crying with tears of honey."

13

End of the Story of Kaametza and Narowé, Which Is an Endless Story

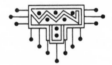

A failing sun, diminished by the lowest hour that hesitates between the last shadows of dusk and the first of night, grants us brightness without light from the windows of the Hotel Tariri.

"It is not true, Don Javier," I lied again.

"You know very well that it is, and nevertheless there is a connection between the sons of the old Cartagena and those of the god Pachamakáite, and an even closer one between Narowé and my friend Babalú. I think that in any case a relationship must exist. Don't you see that random occurrences do not exist? Everything contains a relationship with everything else. We just have to be worthy to discover the hidden connection, the dark springs, the basting thread that connects things and events and people. Why did the conquerors dismember Tupac Amaru, the Serpent God, and bury the parts of his body in the four corners of the unaware universe, in the four nights of the house of Maestro Hildebrando? Are you following me? Why did the body of Juan Santos Atao Wallpa, refusing burial, ascend through the air and disappear spewing smoke? Why do the Quechuas of today, in their stories, talk about the god Inkarri, with his dismembered giant's body, with his head buried with all its hair, all of it, in the approaches of Mount Wanakawre in Cusco, with his dispersed limbs under the earth, which advance year by year, more and more, until some day they will be joined with his wise forehead? They say that when what will happen happens, the god Inkarri, whole by then, will come back from the past to begin again the old struggle and return freedom and lands to all of the Indians of the Kingdom of Peru. Everything is related to everything else. Here in the jungle, it is even more so. This land is made of untold beauty, or of beauty that has been poorly described, which is worse than not describing it at all. For example, you have seen those drawings on the walls of the Hotel Tariri. Do you know that they are only copies of the capes and blankets of our Tzipíbo Indians? But they have been copied poorly, ignorantly. Whoever traced those designs unto the walls thought of them only as decorations, as nice lines. But the matter is quite different to the Tzipíbo who drew the originals—as it is for me, because now I know. In each piece of cloth, the Tzipíbo, with those same traces that appear to be capriciously arranged, they have depicted someone. Each of their tracings is the picture of the soul of a relative, of someone very close. The Tzipíbo are painters of souls, and this is why you will never see two identical designs on their ponchos, even if to the eyes of a stranger all of the designs seem to be similar. Look at the design in this wall: a good-looking one. To your eyes, this surely is nothing more than an attractive drawing. I look at it knowing already what it is and what it has been, knowing that each line that comes down or stops expresses a relationship, an irrevocable connection with behavior and feeling, with particular exuberances or weaknesses of somebody's soul. There is an invisible string, therefore, that one can aim to look for, which one learns and which cannot be seen with the eyes of the physical body. I contemplate this painted wall, but actually I am not looking at a painted wall. There is clearly depicted the face of the soul of a man! There are the features of his soul, very clearly!"

"Lineal portraits," I said to myself; "they resemble maps of cities."

"Exactly!" his voice asserted. "That is what they are: lineal portraits! It isn't that they resemble maps of cities—they are! Yes, souls are cities in movement! The Tzipíbo drawings are maps, but maps of wooded cities, traversed by impossible rivers, not avenues; labyrinths of trenches, not of disciplined little streets; loves and canyons and sadnesses and swamps instead of cold parks and cinemas and avenues! Maps of cities more than portraits of souls! Houses that change locations, the same as days in the life of the jungle, the same as the houses of the Ashanínka who move every year and burn their huts and their farms and return everything to the wilderness, departing for yet another place to rebuild new huts, their plantings, and their life, only to burn everything again a year later to start again and be reborn again! Not like our cities, which are born already knowing their future, chained to the rust of habit, knowing how the days and the homes and the streets that await them will be like! Our civilized cities are born already dead—they resemble the skeletons of tender trees, bored through by worms before they can reach their maturity! Because if the objective of alleged progress, of alleged civilization, is to provide happiness to men, then all of that is a failure. Instead, the Ashanínka, the Campa, are happy. They live in harmony with the nature of the very real and with the nature of dreamed reality, not disputing anyone's space. Thus they become the civilized, the living, the owners of progress, instead of us. Live cities, jungles full of unexpected doors, open only to those who know how to see them, to those who know how to build them, traverse them, and be worthy of them, in dream time and in watchfulness: invisible doors between the wilderness and constant danger, risks that ennoble, danger that fortifies! And there are many more relationships that you will gradually discover. The Bora Indians, as another example, converse by means of fifes and drums. A stranger hearing them playing their instruments will hear only sounds, but to the Bora the music is language. The musical notes entwine themselves in precise words, and to accomplish this they use a decimal sign system. A decimal-musical sign system—can you imagine! A sonorous, numbered writing—can you imagine! Thinking about that, I ask myself whether it could be that the Inkas devised a system of writing as perfect as their architecture, for example, and then decided to do away with it and return to that secret mathematical way of writing suggested by the quipus, the only one we barely know they had? Could it be? Is the decimal sign system of the Inka quipus the same as that of the Bora fifes and drums? What could be the relationship, as yet unknown to us, between those two nations, on the surface so different and distant in space as in time? How many things might a Campa or a Tzipíbo see where your eyes or mine, for example, could distinguish only a nest of ishinshími ants, or a tzangapilla flower, or a sea of little lights in the dark, or fireflies, or otorongo pupils—as when my godson Insapillo noticed thousands of eyes of the dead where you or I could see nothing but the ancient mold that glows in the bark of the dead bloodwood, of the fallen shiwawako barring our way like a wall! And why do the Piro Indians always refer to the Unine River as the River of the Bloody Lips? Do you think that it is because of the bloodwood forests that edge the river as it enters the Ucayali? Can you see anything else? What kind of buried moon, resonating in the bottom of the river, can those eyes see where ours can see only perhaps a hundred lamps breaking on top of the foliage! And what mournful, distant voices will those ears hear, where you or I can hear only a saving laugh emanating from the deep of the woods! Because what no longer is, what has passed, still remains alive in a different kind of life, immune to the loves and the ravages of time. And how many existences against time could a guide be—an Amawaka youth, for example—when he says he would have wanted to be the body of a bullet confronting the irrationality of the rubber harvesters, when he could be nothing more than a spear!

"When I was way up in the tree and felt the biting ants, I became desperate," says Félix Insapillo. "I would have wanted to be a bullet to come down faster! I grasped a vine and began slipping down, cursing. I don't know how the vine broke; with a piece of it still in my hand I fell down all the way to the ground. In the middle of the night I could not tell how far down the ground was, and I hit it standing up, without bending my knees, stiffer than a javelin."

"How could he be anything other than a javelin!" Don Javier tells me. "Can you imagine? Isn't it unreasonable to assume that the Inkas, fantastic in so many ways that we can't even imitate, were never capable of having a written language? Look, here I have copied a paragraph by the Spanish writer Antonio de La Calancha, written in 1638:

> In a place called Cruz de Cailloma, with a type of shells and an herb, mixing the first and making a poultice of the second, the Indians cure cancer.

"Can you imagine? Much of the wisdom of Maestro Ino Moxo has come to him from master to master and from century to century, in sessions of exchange of knowledge, in those astral voyages of ayawaskha, from the time of the Inkas, and even before: from the Urus. They knew that every disease is more than just a disease, as with everything else that exists in the earth's crust. It is fundamentally also a sanction. There is no sickness without a cause. The diseases of men are not like men, who always forgive injuries and never forgive favors. No. Every disease is an indictment, a punishment received by the body or the soul of someone who has caused damage with his body or his soul. Maestro Ino Moxo knows this. He says that everything, absolutely everything, has to do with worthiness. Consequently he cures exactly as the Inkas and Urus did. But perhaps I should say no more. When you meet him, if you ever meet him, Maestro Ino Moxo will tell you what you are worthy to hear. He himself will say what is worthy of being said."

And twisting and gyrating his head as if screwing it in another neck, Don Javier laughingly calls for two glasses of brandy aged in hiporúru leaves, and with the red tinge of clavohuaskha.

"We do not only diagnose the flesh of the material body, just like that, as the doctors with diplomas do. We invoke the vine of the dead to make a complete diagnosis, because ayawaskha knows. And once the decision to cure is made, once we receive permission, the order, we try to make the cure complete. We do not limit ourselves to watching over the palpable terrain of the patient, but with equal attention we channel him in his secret blood, the timeless blood that circulates only during the night when dreams awake."

And smiling again:

"Because you should know, my friend Soriano, that sleep is something that makes me, at least me, close my eyes."

And his eyes and voice returning to a certain shadow:

"That is why we work so hard at fasting, and why we are so careful about curing plants, stone or water or wood plants, charging them with suitable powers, gathering from the air the appropriate icaros, and giving power to those remedies."

"'Maestro Ino Moxo taught me a lot more,' Raul Vásquez, the Jungle Minstrel, tells me. I was very young when I met him, yet I remember as if it were only yesterday. He revealed to me magical songs, which some call icaros and others call bubinzanas. And he showed me something more precious: how to gather the musics that live in the air, to repeat them without moving my lips, to sing in silence 'with the memory of the heart,' as he used to say.

"Giving powers to those remedies that could not have naturally come to them, from birth, increasing them with the chants and potencies unknown to matter. Because if there is no disease that is only a disease, neither can the remedies be only remedies, don't you think?"

"Do you see those hills?" I hear Iván saying.

"We'll go toward them right now, and beyond them lies the Mishawa River, the Amawaka nation," I hear Félix Insapillo saying.

"Ino Moxo lives on the edge of the Mishawa," says César.

"In two days, in the afternoon of the day after tomorrow, you will be speaking with the Black Panther," someone says, I know not who.

"That same day Kaametza and Narowé had four children. They conceived two more on the following day, and still another two on the day after that, until five pairs were completed. The god Pachamakáite had decided that there were to be five girls and five boys and that they would reach full adolescence in barely four hours. He so caused Narowé to command, and Narowé commanded. And the children said farewell, leaving the Great Pajonal behind, and dispersed throughout the world to the four corners of the all-knowing universe. Pachamakáite had decreed that they go out into the world so that from them the first nations could be born. So one pair founded the Tzipíbo nation, another the Amawaka nation, and yet another the Jíbaro nation. The fourth pair reached what is today Lake Titicaca and there founded the Uru nation.

"The Urus, the legendary Urus, much later placed the Sister beneath the Brother, sending them to Mount Wanakawre so that there, on its summit, the incestuous gold phallus would penetrate the Navel of the World and against its sides grow (sacred tremor, pounce of the Puma God!) the outline of stone and silence of the city of Cusco.

"And from there, more astute than silken claws and fangs, departed Inka armies to the four corners of the unknowing universe, to the world grazing in motionless vertigo, in deer-like unconscious beauty. Intentions of double-edged light: if the Sun doesn't freeze you, the Moon will burn you! So it was that those founded by the fourth pair, in turn founded the Inkas, and the Inkas installed their empire, forcing the peoples to be free. So it also was that the Spanish conquerors, teaching loyalty with treachery, founded cemeteries instead of nations. They founded and inhabited cemeteries. With infallible unsheathed sword they beheaded and beheaded until they favored their own neck!

"They all founded everything, perchance adoring the ephemeral while preaching the eternal. If they hatched beliefs, condors, adventures, it was due to fear of earth, not to love of heaven.

"And the Urus were to know everything, which was not enough for them. One of Inganiteri's brothers-in-law, the eldest of all of the old men of the Great Pajonal, told me many things about the Urus: stories that came to him from long ago and far away, from the very mouth of Juan Santos Atao Wallpa. Did you know that Juan Santos Atao Wallpa, in his days as a rebel, lived and preached among the Urus? But they disdained him and refused to rise with him against the invaders. Ah, the ancient Urus, the great founders—they would have indeed risen! Would they have risen? But am I not telling you that he was also going to fight for a woman, as Inganiteri did? Ah, the ancient Urus! They domesticated the giant stones! With icaros, singing, they moved them from one universe to the next! And they did much more in their early times, dazzling generous undertakings, which spread peace and well-being to others. Later they modeled other routes, dried existences, clays that vainly enriched their vain fingers. Not satisfied with knowing everything, they did not apply all that they knew. They reached a state in which they had several bodies in a single life! And for each body, several shades! They traveled without moving, without leaving. They arrived ahead of time, ahead of themselves, like the animals in dreams! They sent themselves as messages to the most distant times and worlds, to the most different worlds and times! And walking there, making This side be the Other, they existed as well in our earth and at the same time in the air, as well as breathing in the bottoms of rivers like moons, with two heads in the bottom of lakes!

"The Urus captured the mysteries, all of the mysteries, and knowledge, all knowledge—not to desire it with respect, to possess it, giving it freedom, but to raise it for the benefit of their misguided purpose, fattening it like a docile herd.

"From that fatuous saliva, without knowing it, the worst tongues of the invaders later gathered the worst. Because the invaders, with a more feeble root but a more luxuriant foliage in their blood, cut, disordered, and gave free rein to everything! They paired in loves with soulless birds, with beasts of burden, with adorning fish! They pillaged and degraded everything! They fell to heaven with open beaks, not like the Urus with their vanity of sages, but like themselves, like virakocha invaders—with only their ignorant greed!

"The Urus were an example to the Inkas of error in disorder, in ambition that falsifies its reasons, to a lesser degree than the Inkas then were to the Spaniards. But they also were the opposite: premonitions of storms as the sowed wind is the announcer of sweet revenges, that harvest which the Ashanínka expect as they await the return of Juan Santos Atao Wallpa, the joining of the body of the god Inkarri, the union of the limbs of Tupaq Amaru with his head of Shining Serpent. The return of Tupaq and of Amaru, of the Serpent, and of what Shines: the time of the Four Corners, Tawantinsuyu, in a single true time. . . .

"So it is, so it has been. The Urus disobeyed the Night: they left it without light and without enigmas. The virakocha invaders disobeyed Day: they kidnapped Mamántziki, the most loved daughter-in-law, and returned her to Pachamakáite worse than a disembodied shade. Juan González knows it; he told me. Juan González is one of the few shirimpiáre who possess the strength to make another time return and be present. He sewed the pieces of that time and made it come down from the air. Traveling among the avatars of his silvery pollen, he existed among the Urus. Juan González told me that the Urus had black blood, were twice as tall as we are in their beginnings, and nothing hurt them. No death touched them, and because of it they confused pride with wisdom.

"They sinned because they were immortal, our Uru grandparents.

"That is why alone, without waging war on anyone, only by being childless and alone, one by one the Urus became extinct."

Finally, after two days of half-sleeping at the foot of the white lupuna tree, we sight the village of Ino Moxo. The young Amawaka stops and peers through some bushes, blinking his eyes. I now notice they have the color of tears, almost being scratched by the tender spines of a maze of garabatokasha, spiny vines hugging the young pomarrosa tree that rises as one of the last boundary posts, one of the last signals, of the entrance to the village. The boy's hand makes a slight gesture and signals us to advance, to pass under the vines, to enter through a sort of woodsy natural door. Above the dark brown hair of the young Amawaka appears a green-and gray-hued wall of bamboo, and beyond that a series of columns of smoke comes from dispersed kitchens. Félix Insapillo juts his square head forward. He barely touches the inconceivable lushness of the native boy's cape, comparable only with that of the Inka Manko Kalli, as Don Hildebrando described, and with the same carvings of the ceremonial vase we saw in his Pucallpa house, the same as those in that q'ero with which César became the sorcerer's ayúmpari. After Félix Insapillo comes Iván, and after him César, pushing aside lianas and cool leaves, and after César, my body enters. My alarmed eyes are on the face of the Amawaka (did I tell you he had dark skin?), and without gratitude we bounce ahead toward the village, leaving behind the boy who was our guide. I notice it and wish to undo it, returning with the intention of saying good-bye. How would one say good-bye in the Amawaka dialect? But by then I find no one under the pomarrosa.

"The chullachaki created to carry harm," repeats Don Juan Tuesta far away in an old night in Muyuy Island, "that chullachaki servant of the Evil One can be identified because he leaves the track of a tiger or of a deer with his right foot, no matter how well disguised in the body of one of

our friends. The other chullachaki, however, is a deceit in the service of truth, he is a good being, and no one, no one, can unseat him, he is perfect in his feet, perfect in everything, humanly human."

The young Amawaka, with dark skin, strange eyes, and always impeccable yellow cape, I don't understand. Furthermore, he disappears in front of our own eyes. I prefer not to think about it and plunge ahead through the squalid opening toward the bamboo wall and the smoke columns.

"Nobody can identify that type of chullachaki," Don Juan Tuesta insists in my memory. "He appears to be a person, but a complete, perfect person. Only very keen eyes can determine that his body is not just one body. More than several persons, several lives seem to inhabit it, as if each part of his body had a divergent existence, diverse existences, which the chullachaki harmonizes into one for the eyes of others. Those chullachakis ignore what is evil. They do not despise people or things. They exist, during the time that they exist, only for the good, to help do good."

My memory pulls me back to the Mapuya River. I see Iván overtaking me on the trail, after not having killed the carnivorous wapapa. I see him advance in front of me, leaving no footprints in the twigs and puddles that broke my back, in the middle of that swarm of insects that pierced my body while ignoring Iván's. I see him arrive at the foot of the white lupuna tree, where Félix Insapillo was talking with César, but I see him arrive dirtied by leaves and cobwebs, his shirt torn by spines, spotted with blood, pierced by thirsty stings.

"Light was thus created," continues Don Javier in a faraway voice. "From shared pleasure was light born. And the Sun, Father Inti, was born together with the Moon, Mother Killa, in a single light—Intikilla—together with the stars. In those beginnings, day and night lived inside a single unity. There was no difference; it was the same time day or night. And in the middle were the happy Kaametza and Narowé, until what happened, happened. Narowé awoke and did not find Kaametza. He did not find her upon his awakening. He fell asleep again. But he did not find her in his dreams either. Again he woke up. He returned to sleep. And he slept and awoke, until his awakening was his dream, his most unique dream—Intikilla—and both were deserts to the eyes of his heart. In the shadow of that pomarrosa he dreamed that he awoke and the

144

pomarrosa had no more shade for him. Kaametza was no longer there. The pomarrosa alone, even without solitude, returned to ashes, just as it was before it was born. Everything turned to ashes, to dust of cold shadow, before the lidless soul of Narowé. His own body returned to a bone ash knife. Narowé looked at the sky. The sky also had turned to ashes. He saw birds, prairies, rivers, and stones, and stones, rivers, prairies, and birds turned to ashes. But that was happening only in his dream. It was worse when he was awake: the world continued without Kaametza.

"In the place of Kaametza, the world only saw a long track of yellow slime sinking in the bushes. It was the koto-machácuy; it was the track of its two heads, slowly heading through quiet spaces to the bottom of all the lakes of the earth!"

And Narowé lunged, desperate and lost in the maze of lies, absences, muddy trails. Somewhere farther on he had to feel his way along, worse than blind, in that brief night the forest provokes when it thickens suddenly, confounding nocturnal monkeys under the matted ceiling of lianas and exuberant foliage. Just at the exit to the thicket forever condemned to night, there where the trail appeared to become a trail again, widening and finally reconciled with the burning sky, we came upon a new obstacle: the incredible bulk of a fallen shiwa-wako, blocking our way like a wall. Narowé surmounted it in an instant, splitting the bark with his hands while his feet made steps as if they were hooks. It took me much longer to climb over my own shadow, chaining it toward that high wall of bamboo and columns of smoke, falling awkwardly on the other side of the rusty trunk on the same desolate trail. Nevertheless, in bad shape, we continued walking. Thick drops were coming down from a sky splintered by a fearful sun. I raised my eyes: the drops were not coming from the sky. Rain from another time overflowed from the eyes of the trees, sliding down in vain like a dead man's tears! My body lunged to a gallop in the trail, zigzagging and bending and jumping over fetid puddles, seeking to reach Narowé. Four centuries I ran without finding him. When I thought I had become lifeless, the husband without a wife appeared behind me. Something like a reproach came out of his eyes. Now I understand that he was just looking at me with pity, because when I advanced, in turmoil, I really was not advancing. I wasn't searching for him or for anyone else. I was running away—running away from my shadow, from the first fear, from this useless rain.

"Maybe the ayawaskha upset you?" says Don Javier. But I don't listen to his voice. Now I can only listen to his mouth, his two lips together making love, quieting each other down, running aground like silver fish.

"When Narowé awoke without Kaametza, day separated from night. And Narowé knew loneliness. After the second solitude he knew anger. When he was initiated into rage, he made the first bow and arrow. And with a single shot he brought down the moon, the first moon our world had, because you should know that the moon we see now is the fourth moon our world has had."

Peeking behind my visions, Don Javier pushed aside blue, mute, orange bamboos.

"He shot it down in pure rage because there was no koto-machácuy and there was no Kaametza. The moon was then a hollow trunk. Narowé shot it down and began beating it with a club. And the moon sounded; it resounded strongly, far away. It was the first manguaré of our jungle. Have you listened to a manguaré, that hollow drum the natives strike to communicate, to send invitations to wars or to celebrations? The moon was the first one to sound in this earth, under the fury of Narowé reclaiming his wife and invoking vengeances that still go on. And the time was spent in vain. That was when time became tame and divided, just as the Sacred River did: the Urubamba, the Wilkamayu of the Inkas of Cusco, father of the Ucayali and grandfather of the Amazon, which has no relatives. Time passed in vain, and no one responded to Narowé. And Narowé knew the flavor of tears. He knew sorrow. In the pain of abandonment, he began to weep and curse endlessly. When the two souls of his face dried up, Narowé was already at the bottom of a fathomless river. That was how the Amazon was born, not in any other way. From the orphaned eyelids of our first father came the Amazon River. Inganiteri told me exactly this. And telling me—I'll never know why—he turned away to hide his tears. Now I think he did not wish to cry only so that I wouldn't cry myself. As if my eyes were in his face, imagine. Of course my eyes were in his face at that time!"

And Don Javier, finally with a voice I can recognize:

"Narowé is at the bottom of the river right now, risking the floods, the tides, forgiving the moon, making music. Because the real moon continues in the bottom of the river-sea, down below. And that other one we see in the sky is only its reflection."

"And the fifth pair?" I insist. "If one pair founded the Amawaka nation, another one the Tzipíbo nation, another one the Uru nation, another one the Jíbaro nation, one pair is missing. Did they found the virakocha nation?"

Don Javier hesitates, looks at the tape recorder, clears his throat, clears it again with force, and finally surges ahead:

"The fifth pair was lost. No one knows."

And again, going away, I think forever:

"My friend Inganiteri, at least, told me he didn't know."

"But it was not Iván who returned looking for you," says Don Hildebrando, with his lowered head pushing aside colored bamboos, visions that have just inhabited the lobby of the Hotel Tariri.

"What he thought was reality was only its reflection," Don Javier says in support.

"It was the reflection of another reality," corrects the deceased Inganiteri from the air.

"The real moon is not in the sky but in the heart, in the memory of the heart," says Juan Santos Atao Wallpa.

"It is more than a hollow trunk, a manguaré, an instrument I touch from the bottom of time," confirms Narowé.

We sight the kitchen smokes of Ino Moxo's village. Our Amawaka guide stops under a pomarrosa tree hugged by a maze of garabatokasha and makes a slight gesture with his arm, inviting us. Without gratitude, we surge toward the village, crossing a sort of doorway of branches, leaving behind the boy who brought us here. The first huts appear; they have gray and desolate roofs and are protected by a natural wall of bamboos. Félix Insapillo goes ahead, followed by Iván and César, moving toward the village. I restrain my anxiety and turn around in vain. The little Ino Moxo has disappeared.

"He has gone to look for you. It is because of you that he has left," says a voice inside me that I confuse with Don Javier's. "And in reality it is not a boy, not the chullachaki boyhood of the Sorcerer of Sorcerers. It is timeless time, and not this time, which builds ruins and leads lives to death, but the guide of the death that lives. This boy is the guide of the lives that never die, the eternal maker of beauty and happiness."

And a little farther away, in front of me, the voice adds, without stopping to walk:

"He is gone because he has just heard your shot. He will never find you now."

I hurry on along the squalid trail, overtake the others, and enter the Amawaka village with them.

III

INO
MOXO

I

And We Were Granted a Meeting with the Black Panther

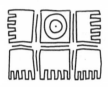

Ino Moxo's hut is distinguished by being different rather than large, and while we figured it would be at the center of the village, as a foundation for this dispersion of columns of smoke and huts with yellow straw sunshades, it actually occupies a timid end of it, almost out of it, on the way to the Mishawa River. And to the Mishawa we returned, sooner than we anticipated, after greeting the old chief of the Amawaka. Our hands trembled in his; our eyes did not dare meet his. We accepted a chicha tea made of chewed manioc and female saliva, the forced and fraternal masato, spiced by certain natives with a flour made of their ancestors' bones.

I don't know the exact moment when he rose from his mat, inviting us to talk by the shore of the Mishawa, as the pona palm structure of his hut creaked. From the other huts sad bare breasts peered timidly. Women in loincloths were behind a herd of tame trees: chimicúas, shapájas, capironas farther down, and behind that the face of a sapote, an espintana, three wakapúranas, an ojé of shocking green among the late clouds. I don't know at what moment we came down the three coarse steps of his house, pushed aside the pashakula vines framing the door, discovered a trail zigzagging to the river, and walked in a single file behind the sorcerer. We were unable to conceive that whiteness under his skin, tanned by the jungle. We were amazed at his strict Castilian pronunciation, his imperturbable drill pants under the native cushma, and his energetic, charmed gait, that of a wild cat—impossible if one considers the Black Panther's ninety-plus age. Now he slowed down, absorbing the sun's peace, and seated himself on the leg of a trunk devastated by fungi, dissolving his cinnamon eyes beyond the hungry hills of mahogany, bananas, and egrets and canoes piercing the shores of the river.

There is a sudden noise to my right; I turn around. A black crocodile shows himself among the trees in the muddy waters and floats closer, poorly pretending. Ino Moxo bends over and pushes him away with his hand. The enormous lizard changes course toward dusk and disappears under the bare branches of the renaco tree, which I only then notice in the center of the Mishawa as a sort of dead forest stripping the current with its roots drowning in the air. The Sorcerer of Sorcerers contemplates the renaco anchored in no one, helpless in the torrent, without flowers and without fruiting branches, hugged only by its own roots. He turns sadly to me, and I respond:

"Could you tell us how you became chief of the Amawakas, not being an Amawaka yourself?"

He was silent.

"Your skin is not that of a pure Indian, and you speak better than a white man."

"I am an Amawaka," he interrupted. "Very pure Amawaka. Son of a native more than of a virakocha, son of an Andean more than of a white man, it is true, but also a descendant of the Urus from my mother's side."

"Don Hildebrando said that you . . ."

"I am a legitimate Yora, he said, mortified. "A Yora, whom you know only as an Amawaka. Ino Moxo, that's who I am." And out of the dull neck of his cushma, the painted poncho that scares the sun and the unpredictable Amazonian downpours, he extracted from the pocket of his white shirt a crestfallen cigarette, a shirikaipi made of strong leaves of wild tobacco. "The problem is that I was not before what I am now," he says. "I had another name and another life before." And he lights the cigarette and the torn light tinges his profile pink. "I was not Ino Moxo before and will probably not be tomorrow." His features get lost in the fragrant, teary smoke. "It is a long story, very long— a story fully known to very few." I looked upon other kingdoms while Ino Moxo smoked, as if he were inwardly remembering, there at night on the golden edge of the Mishawa.

"You will be granted knowledge about the way in which the children devoured their parents," repeats Don Javier.

From above, upriver in the Kashpajali, erupts an end-of-afternoon sky. Almost five hundred men, more white than mestizo, have gathered with guns, with pillage, and with fear. They go down river trying to be silent, hundreds of carbines in their hands and in boxes, and with more crates of ammunition, to the mouth of the Sutilija River, overflowing it with the weight of barges. Five hundred mercenaries, collected no one knows where, split currents that were recently peaceful, push waters that climb up the ankles of trees on the shore. These people are seen for the first time by this forest and the sky. The Mashko Indians who inhabit the mouth of the Sutilija River in a few houses are also surprised; they do not believe. But they already know that the virakocha, the white men, have no pity when better armed. The Mashko angrily get together, no more than twenty males, and attempt to board their canoes. Surely they intend to head to the Manu River to join their kindred and confront the virakocha in larger numbers, to throw the virakocha out of their violated territories, since the largest village of the Mashko is on the Manu, and there are three hundred invincible warriors on the Manu River. Their attempt is in vain. The astute virakocha have posted guards on both shores, and the twenty brown unarmed men cannot get through to pass the alarm. Their empty canoes float down the middle of the river. Under the red sky the water is red water.

"We had one-half hour of fierce combat," says Zacarías Valdez, one of the five hundred mercenaries. "Toward the end, we inflicted many casualties among the savages, who had to retreat in face of the energetic attitude of our combatants. The Mashko Indians lived in the Colorado River and were also spread along the shores of the Madre de Dios and the Manu Rivers, but in view of hostilities from our people, the people of the great rubber baron Fitzcarrald, they had to pull back up the Colorado River to their original territories among the headwaters of those rivers which in their language are called Piuquene, Panahua, Cumarjani, and Sutilija, all of them tributaries of the Manu. I must tell you that a distinguishing characteristic of these savages is that they are very tall and carry beards, many of them quite thick. Fitzcarrald decided to punish them and arranged to attack their big village located some distance away down the Sutilija River. Once our personnel boarded many canoes, we set forth, and eight hundred men came ashore at the bend of the river just above the village, in order to surround it by land, giving a signal once that was completed. Meanwhile, the canoes slowly continued down river. At four o'clock in the afternoon, we heard a heavy volley: it was the signal that

fighting had begun. When we arrived at the site of the village, it was
already in the hands of our people. The Mashko lost many warriors who
stayed behind to defend their houses, while women and children had been
moved out in time. Once the first encounter was over, the bodies were
collected and cremated. Because of this funeral proceeding, the Piro
Indians who were in our party named that place Mashko Rupuna, *which*
means "Burned Mashko Indian." But the fight wasn't over. We had to
continue attacking the savages. The fighting was extended. Combat took
place in several locations, resulting in many casualties in a war to the
death, to such a degree that many bodies floated down the Manu River,
and its waters were no longer potable. Finally, we dislodged the savages
from the Manu, even though incompletely, because the Mashko continued
their incursions, harassing our workers, until rubber extraction activities
had to be discontinued in those areas, moving to other more peaceful
ones."

"It is a long, long story," says Ino Moxo. "I was thirteen years old, and at
that time the chieftain of chieftains was old Ximu, a truly wise man, great and
wise, giver of orders to gods and to souls."

We have barely slept the previous night, this being our second day with
Ino Moxo. We breakfast on the meat of big monkeys, a species called maquisapa,
salted and unsalted. Whole bodies are kept in a basket hanging to the side of
the door of the sorcerer's hut, from which we learn they pluck a piece of leg, a
joint, a shoulder, sometimes peeled like that of an adolescent, our only sustenance for four days.

Once again by the shore of the Mishawa, Ino Moxo looks at me.

"We Amawaka are few in number, very few; you have seen it. Including
the ones living here, as well as those farther down in several places, we don't
exceed two hundred families. Did you know that there were thousands of us
in Ximu's time? The virakocha gradually exterminated us. They reduced us.
They killed us only to take our lands. And they killed people of other nations
as well—Jíbaros, Yaminawas, Aguarunas, Tzipíbos, Mashkos—because our lands
were full of rubber, they were areas with many rubber trees, nothing but pure
fat rubber roads. And the virakocha rubber men needed that rubber, they say
for the progress of the country. They still say that. In the name of progress
they pillaged and shot us."

And turning his face toward the renaco tree that shines in blues and or-

154

anges, erecting a labyrinth of branches against the current, in the middle of the river:

"It is a long and bitter story. If I were to tell you everything, surely you would not believe me. It is a story that is part of me, which brought me here, which rebirthed me as an Amawaka, Yora, as a Yora chief. Because my father came from Arequipa, where I was born. Where I was born the time before the last time."

"Were you then born in Arequipa?"

"The time before last."

"What do you mean?"

And he, without listening to me:

"My father came to become a rubber worker, and my mother, unwillingly, also came. As for me? I wanted to come and didn't want to. I was very young, although I think I already knew; I sniffed things, as I was to sniff destinies. Worried and happy—that is how I came, I remember. By that time, the Amawaka were already suffering too much. Whole villages died at the hands of the virakocha. It was because of it that old Ximu made me come. From the air he ordered, disposed, commanded. He brought me, as I found out later. But this story is a long one."

A young Amawaka appears to the right, among the trees to my right, carrying a black pukuna. He says something to Ino Moxo. Ino Moxo makes a gesture and the Amawaka speaks with Iván, who rises and says he's going to look for César and also Insapillo, to bring food. They leave me alone with the Black Panther, whose eyes wander away as he talks to the renaco, which seems to concede and makes a stand under the sun of long waters.

"Taking ayawaskha, one becomes something like a crystal," says Ino Moxo distractedly, but I am not distracted. "One becomes a crystal exposed to all the spirits, to the evil ones and the true ones that inhabit the air. That's what the icaros are for—icaros for protection—but there are also curing icaros, fundamental ones, songs that call upon a particular soul to descend and counteract other ones. With one of those icaros, Maestro Ximu made me come with his calling. He made me come as if I were a protective spirit. And before airing his icaro for me, Ximu had to fast. Because ayawaskha, like any conscious plant, has four requirements—no salt, no sugar, no fats, no sex—during all the time taken for its preparation, ingestion, and effects. Ximu had to fast so he could call me, then he ingested ayawaskha and sang the icaro. And I came. I had no choice but to obey. Because we are dealing with centuries-old wisdom, many

155

have mistakenly died while fasting. From the time of our Uru fathers, since before the Inkas, many are dead."

*Under the red sky, red water. All of the mercenaries of Cumaria,
Cuenga, from the Unine, sail down the Urubamba. Hundreds of canoes full
of supplies, boxes and boxes of Winchester 44-caliber carbines, respond to
the war call of Fermin Fitzcarrald.*

*"Winchesters against arrows, imagine that!" mutters the Spanish
cattleman Don Andrés Rúa in Atalaya. "Repeating guns against wooden
spears!"*

*"We were not short of fine liquors either, such as cognac and cham-
pagne," Zacarías Valdez, the rubber worker, tells us.*

*The expeditionaries hurry along, arrive at the landing place in the
Camisea River, and come ashore. Their mestizo and Piro Indian servants
take the French boxes out of the canoes, containing tinned meat and
wines, and deposit them on shore. The rubber pioneers, agents of
progress, have lunch, laugh, and make toasts to war—Winchesters against
arrows—which they know is already won. Then they again board their
canoes, leave the landing behind, go up the Manu, and arrive tired at their
general headquarters at the mouth of the Kashpajali River. They arrive
just in time, because a Mr. Maldonado, a representative from their leader,
informs them that because of the Indians, so many dead barbarians, the
rubber workers in that area have consumed their allotment of ammunition
ahead of schedule.*

*"During that interval," says Zacarías Valdez, "since the savages
insisted on attacking the rubber stations, we initiated forays against their
own villages, sending hundreds of very well armed men to the Sutilija,
Cumarjani, Panahua, and Pinquene Rivers, surprising the savages while
they slept. Our combatants, as unequivocal proof of their actions, brought
back two Indian boys as prisoners, and pieces of gold they found in those
regions. Once things calmed down, and after a few days' stay in
Kashpajali, a new expedition was organized. Before setting off,
Fitzcarrald called together all the rubber workers and told them:*

*" 'Those who have decided never to return to their homes, step
forward!'*

*"Of hundreds of men gathered together there, the first ones to step
forward were Alfred Cockburn and Pedro Sarria, from Lima; Erasmo*

Zorrilla from Ica; Carmen López from Moyobamba; and I, Zacarías
Valdez, born in Huanta, in addition to thirty Piro Indians selected as
consummate warriors.

"The guns we used were Winchester carbines, constituting the only
means of imposing the law of the strongest, which later on became the
law of the rubber workers.

"Well into the Madre de Dios River, we discovered a tributary to the
right, which was named the Colorado. This is what happened: we landed
somewhat above a Mashko village. The Mashkos were fierce and tall, as I
have already said, and we could not risk direct body-to-body combat with
them. They came quickly to attack us but faced thirty gunmen firing point
blank at them. Since they had never seen guns, the loud shots of the
riflemen and the death sowed in their ranks kept them at a certain
distance, from where they started shooting arrows at us. The fight lasted
about two hours, and we won thanks to our guns. The Piro warriors, able
gunmen trained by us and totally loyal to our cause, were the ones who
ended the fight, pursuing the savages to their houses and finding nothing
but dead and wounded, among which was a boy so brave that when food
was offered him he tried to bite us.

"In that place Fitzcarrald planted the Peruvian flag and baptized the
recently discovered river as the Colorado: the red river, because its turbid
waters were tinged with blood."

"This is a long story; I warned you," says Ino Moxo. "If I told you everything you would not believe me, because one can never believe everything.
You can never, never listen to everything. Take, for example, the jungle. If you
try to listen to every sound in the jungle, what do you hear? You hear more
than land animals, water animals, animals of the air, even when it is no longer
possible to hear the song of the fish that gladdened the waters of the Pangoa,
Tambo, and Ucayali Rivers. Those musical beings who foresaw the arrival of
the great black otorongo, fled beforehand, and saved themselves, even though
they can no longer sing. Or if they do, that is if they can still sing, they surely
do it soundlessly, with notes our ears are not accustomed to. They might sing
in silence, in another dimension. And the plants also make sounds, the stone
or wood plants. Each and all make their sound, the same as the stones.

"And more than anything else, one hears the sound of the steps of animals we have been before we were human, the sound of the steps of stones

and of plants and of things that all human beings have previously been. And also what we have heard before, all that you can hear at night in the jungle. Inwardly we hear, in memory, what we have listened to in the course of our lives: dances and flutes and promises and lies and fears and confessions and war cries and moans of love. True stories, stories of tomorrow—because you also hear what you will listen to in the future, what you anticipate, in the middle of the night in the jungle, in the jungle that sounds in the middle of the night. Memory is more, much more—don't you know? True memory also holds what is yet to come. And what will never come: it also holds that. Imagine. Just imagine. Who on earth could hear all of it—tell me? Who could listen to it all at once and believe it?

2

Ino Moxo Was Born When He Was Thirteen Years Old

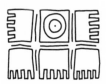

The Amawaka youth has returned with the others, empty-handed, the used blowgun on his right shoulder. I believe that at that moment we are all straining to hear. At my side, César smokes to discourage insects and looks at the opposite shore and at the reflection of uneven profiles, broken trees moving over the sharpened waters, cooling down against the brilliance of the Mishawa. Some meters away from the river, on high ground, Insapillo and Iván, kneeling on an abutment of dry ground, carve a porous quietude, the muteness of a town square without statues. For a dizzy second, I believe I was hearing everything.

"I would like only to hear something about you, Maestro Ino Moxo, whatever you might well consider telling me about your life."

"It is almost night," says the sorcerer, "and of all the things that live in the night, in the doorway to it, all you want to hear is about the Black Panther?"

"If you think it's possible."

"A lot of things seem possible to me; I'm not sure yet. But I read something in your interest. I sense something very gentle. I will say things to that piece of your soul, to that *other you.*"

Assuredly then, setting aside the onset of night and using it to cover the past moments to come, I listened. The sorcerer was looking at me sideways, with satisfied mourning, satiated with smiles that never fully took flight. I had an the intuition that I was following his orders. A family of macaws screamed behind us. I did not hear them; I was their scream. I was the creaking of branches besieged in the dark by winds, I was the wind, I was the dark. No more the helplessness of the renaco tree amid the current, but the current itself, the flow of the river, and the voice of Ino Moxo facing the river:

"You will not leave as you have come. I will tell you things. From Ino Moxo, the Black Panther, I will tell you some of the things that you are seeking."

The screaming of the macaws was dissolved in a long and invisible flapping of wings. Did the wind stop? It seemed rather as if the jungle ceased to walk under the wind, as if the whole earth, bent under the dark breath, was a river of birds and enigmas and openings between branches and gentle dangers. A motionless and forever fleeing river, I thought, as if I had come back from the future, from that timeless time that Don Hildebrando and Don Javier spoke about.

"This river," says Ino Moxo, "is lined with ocean fossils, just as the Mapuya River is. All rivers around here are the same as roads, paths in a sea that no longer exists and will not exist in the future."

"Happily for us, the Mashko we had punished to set an example had no canoes to pursue us in," the expedition member Zacarías Valdez continues his story. "They did not have canoes, but only some logs, hollowed out with fire, that weren't of much use. Modern tools had not yet reached them. They only used stone axes with a primitive shape. One day later, we found a village different from those of the savages. For a moment we thought they might be Brazilians at the border. When we were five hundred meters away from the landing, the inhabitants hoisted a flag to imitate us, since we were flying the bicolored Peruvian flag from our stern. Fitzcarrald, armed with his telescope, realized it was a Bolivian flag and exclaimed with feeling:

"'We are navigating the Madre de Dios River!'

"The Bolivians overwhelmed us with greetings, setting out a royal banquet with generous portions of wines, including lachrima christi, muscatel, Malaga, Bordeaux, and champagne, contributed by our leader Fitzcarrald. I will not overlook mentioning that our hosts were surprised to see how many fine liquors we had with our supplies. They could never have imagined that. We were received magnificently and feasts were held in our honor for several days, during which we were treated like kings, as we remembered our life on the coast and in the sierra, where we were

happy and had good times. But since we could not remain there forever, the time came to think about our return, much against our will. Mr. Jesus Roca, a partner in the Bolivian enterprise Suarez-Roca, a powerful rubber company, provided us with good boats. Once we were under way, twenty-five Piro warriors went on foot through the forest, tracking and protecting the boats from possible surprises.

"We had to help these twenty-five scouts in the runs—that is, in the straight sections of the river, at the end of which there always were savages on the lookout—but our people surrounded them by land and dispatched them while they were still confidently awaiting our boats on the shore. In this manner we won every fight without human casualties.

"Not wishing to rest, Fitzcarrald planned a second expedition to the village of Carmen. His objective was to clean up all of the Madre de Dios River from Mashko and Huarayo savages, which forced him into many new skirmishes during the trip. But his men were already used to fighting and were hardy, so his efforts were always successful and he was able to dislodge the savages from the shores of the Madre de Dios River, so much so that the Huarayos retreated to the Inambari, and the Mashko to the Colorado!"

"Did you ever fight the Amawaka?"

"Of course!" Zacarías Valdez prides himself, "we fought those cannibals several times. I especially remember one time, about eight in the morning, in a straight run of the river, the Amawaka began to attack us with arrows from both shores. We responded with carbine gunfire. Our boats continued past the site of the encounter. At four in the afternoon, the fiercest fighting took place, during which one man was killed."

"A single man?"

"Just one, no more."

"Were any Amawaka killed?"

"Ah! We killed at least two hundred of them. When we saw them lost, we landed and surrounded them. Strangely, we found no one—I mean no one alive. It was as if the earth had swallowed them, as if they had become invisible. We again won because of our firepower. But the savages reappeared as if by magic as soon as we boarded our canoes, and stopped attacking us only when they ran out of arrows. The Amawaka were as brave as the Campa or even more so. The warrior spirit inherited from their ancestors, the Inkas, was reflected in them."

"Maestro Ximu set a spell on me by singing an icaro with ayawaskha to make me come. He knew more than he knew, and he also divined what would not happen and what could be avoided," Ino Moxo tells me, contemplating the Mishawa River in front of us. The river lost itself in a great bend, giving itself up in a search for the Sacred River of the Inkas, the Wilkamayu, which was reborn, like Ino Moxo, and today lives and flows under its older Uru name: Urubamba. Land of red water under red sky. Red pampa, water pampa, pampa of the Urus: Urupampa.

"Maestro Ximu made me come because he knew the Urus were going to become extinct. It was the time of rubber, a scattering of deaths, of pillaging, of violated girls, of nothing but bullets, and we were armed only with arrows, with pukuna darts. Bullets and fear—I remember the confusion. The chief Ximu, a great wise man, knew that only with white men's firearms could we face white men's ferocity. Only with guns could we stop the virakocha and defend our lands. Only with Winchesters could we protect ourselves from the greed of the rubber workers. Because arrows were useless, in vain did our warriors use their blowguns. The darts never reached their targets; they strung their bows without result. They fought only to die, open forehead and bare chest against bullets from the ambushers. Ximu foresaw all of that."

Lighting another shirikaipi and smoking it: "Then who was going to sell firearms to the natives? Same as now, it was forbidden, whether the Indians promised all the rubber and all the gold in the world. They sold carbines and bullets only to traitor Indians, teaching them to fire against their own people. I remember one of them, called Hohuaté in Campa but Andrés Avelino Cáceres y Ruiz in virakocha, a pure Indian traitor. And I remember another one, still alive today, a Piro Indian called Morales Bermúdez in Spanish, but in Piro language he would be called something worse than traitor. And I also remember his bosses, the insatiable Fermin Fitzcarrald and his brother Delfin. You probably know how Delfin Fitzcarrald was sentenced and died. Some say he was a great fool; others said the same. I think he was a good man not by vocation but by exhaustion, out of tiredness, the same as snakes that have lost their fangs.

"Therefore, Ximu decided that the Amawaka were to have a mestizo chief, someone who would be able to provide them with carbines, rear-loaders, rifles, and ammunition so that their nation might survive. Chief Ximu consulted the spirits and called upon the spirits of the water and the wind—all of the souls of the jungle and beyond. He consulted. He drank the sacred juice of the vine of the dead (oni xuma is its name, which you know as ayawaskha) until finally, meditating, dieting, fasting, and making icaros, he selected a successor: a half-white youth, barely thirteen years old, son of a Uru mother and a virakocha father, a rubber collector from Arequipa. That is how the great Maestro Ximu chose me, directed by the souls that are different shadows of the god Pachamakáite, even though Pachamakáite does not now have a body. He selected me by order of his powers, and through the oni xuma; that is how he chose me.

"They kidnapped me, I remember well. Later, I found out that Ximu himself had directed the group of seven males who took me away. But I didn't see him. Ximu directed all of this from afar, from within the forest, fasting and making arrangements so that all would turn out well. That day, my father had sent me away with a Campa servant girl to the hut next to the big house, to the hut used to house guests, a custom usual in the Unine area but not here. It was precisely on that day that my mother was going to give me a sister, and my father was helping with the delivery of the baby. I was playing, throwing pebbles and seeds at a tiwakuru whistling atop a wimbra, surrounded by tall flowers, when my father came laughing out of the woods. I wanted to be surprised. I had just seen him inside the house, dressed differently, playing the role of midwife! But there he was, right in front of me, laughing. I didn't know what to think, because my father was completely naked. He carried a tanishi string around his waist, with all of his face and chest painted red. He took my hand in silence. I almost resisted him. But his face was my father's face, perhaps only darker, and his body and his voice. "Let's go," he said—all of him was my father! The Campa girl who was taking care of me never made a move. She said nothing but remained in the hut looking the other way, as if no one were there, as if she had seen nothing. That is how it was. A chullachaki dressed in my father's body took me, while at that moment my father was delivering my baby sister. I walked for hours with my other father, the Amawaka, until we joined six others in the forest. Many hours went by, before and after, because at the beginning of the second day we arrived at this village. A little old woman received me, named Rosa Urquía. She removed my clothes, bathed me, sang strange songs to me, put a yellow cushma on me. I was alone with the old woman, locked in her hut for seven days. She fed me with plantains broiled over a fire. She calmed me and chased away my remaining fears, and made me sleep happily with the juice from the stems of tohé. Day and night I slept, watching beautiful sights, dreaming beautiful dreams, with eyes open during the day, and with eyes closed, looking inside, during the night. A week later, I met Ximu."

Insapillo and Iván remained motionless. César rose and approached Ino Moxo. His eyes were distended in the fading light. The bustle of his turning voice was darker than air, as if it came from the arms of the renaco tree fighting in the middle of the Mishawa River. "Always seven," says my cousin César. "Seven men kidnapped him; seven days later Ximu appeared." And, lighting a match and looking at his watch, "It is now seven o'clock in the evening, and today is the seventh of July."

Maestro Ino Moxo, without listening to him:

"On that day I stopped being who I was, the son of my father and mother, and I began to be an Amawaka, a Yora, son of Ximu, disciple of Ximu, heir to Ximu."

3

Life, Betrayal, and Death of Chief Hohuaté

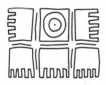

"There was a Campa witch doctor," the rubber collector Zacarías Valdez informs us, "a witch doctor friend of ours. His name was Hohuaté. It was Hohuaté who accompanied Colonel Portillo on his expeditions as directed by La Fuente, together with other Indians from his Ashanínka tribe. When Colonel Portillo, distinguished leader of our army, who later became Prefect of Loreto, arrived at the Ucayali River, in gratitude for the services rendered by the witch doctor, he gave him some firearms, a revolver among them.

"During the return, at the confluence of the Ene and Perené Rivers, during a feast given by the Campas from the Tambo River with our witch doctor Hohuaté in attendance, a fight started because so much masato had been consumed. Hohuaté discharged his revolver and wounded the witch doctor of the Tambo River Campas, leaving him blind in one eye, while he himself embarked and continued the journey with the rest of his companions. This incident started a hopeless enmity between both Campa leaders.

"I'll tell you something else about the life of the witch doctor Hohuaté. When General Andrés Avelino Cáceres visited Ayacucho, his native land, he crossed the Apurimac River, staying as a guest in the house of Don Manuel de La Fuente, who knew him well because Cáceres had been Sergeant Major when La Fuente was President of the Republic,

and both had been together during the La Brena campaigns in the war
with Chile. General Cáceres asked La Fuente to give him Hohuaté as a gift
so he could baptize him, a request that was granted. Hohuaté was taken to
Ayacucho, where he was baptized by the bishop. General Cáceres and
Senator Ruiz were godfathers in the ceremony, and Hohuaté was given the
Christian name of Andrés Avelino Cáceres y Ruiz. Laden with gifts from
his godfathers, our Campa friend returned to the Apurimac.

"As I was telling you, La Fuente arranged to have his witch doctor
accompany me on the journey, since he had extensive knowledge of river
conditions. One of the first things he did was to warn me not to travel
down river unarmed, because the Huncuninas, savages inhabiting the
shores of the Tambo River, were waiting there to attack us. Following the
advice of this excellent guide, I returned to Huanta to buy a regular
amount of firearms, which the merchants had reserved for us in their
warehouses: carbines, Winchesters, Remingtons, etc., and a sizable stock
of ammunition.

"Returning to the Apurimac, I ordered six large canoes to be made
ready, an operation that consisted of installing buoyant tree trunks on both
sides of the boats, which provided great stability and prevented capsizing.
Preparations were completed, and we continued the journey with over
one hundred men. Three river bends before we arrived at the confluence
of the Ene and the Perené Rivers, Chief Andrés Avelino Cáceres y Ruiz
insisted we land on the beach. We were to spend the night there and
continue the voyage early next morning, a moment he considered
appropriate to pass the mouth of the Perené and avoid the vigilance of the
opposing chief, who was surely waiting for him to seek revenge.

"So we disembarked and established camp. It was interesting to see
Chief Andrés Avelino Cáceres y Ruiz take off his boots and the civilized
clothes he was wearing, to put on his cushma anew and paint his face
with achiote, meaning he was again becoming Hohuaté, getting ready for
possible combat. I ordered bamboo canes to be brought, split into strips,
and woven into mats to build pamacaris, low roofs over the six canoes, as
we did in the exploration of the Madre de Dios River. To me it seemed
very natural that Hohuaté, after scouting out the territory, announced that
there was no danger. We embarked at three in the morning, moving to the
center of the river, and noiselessly passed the mouth of the Perené at half
past four in the morning without the savages noticing us. At six in the

morning, two river bends farther down, we sighted two Campas fishing.
They asked who we were. I did not answer and neither did anyone in our
company. But Chief Andrés Avelino Cáceres y Ruiz shouted, 'Hohuaté!'

"Hearing that name, the two Campas ran to get their weapons and
returned to the landing, boarding their canoes and rowing at full speed to
alert their nearby colleagues to our presence. Our boats, since they had
the added tree trunks on their sides, moved slower than those of the
savages, which allowed them to surge ahead of us. About eight in the
morning, while we were going down a straight section of the river, they
began attacking us with arrows from both shores. Although two of our men
were wounded, the pamacaris defended us well because arrows did not
manage to pass through the thick mat of bamboos, reinforced on its inner
side with ponchos and blankets. Our people responded with random
carbine shots. They could not see what they were shooting at because the
natives were hidden by the forest, having already tasted gunfire. Chief
Andrés Avelino Cáceres y Ruiz jeered at his adversaries, dancing on the
stern of the canoe, avoiding the arrows by moving his body and shouting
at them to come out of the woods and let themselves be seen. The
attackers shouted back, asking us to stop the carbine fire, bullets of which
they couldn't see and thus could not avoid, as Hohuaté was doing with
their arrows, and telling us they would come out into the clearing and fight
anyone as long as it was equal to equal, face to face, and arrows against
arrows.

"We again succeeded in taking control of the situation thanks to our
firearms, but the savages stopped their attack only when they ran out of
arrows. They shouted for us to wait until they went and brought more
arrows. We continued down river and camped on a beach about six
o'clock in the afternoon. Guards were posted through the night. And night
passed uneventfully, we thought, since we had left the dangerous region
behind us. Night did indeed pass uneventfully, but only for us, the Peruvians. The Indians who accompanied us, savages from Hohuaté's tribe,
woke us up early with their screams: Chief Andrés Avelino Cáceres y Ruiz
had been killed by a poisoned dart driven through the center of his chest,
something we couldn't understand because he had slept that night inside
our canoe, as a special exception, well protected by riflemen who had not
moved from their guard posts.

" 'Inganiteri, Chief Inganiteri killed him with a virote!' screamed the *oldest Indian from Hohuaté's tribe. I asked who Inganiteri was, planning to take revenge upon him, since I thought he was one of the Campa accompanying us. Hohuaté's assistant informed me that Inganiteri was a great sorcerer, a shirimpiáre, precisely the Campa chief who had been wounded by Hohuaté's revolver and lost an eye in that celebration, long ago."*

4

Chief Ximu Orders;
the Rivers Obey

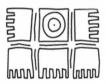

I saw the great maestro Ximu, when I was a child, right after I was kidnapped. He made me witness it as my first apprenticeship: he began to think strongly, strongly, calling the spirits and initiating rites of vengeance. He fasted in the woods, dieted without mercy to his body, drank oni xuma every day: ayawaskha mixed with tohé leaves to nourish his visions, and with coca leaves for divination. He had silvery visions, golden but very real, natural. "Quitaitre! Quitaitre!" called the sorcerer. "Quiet! Quiet!" he called. And he drank wankawisacha to cleanse the soul, so he could separate the soul from the body and send it far away, far away in time. He drank it together with oni xuma, and he also drank chirisanango and sometimes uchusanango. I, a boy, barely thirteen, learned to see the visions he was seeing. To teach me, he told me about each of his visions. The last time I looked at the visions he had summoned, his visions of vengeance against the virakochas, my body became stiff. I became lost in some very dark spirals, and without sweating, my blood pressure went down. Chief Ximu had to throw me head first into the Mishawa River to make me come out of it. I continued seeing the visions without interruption, my body returning to normal but not my soul. That was the first time that Ximu separated me. My soul was seeing. My soul separated from my body and was letting me see, from the air, the vision of a sinking ship. My soul was taking me flying over a wide river, with golden brown waters, seemingly motionless. "It isn't motionless," my soul told me; "it is just pretending." As my soul flew with me from one place to the next, it said, "It is really going back in time; it is returning." And I could determine that the apparently motionless river was the Urubamba, the Sacred River of the Inkas. In a stretch further down, my soul was carrying me by my shoulders, as if I were its prey, my body dangling from the claws of my soul. Further down it showed me the sinking vessel. The ship was sinking and all passengers were saved except two. They all had jumped overboard from the ship, which was heading straight into a giant whirlpool, a muyuna. The ship's pilot was a boy of my age, like me, and he was saying, "My name is Aroldo Cárdenas." I clearly remember that, and his voice. The pilot was steering the ship into the whirlpool, raising his eyes to me, to my soul, and shouting.

"Severo Quinchókeri, the Campa Indian," Ruth Cárdenas, Don Javier's wife in Iquitos, tells me, "Severo Quinchókeri told us that thanks to ayawaskha, he has been able to see how the wizard Julio Valles stole my little brother Aroldo by deceiving him, disguised in my mother's body and voice."

"I am Aroldo Cárdenas!" yelled the ship's pilot, while steering it into the whirlpool.

"A chullachaki is no longer a person," continues Ruth Cárdenas. "A chullachaki—Aroldo, for example—has the appearance of a person but is really not one. He is an empty container filled by the sorcerers at their convenience, giving it the appearance of any body they want, the body with which they want to deceive. Within the emptiness of a chullachaki, which nevertheless has great powers, they place the persons they want us to believe in. I don't know if you understand me."

"I am Aroldo Cárdenas!" he shouted. And he jumped into the water as well. Just before the ship was swallowed by the whirlpool, that boy jumped and joined the others swimming to the shore. I saw it. Then later he returned to the water and slowly walked away along the bottom of the river. And as his body went further away from the survivors, it began to change: it began to grow older, very old, bent over and old. And everyone was saved except two, who were inside a stateroom in the ship's hold. They were talking and laughing, unaware of what was going on and alerted by no one. Both were quite drunk.

That is what I saw in that vision.

"The next day was the ninth of July," bitterly says Zacarías Valdez, the expedition member, in a booklet issued in 1944, a work called "The Real Fitzcarrald in History." "The following day Fitzcarrald started the journey aboard his ship Adolfito. *After navigating for several hours, they arrived at the Mapalja rapids of*

the Urubamba River. The shallow-draft ship was going at full speed, close to the shore. In that manner, upon reaching a sharp turn of the the river, instead of opening up the prow to enter the main current, it continued to navigate close to the shore and thus received the full force of the river on its side, which made it deviate from its course. The pilot, a little old man named Perla, maneuvered to recover the ship's course, and in that effort the steering wheel chain broke, resulting in a loss of control. The crew, realizing the ship was rudderless, jumped overboard and swam, all being saved except Fitzcarrald and the Bolivian rubber magnate Vaca-Diez, both of whom were in the stateroom, ignorant of what was happening outside, celebrating the agreement to merge their respective enterprises to exploit all of the Amazon area.

"The rudderless ship was abandoned even by the pilot, who instead of warning the two moguls only saw fit to jump overboard without even stopping the engine. The Adolfito churned at full engine directly toward the whirlpool, entered it, turned upside down, and sank.

"After the tragedy and once the survivors were counted, old man Perla, probably dead as well, was not to be found. Our Piro oarsmen were ordered to search for the missing bodies, and two days later they found the body of Fermin Fitzcarrald in a backwater full of vegetation.

"The bodies of the Bolivian rubber magnate Vaca-Diez and the pilot Perla were never found. The tragedy was bigger than you might think, Zacarías Valdez tells me, because in that stateroom of the Adolfito the two greatest rubber men of Peru and Bolivia were celebrating the merger of their strengths, to better exploit the rubber business and bring more progress to the Amazon and to our country.

"The body of Fermin Fitzcarrald was burned right there, in the mouth of the Inuya, that accursed tributary of the Urubamba. The savages took advantage of this opportunity to attack the rubber workers. The Amawaka Indians started it by murdering no less than Delfin Fitzcarrald, brother of the unforgettable rubber baron, in the Purus River. And the Piros, our old allies, followed with more of the same in the Curiyane, a tributary of the Las Piedras River, by killing Carlos Shonfe, Leopoldo Collazo, and all of their employees, leaving only women and children alive.

"By that time, the savages were using firearms. Someone had already taught them how to shoot."

5

Ino Moxo Says That Words Are Born, Grow, and Reproduce, but Not in Spanish

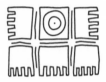

"The truth is not *the* truth, but *our* truth," exclaims Maestro Ino Moxo with a hard and dark voice. "It is the truth of oni xuma, the truth of the chullachaki, the curse of Ximu!" I see him angry for the first time, breathing strongly toward the Mishawa, which slides into the night. He slightly lowers his voice.

"Ximu dedicated himself to teaching me all of our truths."

And overcome by darkness:

"I would lie if I told you that I easily adapted to Amawaka existence. I would lie if I simply told you that I adapted. In reality, it was as if I had always lived here, rising early in the morning with them, going hunting, fishing at midnight, feasting, warring, loving, cutting down trees for canoes and branches for firewood, accompanying women to capture turtles and cupiso eggs under the sand, learning to row without the sound of a single drop, preparing arrows and their poison, polishing blowguns, great bows, and blowing darts without letting the air know about it. And above all else, being always near Maestro Ximu, going everywhere with him, witnessing his fasts, his intoxications for invocation, of call, of exchange of knowledge, spelling out his icaros word for word, as if I were his third lip, and listening to him always. He taught me what one can know, what one should know for the benefit of human beings, of human men and things and animals, of all humans. My initial apprenticeship with Ximu lasted until I was fifteen, then it continued with other chiefs who came to teach me from afar and to practice. But at that age, the great maestro died, shortly after naming me his heir. He donned his ritual cushma when he felt death near. To enter death he donned his yellow cushma. He said farewell to me, saying nothing to the others, and he went into the forest. Ximu's body disappeared spewing smoke."

It has been four days since we arrived at Ino Moxo's village. It is almost noon. Several black lizards bask in the sun, in front of us and to our side, on the shining pebble beaches on both sides of the Mishawa. The river right at this moment is about to win; it pulls out and carries away the remains of the renaco tree down river, to the vast and sacred Urubamba.

"Some of those things, only some of them will I tell you," says Ino Moxo slowly, gazing at the renaco, which sinks and resurfaces, stumbling, grasping the water, which dislodges it beyond the muyuna. "Maestro Ximu returned me to my true nation and its wisdom. He taught me that the miracle is in the eyes, in the hands that touch and search, not in what is seen, not in what is touched."

The childhood of the kidnapped boy passed in a long celebration, a noisy ceremony of potions and fierce nostalgias, in the climax of which he was re-baptized. He stretched his arms, and from the high bush his new life rained down. "Ino Moxo," said the branches above, struck by a heavy downpour. "Ino Moxo," as a talisman made of roots and darkness. Ino Moxo: Black Panther.

Enrolled in the wisdom of plants, warm animals, absent animals, things, stones, and souls; expert in conflict and in counsel; worthy of being listened to by shadows and the bodies of shadows, as Ximu intended, the kidnapped youth was to reach the loftiest depths. Disguised in his former identity, with mestizo clothes and manners, he would deceive the deceivers and obtain carbines and bullets from the white merchants. Later, returning to his real life, he would demonstrate how these iron blowguns, which spew thunder and explosions, were to be used. So Ximu ordered, and so it happened. He trained the youth starting with a first night he has never forgotten. Naked and white, among naked coppery men, surrounded by the bodies of the tribe, he received his destiny at the end of a ritual ayawaskha session.

"Visions . . . begin!" exclaimed Ximu, while calibrating the hallucinogenic apparitions in the mind of the young man, and with those two words taking over his emotions, his soul, his life. The youth learned that all barriers, all *walls* between his existences and those of old Ximu began to disappear. The slightest gesture of the old man developed in his consciousness the caresses of an order. Whatever Ximu thought was seen and heard by the boy. They understood each other through flashes of lightning and through shadows, amid slow visions and colors, and Ximu began to confide his patience and his strength. The boy was told which orders to accept from the souls that live in the air, which directions to ask for and listen to from ayawaskha, which intentions and operative words. He was fertilized with the capacity to carry out these orders and to transmit them, to heal bodies and souls, to mold his own life with hands of service. First of all, the youth had to learn to know dark, unclear forests in full detail, to understand the jungle, and to recognize plants one by one—their uses, spirits, and names. Because each plant has a spirit and a vocation. The same applies to animals, even the most useless ones, one by one, even those that don't exist. He started with the birds, overwhelmed by the ayawaskha, in that first Amawaka intoxication.

"Do you remember what a panguana, that lovely partridge, looks like?" Ximu insisted. "I want you to visualize one now, for me."

And the youth closed and opened his eyes.

"And there was the panguana!" Ino Moxo tells me with a bright smile. "There it was next to Chief Ximu and next to me—the panguana. I could see it perfectly well, tailless, with its green plumage spotted with brown. The colors of the bird were one with the reminiscences of the light, with the shades moving behind the torches, upon the leaves on the ground. I could see everything without limits. Never again in my life have I been able to see like that, with so much clarity, with so many details."

"The panguana will begin to move," Ximu alerted him.

And the panguana moved, began to turn around the youth's field of vision. Ximu invoked and produced a male panguana from the air by willing it, and the two partridges began a courtship dance, flapping their wings and gently pecking each other. A shadow appeared between the two partridges, something that made a nest on the ground, and five eggs. The male panguana sat on the five blue eggs.

"It is the male that incubates," says Ximu.

"And I saw how the eggs began to crack open!" exclaims Ino Moxo, "and from each egg grew two panguanas, big ones, adult ones!"

"It wasn't a man, it was a woman," says Don Javier to my memory. "Because the god Pachamakáite had ordered that Kaametza and Narowé were to have five . . ."

Ino Moxo interrupts him: "Later, by just gazing at Ximu's visions, I learned that there are several classes of panguanas. I learned about the trumpet birds and the wapapas, about many birds, all of them—all the birds. Chief Ximu went about imitating their song, and they would appear and enter my field of vision: day animals, night animals. Later they sang on their own, alone, and their songs passed into my life, forming that other part of my repertory forever. Lovely languages—I still remember them. Chief Ximu put them in my heart and my mouth in those years, in the voice of those years—my spiritual body and my material body. He taught me all the languages: the speech of the birds, the languages of the plants, the more complex ones of the stones. He taught me to tame the powers of the plants and of the stones, the dangerous and honest vocations of herbs. More than anything else he taught me to listen. He taught me to listen to them; he put my ear to their powers, their knowledge, and their ignorance, using ayawaskha. Now, if I come across a root, a flower, or a vine that Maestro Ximu did not show me in his visions, I can listen to that root, to that bush, flower, or vine. I am able to determine its soul, which solitude rules it or which company it keeps, how it was born, what it can be used for, which disease it can banish, which ills feed it. And I know with what diet, with what icaro you might increase or diminish the powers of that plant, with what songs I can nourish it, with what powerful thoughts I can graft it. The same applies to people—Chief Ximu taught me the same things about them. Something for better or worse: Ximu taught me to distinguish the days of the plants. Because on some days a plant is female and is good for certain things, and on other days the plant is male and is good for the opposite."

"If I get to a large river, I'll be safe," said the absent renaco in my vision. Later. Now, I listen to the sound of the site where its branches defied the current, and hear myself inevitably saying:

"Ayawaskha, in the Amawaka dialect—how did you say it?"

"Your question is not fair," interrupts Ino Moxo, with pity in his voice. In the *language* of the Yoras—not a *dialect*—in their language, phrases can go away forever, join together, intermingle and separate for all time, further away than infinity itself."

And turning his face away, nostalgic, losing himself in the absence of the renaco in the middle of the Mishawa:

"Perhaps because of the character of these jungles, this world of ours is still in its formative stage, like rivers that suddenly change course or increase or decrease their flow in a few hours. You must have seen it: if you tie down your canoe without taking it out of the water, you will find it next morning hanging in midair, if you find it at all. The river will look at you from below and you see nothing but stones, all of last night's water has been converted to stone. The

175

reverse may also happen: your canoe may be gone with the currents, which increase without warning and give you no time to react. This world is still being formed, carving out its niche, putting in place its future, falling with the canyons. The gigantic trees, sprouting in islands that today sleep here, like the renaco, tomorrow may wake up far, far away, and in a few moments be again populated by plants, animals, people. In order to see and understand and name a world like that, we must be able to speak in that same way. A language that can decrease or ascend without warning, containing thickets of words that are here today and may wake up far away tomorrow, can in this very instant and inside the same mouth be populated with other symbols, other resonances. It will be hard for you to understand this in Spanish. Spanish is like a quiet river: when it says something, it says only what that something says. It is not so in Amawaka. In the Amawaka language, words always contain things. They always contain other words."

And with a voice that only now I recognize, Ino Moxo said, in the voice of those times in the Hotel Tariri in Pucallpa, flowing from the closed mouth of Don Javier:

"Our words are similar to wells, and those wells can accommodate the most diverse waters: cataracts, drizzles of other times, oceans that were and will be of ashes, whirlpools of rivers, of human beings, and of tears as well. Our words are like people, and sometimes much more, not simple carriers of only one meaning. They are not like those bored pots holding always the same water until their beings, their tongues, forget them, and then crack or get tired, and lean to one side, almost dead. No. You can put entire rivers in our pots, and if perchance they break, if the envelope of the words cracks, the water remains: vivid, intact, running, and renovating itself unceasingly. They are live beings who wander on their own, our words: animals that never repeat themselves and are never resigned to a single skin, to an unchanging temperature, to the same steps. And they couple, like panguanas, and have offspring.

"From the word *tiger,* coupled with the word *dance,* may be born *orchids* or perhaps *tohé poison. Night,* inseminated by *gull,* gives birth to *lightning,* a twin brother of the word that in Amawaka means 'silence-after-the-rain.' Because not just one silence exists in Amawaka, as it would in your generally quiet language, which says nothing. In Amawaka there are many silences, as there are in the jungle, as there are in our visible world, and also as many silences as exist in the worlds that cannot be seen with the eyes of the material body.

"Words, therefore, have descendants.

"And your question is unfair. I believe it comes more from virakocha prejudice than from insolence or ignorance. Even then, I will not let it go unanswered. In the Amawaka language, *ayawaskha* is *oni xuma*—write it down. But *oni xuma* does not only mean 'ayawaskha.' You shall see. *Oni xuma* may mean the same thing, or something else, or its opposite, depending on how you say it and for what purpose, depending on the time of day and the place where you say it. If I pronounce it like this—oni xuma—with a thin voice, shining, as if spelling bonfires instead of words, in the dark, *oni xuma* means 'cutting-edge-of-flat-stone.' And pronounced another way it means 'sorrow-which-does-not-show.' And it means 'arrowhead-of-the-first-arrow.' And it means 'wound,' which also means 'lip-of-the-soul.' And always, at the same time, it is ayawaskha.

"Ayawaskha, for us, is not fugitive pleasure, venture, or seedless adventure, as it is for the virakocha. Ayawaskha is a gateway—not for escape but for eternity. It allows us to enter those worlds, to live at the same time in this and in other realities, to traverse the endless, unmeasurable provinces of the night.

"That is why the light of the oni xuma is black. It doesn't explain. It doesn't reveal. Instead of uncovering mysteries, it respects them. It makes them more and more mysterious, more fertile and prodigal. Oni xuma irrigates the unknown territory: that is its way of shedding light.

"And when we invoke it with urgency, with hunger, and with respect, with that intonation of finite waters, waters passing between the embrace of two round boulders, oni xuma is 'flank-of-a-stone-knife.' We cut the fingers of the Evil One with it. With it, we separate the body from its souls. If a soul is ill or in danger, we divorce it from its hard matter and negate the contamination. We energize it. The ayawaskha shows us the origin and location of the problem, and tells us which herbs and which icaros to use in scaring it away. Likewise, if a body is sick, we pull it away from its soul so that it will not putrefy. We also isolate the location of the damage. We know which roots keep the spiritual body and the material soul away from each other, until the flesh resuscitates in the very heart of its health. Until its double in the air and in the shadows grows again in the body as a renaco would: innocent, not knowing only what the flesh knows, not caring whether it is happy or immortal because both states mean nothing and belong to everything. It is all the same whether it is eternal or fleeting to him who enjoys it. And this, which is nothing, is everything. There are gifts, there are powers, there are commands. There are no miracles in the sense you are now thinking about the word miracle. There is no miracle in the cure or in the invocation, neither before or after oni xuma. There are roots and the juices of roots; there are barks precisely used for this and that, several types of rains which one drinks, and also certain stones. In what manner and in which cases to use them, when to gather them, and how to prepare them—that is what ayawaskha knows and will reveal to us when it deems proper, if the soul or the body is worthy of it. To give you an example: If you live only for yourself, you already have chosen to die. And since nothing will cure you, even though on the outside you may appear to have been born and continue living, you will die, you are already dead. But if you remain in your place—if your soul is in its place, and your body is in its place, snatching away from nothing or no one their rightful living space—then there is no illness that can survive. Oni xuma advises me, dictates the plants, the strong thoughts, the exact medicine that will cleanse the earth and the air belonging to a body. Oni xuma is necessary for that so that the sick person will not advance, will not retreat, and at the same time will not stand still. So that the secret blood of the patient continues flowing. I'm speaking of the blood that feeds the dreams without boundaries, as the existences of the Ashanínka, the Campa, once circulated in the time of men inside their dreams, the time of men in the perfect time.

"That is everything, and as I told you, it is nothing. When you know how to call upon ayawaskha, the impossible becomes easy. There is no mistake; there is no miracle. There is what we deserve to know, and what we deserve to remain ignorant about. That is what the Urus in their wisdom forgot. Everything depends on worthiness. Each ailment, each disease, comes to the world after its remedy. What happens is that there are bodies that deserve to be one with their souls, clean to such a degree that you can't even detect the junction. There are others who deserve a constant lack of equilibrium, always orphaned in something—widowers, lacking in something, stuffed into themselves like a cave within a cave like blind men who are also only one-eyed on top of being blind. They are incapable of contributing anything to the world, never learning that souls are nourished by offerings, that they are nourished by offering themselves, that they become more themselves the more they give of themselves. And he who gives what he has does not really give. He who really gives is he who gives of himself, he who gives from his own life in the earth of this life. Yes, my friend Soriano, souls get nourished by giving nourishment. And ashes turn to water when the thirsty kiss them. But there are those who forget it by remaining unaware, without affirming or denying it. Those bodies do not deserve to be bodies; they occupy a void in this world, in the infinite existences of this world, and that is why they always lack something. They lack air, a slice of soil. Their souls are in disarray and useless; their flesh ray. Oni xuma knows how to untie them. That is why it is the cutting euge ui a flat stone, it is wound and knife and arrowhead of the first arrow of the last rib, and it is a needle that mends or tears apart. It knows how to separate the bodies from their souls and then return them. It knows who says yes and who says no, who is worthy of this life or deserves another one, or deserves none. I can only obey. Without the black light of ayawaskha I am not even ignorant. I can't even make mistakes; I simply hit the target in reverse, which is quite different. Ayawaskha makes me its most wretched instrument because it is so powerful. If there is much that I don't know, that I don't quite see, it doesn't matter: ayawaskha knows. Everything depends on worthiness. Ayawaskha orders or disorders; I obey. If it doesn't order me to do anything, I obey all the same. And if it orders me to postpone a death, then I certainly transform any damaging spell into a mere memory!

"I have probably said more than your question asked for. Do you see it? Words start other words moving; they unleash powers, liberate other energies. If the person who hears my words can only hear my words, what a waste— but no matter: the powers are already unleashed to roam in the air, traveling and transforming the world. Can't you see? I told you. Everything depends on worthiness."

"You mean to say that ayawaskha opens the door to health?"

"Everything depends on worthiness, my friend Soriano." He half-gyrated his face again and again, scattering gazes upon the floor, under a pomarrosa tree I had not noticed until yesterday. "Look at these small ants—they are called citarácuy. Do you know that they forecast the future?" I, in silence, wonder whether he is making a fool of me. "Look how they run to protect themselves from the rain," says Ino Moxo. "They hurriedly run pell-mell looking for their nest, ungrateful, leaving behind the time that guided them. The citarácuy know that shortly, within five to seven hours, it will rain heavily. But considering their life span, five to seven hours to these ants represents ten or fifteen years to us. What man could predict exactly when it will rain and at what time of day, fifteen years in the future? Many animals around here know. Even certain flowers know: they close and hide long before the rains come. Other things are foreseen here. I have learned, taught by the air, that human beings in ancient times could also foresee the future as they could see what had already happened. I have seen them in timeless time. In time perhaps, and in the night, they began to lose those powers. Now only some people can do that, gener-

179

ally children or shirimpiáre—sorcerers. Newly born, we all possess those powers and many others as well, but as we get older we retreat for whatever reason and gradually lose them. Speaking, for example. I am now speaking for you. Otherwise, I would surely do so in a different way. I would not develop the concepts in order to fit your understanding. But I'm forced to use your words. I have to fit my words inside yours and adapt my thoughts, silencing others that do not fit, that rebel against that confinement you call coherence. If we had enough time to be worthy, perhaps I might show you how to use my eyes, to speak with my mouth. Maybe you would understand. As it is, I have to reduce everything. The obstacle is time."

And Maestro Ino Moxo, as if distancing his mouth but not his voice from my increasing interest, spoke from his own body seated on the log in front of the Mapuya River, making himself weaker and slower in his words:

"Within a short time I will have to go. The problem is that of time, this time. No matter how long you wait, you cannot wait for me. My time is not your time but the time of Chief Ximu. Last night I dreamed about Chief Ximu. I have seen him again, and he disappeared spewing smoke, the time of his body, a great yellow smoke."

6

The Slap That
Set Petroleum on Fire

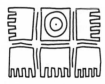

I know who slapped Severo Quinchókeri this morning. It was a foreman named Eulalio Vargas, furious because a container of sugar had disappeared from his backpack. It happened in the French petroleum camp upstream, near the Sepawa River. It was even worse: the foreman insulted the Ashanínka Severo Quinchókeri in front of two Piro Indians, two people from the tribe most hostile to the Ashanínka! And Severo Quinchókeri was not only an Ashanínka but also husband to the favorite granddaughter of old Chief Ximu. The insulted man did not utter a word or make a gesture, but right at that moment, even before the punished expression developed on his face, the severe silence of Quinchókeri had already sentenced the foreman. The Piro witnesses knew it, called their warriors, and prepared for the inevitable. They alerted the oil workers in vain. Ignoring the risks, the latter kept on working as if nothing had happened.

On the following daybreak the men of Ino Moxo stormed the virakocha camp, dancing. They used blowguns and some dark flutes they call "songárinchis." A face with only one eye, unmistakable, added his skill to the magic fury of the Black Panther. The people of Inganiteri, the Ashanínka, forgetting old disputes, joined the Amawaka of Chief Ximu and Ino Moxo in setting everything afire. The petroleum tanks burned for hours, redder and blacker than an explosion of heaven itself. The foreman

*Eulalio Vargas was killed, as were the engineer Mauricio Berrios and
another engineer, a Greek by the name of Sotiris. Late that afternoon,
uniformed men from the Atalaya post arrived with guns. They found
nothing in the petroleum camp and nothing in the adjoining village where
the Amawaka lived. The only thing they found in shallow pits were what
resembled tombs, with remains of half-eaten corpses.*

*So they wouldn't have to deal with uniformed men, because this was
not a matter for uniformed men and only because of that reason, the
Amawaka decided to move farther away. They went to an island some
call Chumichinia, in the middle of the Ucayali between the villages of
Bolognesi and Chicoza near the mouth of the Puntijau canyon. The
surviving oil men have no wish to return—we don't know why. The
Amawaka are still installed in their new site, led by a Campa, the
Ashanínka Severo Quinchókeri, living as before and as always, in peace.*

And this happened recently, in the middle of 1976, Ino Moxo tells me, coming
into the village of Muyuy Island, crossing Rumania Plaza, already being erased
by the night.

7

Maestro Ino Moxo Says Farewell

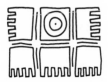

"Is there a memory of the heart?" answered Ino Moxo the following day. "There must be. It must be from that memory that the face of Chief Ximu appeared to me, as I was still dazzled by the lights of ayawaskha, features I confuse with those of the Inka Manko Kalli holding that wooden vase. All of Ximu's body, his feet formed by the buttressed roots of a lupuna tree, his body lean and hard under the cushma which high above, like a moon, is giving rise to clouds in his head of wide leaves. He looks down on me from his crown, modeled by lost Jíbaros, his enlarged head impaled on a stake, and from his body made of a yellow lupuna tree."

"I must go," says Ximu regretfully, slowly leaving my field of vision. And it is not Chief Ximu. It is Chief Ino Moxo. I strain to listen to him; I barely listen to his body, the empty icaro of his skin. Through a tunnel of paka vines with generous thorns I observe his words, like butterflies moon-spotted with black, flutter toward me. I must go, repeats Ino Ximu, repeats Ximu Moxo. He is getting closer; his face with cloudy filaments in the bleaching dark brown hair falls from the lupuna tree. I try to revive; I tell myself I'm fully conscious, but for nothing. Hours of years went by. I saw the boat devoured by the whirlpool of hummings and shadows, thanks. Ayawaskha and tohé, thanks, a thousand thanks. I saw Kaametza on the shore watching over Narowé's sleep: thanks. I saw Narowé awakening in that lake, which was again a river. I saw the male panguana hatching five blue moons—or were they orange?—in the black entreaty on that early

,ning. Hand of the Amazon: thanks. Five-headed koto-machácuy stretching
ɔward the hut of Don Juan Tuesta in Muyuy Island: thanks.

And from the five moons, cracking open the shell made of feathers with
scaly wings, I saw the sons of my sons come out, heading to the four corners
of the universe to give rise to nations. I saw when everything in the world was
ashes—the ocean, love, air, promises, the moon, the ancient youthfulness of
things. And I saw a bolt of lightning strike the pomarrosa tree. "It is Kaametza,"
I saw the god Pachamakáite say. "It is the first human being, the first man," I
see Don Javier say in the lobby of the Hotel Tariri, entering the river, entangled
in deep laughter. I see the drawings on the walls of the hotel and I see no drawings. I see the faces of souls, maps of cities, cities that are souls in movement.
I distinguish clear features, familiar faces of forested souls! I see houses that
change locations, live cities, unexpected forests that open in midair, their thickets
invisible amid the constant danger! A black woman tells me something with
her closed mouth; I draw nearer and discover a musical cajón at her feet. I hear
the cajón resound without being touched by human hands, and its notes are
words, voices, that flee from the skin of the traitor. A lost language is flowing
from the drum of the Bora Indians. And I see that I recognize those words: they
are the wind of the Quechuas, outlining themselves against the cobweb suddenly shining and erasing the white woman, carved in the bark of a bleeding
renaco. And the renaco is the drum skin of that drum, and from its skin emerge
the words, drop by drop, from the earth to the sky, a golden shower crackling
in the air and entering my nostalgia:

> *Apu miski yawar*
> *Qespichiway yawar*
> *Auqay kunamanta*

They come in one by one: *Apu*, omnipotent, *miski*, sweet, *yawar*, blood.
Omnipotent sweet blood. One by one: *qespichiway*, couple me with crystal, make
me crystalline, free, pristine. *Auqay*, enemy. *Kunamanta*, all men.

> *Omnipotent sweet blood:*
> *make me crystalline, purify me,*
> *free me from all men who are my enemies*

Those words pour gold in my ears. And my head becomes transparent—
thank you—becomes a sparkling earthen bowl full of rainwater. And in the bowl

of my head I see another floating head, with a stubborn beard of steel like a conquistador's armor. Behind the beard are hard golden lips like the beak of a wapapa. Hurriedly, I take the head out of the bowl before the water boils and rest it on the sand. I form a semicircle of warriors, silences, shadows, who are already shrinking their trophies. I model mine with hot ashes, with flour made from my ancestors' bones. I begin to give it features I have never seen before, and which I know: they are the Inka Hohuaté's. It is the traitor Morales Bermúdez, the reborn head of the traitor; it is the Piro Atawallpa, who drank to his victory from the skull of his brother Huáscar. And the water in my bowl turns red like the Pisacq moon, like the sun of Pawkartampu: thank you. My head is full of the sun's sperm, bleeding crystalline blood. Don Javier peers out from behind it, and the joyful Christ soars like a condor, the claws of his soul covered with scars, and the condor rescues me from the earth and takes me to the skies. I see myself flying even farther away, and simultaneously I see myself here in the house of Ino Moxo, next to Iván and to Félix Insapillo, with closed eyes sweating in the corners of the floor made of scratched pona boards. Suddenly Insapillo and Iván disappear, and in their places a new landscape is born, which I have never seen before. I see myself walking between boulders, great rocks carved with the images of monkeys, dinosaurs, symbols I do not understand— and I am the human footprint on the rock. I am sixty million years old. In the sorcerer's house, Iván sits up and comes near Ino Moxo, crossing the room like a serpent formed of smoke:

"Perhaps the mixture with tohé has affected César."

And the serpent made of smoke has wings and escapes, flying and smoking to the forest. I feel quieter; everything is all right. I look with my eyes and know that what I see is not what I see; I know I'm observing *other* things. An Amawaka boy climbs the steps to the hut and smiles. It is Ino Moxo's envoy, the child who led us here! I stand up and go to him, wanting to embrace him, but the vision retreats into the jungle. He is Ino Moxo as a child. It is the ancient childhood of the master, Black Panther as a child who goes away and dissolves under the pomarrosa tree among the garabatokasha vines! I turn my face to the smoke, go through the shirikaipi being smoked by the sorcerer, and I see: the Mishawa River is traversing the hut, its green-black waters pounding the pona boards, escaping through the door of the sorcerer's house, tumbling down the wooden steps, which have now turned to stone, and pouring down in a tame waterfall. The floorboards rearrange themselves, seeking another configuration; they are stone medusas, strange fossils of giant fish and shells.

I lean forward, pick one of them, and place it in the floor to my right, next to the wapapa, which is devouring entire cities, cultures, true civilizations, flesh-and-blood men, small like the fruit of the aguaje palm. The wapapa tears up their backs and drinks their eyeless, shrunken heads. The Colorado River flows from its beak; the life of the Mashko is still flowing. I see my cousin César Calvo stand up, lift the carnivorous wapapa, and pull its head off—thank you—with both of my hands. I now see the Mapuya River flow from the torn neck of the wapapa under the sun of another time, move in the direction of the Urubamba River, climb the mountains—thank you—and become narrower in the Sacred Valley of the Inkas, amid snowy summits. And I fall asleep with distant and content eyes: thank you. I keep on seeing other visions while asleep. And I know that I'm awake, dreaming a much more real dream.

8

Jose Maria Arguedas
Kisses the Mouth of a Dart Gun

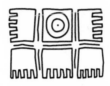

And I could not see anything else. I woke up. Seated on an espintana log to my right, Don Javier sat shining like a dead man's letter. Narowé sang in front of him in my vision, but his voice was that of Don Hildebrando in Pucallpa, the mouth of a white guitar, which repeated Raul Vásquez's verses from high up in the air, behind a rainbow palisade:

> *And you leave me alone*
> *as the sleeping sky,*
> *as when the rain*
> *goes writing forgetfulness,*
> *in the same way as the canoes*
> *which will never see the river.*

"From now on, you will sing no more!" Don Hildebrando commands Narowé. "From now on, you will be the song!" and the Minstrel of the Jungle becomes the jungle—I saw it with my own eyes. I saw him going toward the Amazon, immerse himself, and then return with the moon held in his arms. And the moon sounded like all the musics of man upon the world. "Manguaré! Manguaré!" said Narowé with closed lips, singing inside a river of return that went up the Urubamba, the Wilkamayu, upriver in time, taking forests with him as if they were pebbles in his knapsack. Colored fish, great boulders from large fortresses were moved

by Narowé with quiet songs, pushed only with icaros, singing and thinking, raising the impossible against the virakocha ships, a palisade made of souls, an invincible bamboo wall against the voice of the sea.

"But they are not bamboo," says Don Juan Tuesta, seated on the espintana log.

"Leg bones of tanrilla, penises of achúni—that's what they are," says Don Hildebrando from my left.

"No bird is more sought after than the poor tanrilla; no fish is more envied that the innocent achúni. The achúni is the only being in the world with a permanent erection, even if doesn't want it; a powerful, bony pole advances within its phallus. And the tanrilla is forever condemned to live in the air: if it descends to the ground, it loses either its legs or its life. There is no better love philter than the leg bones of a tanrilla," smiles Don Juan Tuesta.

And Don Hildebrando agrees: "Sorcerers deceive the tanrillas; they attract them singing like herons. The tanrillas descend and return to the skies minus two legs, walking thereafter on two absences, on two threads of blood, like the loves they unleash. The shirimpiáre cure their severed legs and sing icaros to them; they fast and store them buried under the soil. After a suitable time elapses, after that silvery pollen falls from the clouds under whose shadows they forget, the bones by now are bare and pure. They take them out; they unearth them as thin, hollow tubes, like dart blowguns. If a disdainéd male can sight the naked woman who refused him through a tanrilla leg bone used as a telescope, after three days he will no longer have to court her—she will pursue him.

"Pukuna of love—that is what the leg of a tanrilla is, through which you can project infallible looks as you would a dart," says Don Hildebrando.

"Essentially, the sorcerers use them as mouthpieces in the pipes they use while they sing icaros," adds Don Juan Tuesta. "When he casts spells, every sorcerer bites on the tanrilla leg bone, a bony blowpipe that works in reverse: you aspirate through it rather than blow into it."

And Don Hildebrando: "Because the true shirimpiáre do not smoke when they smoke: by means of tobacco, they inhale souls, forces that the tanrilla knew how to extract from the air when it walked in another time, when it only stepped upon transparent paths rather than in buried tracks, or impious and smoky pupils and mouths."

I could no longer hear them. I was awake. With my eyes sealed by who knows what dreams, I looked. Jose Maria Arguedas was walking back along the river, from the foggy "Second of May" docks in front of the island, wearing a flaming yellow cushma. Death was looking at him through a pukuna made out of tanrilla leg bone.

"Tell me what can I do!" grieved the rough, gray voice of the Amazon River. "Tell me what I must do, Jose Maria Arguedas, so that you will not abandon us, so that you will not submit your forehead to the dart blown at you by the enemy!"

And in a stretch farther down, in front of me, without stopping his walk, Jose Maria Arguedas replied:

"Return to the Urubamba!" he said. "Take me back upriver with you! Advance four centuries! Go back, Amazon, four centuries to the Sacred River! Prevent the barbarians, the virakochas, the conquistadors, from landing!"

"From now on you will see no more!" interrupted the voice of Don Juan Tuesta. "From now on, Jose Maria Arguedas, you will be the vision!"

Narowé, the first man, obeyed and put on the red poncho of his yellow cushma. "Yawar fiesta!" he shouted. "Raymi-yawar!" he sang, and he headed toward the wings of the burning bull, toward the horns of the condor. Jose Maria Arguedas came near the shore, walked again upon the water, and squarely faced the mouth of the black pukuna.

And his body disappeared spewing smoke.

I saw it in my vision.

9

Maestro Ino Moxo Disappears
While Spewing Smoke

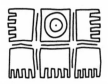

"You will never learn that it is not simply a matter of just wanting to learn," Ino Moxo accuses me. "If I were a tree," he says, "if I were a tree and wanted to walk like a human being . . ."

"You couldn't, obviously."

"Do you see?" He becomes impatient. "Of course I could walk, yes: I would walk!" And erasing me with a flash of his brown eyes: "But I would walk as a tree, not as a human being! The same thing happens with you, the virakocha: some have the will of language but lack a mouth. I could tell you many things; you will listen to none of them. And if you listen to any of them, you will do so in your own way. You will hear them as a tree, not as a Yora, not as an Amawaka. The most difficult problem is not that of wanting to learn. It is time. With enough time you might learn to listen and to walk. And with enough time I would listen to you, and walk your way without undoing mine. With sufficient time everything will again belong to everybody. We will be able to exist in our life, and at the same time in the life of all persons who were once things, and in the life of things that later are to be persons. All existences, including the nonlife of the chullachakis, the lives invented by Don Javier, invented by me. What passes for a life, as in the case of my godson Iván Calvo, is so identical to his true life that if you come up against him in the jungle returning from the Mapuya, for example, you will never doubt that you're dealing with Iván Calvo. Even more, with time, the simulated life of that Iván Calvo will lead your own life—are you following me?

"Because the virakochas structure their knowledge so that it includes only the intimate realities that define a person, not the universal and infinite ones, I don't know what words to use to explain this to you. The virakocha accept that our river is not the only one. They say there are many other rivers. As if rivers were all that existed, and as if all rivers were made of water, and all had only two shores that eventually led to the sea. They cannot conceive that a river could have one, or three, or five shores. Neither can they conceive of a river with still waters, or with waters that run upstream. They say it is impossible for a river to flow without water, to advance between two landscapes without moving, that it is impossible for the landscapes themselves to move toward the sea. They do not see the worlds that create this world, the worlds that oni xuma reveals to us, for example. Some virakocha, a minority, tolerate certain of our wisdoms, only the knowledge relating to plants. But they do not see that the plants are only the visible portion of the healing. The virakocha use our plants, and they fail, without good results. Plants mean nothing unless they are inserted within a whole, in the totality of knowledge we have inherited, in that infinite architecture of sacred realities, each one having very precise gateways. They don't know that those doors are really only one, a single one with a multiple key—and that that key never repeats itself and is always oni xuma. For them it is toxic: ayawaskha is a drug, they say—a hallucinogen. And they experiment, they play. They have played with everything like this, unknowingly, wasting it. In time they will come to accept us in our full truth. They will accept not only the very last leaf of the crown of the tree but also the whole tree: its roots, the soil upon which it rests, and so on until the infinite, in that time which repeats and repeats in the mind as if always for the first time, in the mind of men when they think about existence. Perhaps some day the life of mankind may occupy a yellow void, a reflection of ashes in the air, or it may occupy another state, another existence, a sound, a stone shell without memory. Because things are not only truly real, or only mere illusions. There are many categories in between, where things exist: many categories of the real, simultaneously and in different times. And you will see that. For example, it may be difficult for you to accept that we, the Amawaka, survived not only because of bullets and Winchesters. We were also allowed to become invisible. Ximu knew how to chant icaros in order to make his warriors invisible so the destructive rubber collectors could not see them. They vanished. He also chanted me into invisibility when I was thirteen years old. That's how I survived. The rubber people went right by me without seeing, looking for me with their carbines and seeing nothing. There was no one in my place. I laughed at them, laughed at their bullets whistling past me in the air. I still remember the cruelty of Fitzcarrald and his mercenaries. And to think that those genocidal criminals were men! Even now, at times, I am tempted to better declare myself a snake, or a piece of bloodwood, or a stone from a canyon—anything other than a man."

Two Amawakas pass in front of us, carrying sparse boxes filled with even sparser provisions. Ino Moxo looks at them:

"Those two, for example, my first godsons, were chosen to punish the younger brother of Fitzcarrald. Ximu sang icaros to them, magnetizing them and empowering with precise and sufficient powers. On the proper day, at the proper time, the two of them took their clothes off and entered the Mishawa River. As if someone were entering into the space below a mosquito net, they entered the river and went quietly, walking over its rocky bottom. They surfaced in the Purus River. There they executed Delfin Fitzcarrald. Then they returned to the river and walked back quietly without getting wet."

Asleep, I continue seeing visions. Someone, perhaps Insapillo, pours cane juice over my pupils, and I see again. I am here again, never having left, in the hut of the Sorcerer of Sorcerers, on the shore of the Mishawa. It is daytime.

"This moon shining on us from the bottom of the Amazon River is the fourth moon that has accompanied the Earth," said my cousin César, who heard it from Don Javier, who had in turn heard it from Inganiteri. "And he says that the prior moon wasn't a hollow log but an otorongo, a tiger made of ashes. That black moon—that luminous, round tiger—was condemned by the god Pachamakáite to be knocked down, without blame or reward, sentenced to lose its stature and fall into the lives of men. The forests of the Great Pangoa were the site selected by Pachamakáite for the moon to fall like the paw of sin on the flanks of the earth of men."

"You should know that the Pangoa River empties into the Perené River," says Inganiteri to Don Javier. "Also remember that the Perené and the Ene Rivers form the Tambo River, and the latter merges with the Urubamba to give rise to the Ucayali, which together with the Marañón, beyond the bloodwood forests, are the two eyes of Narowé that created the Amazon. Seven kilometers from the point where the Pangoa joins the Perené was a village named Puerto Ocopa with a Franciscan convent—a school created to teach the inconveniences of Western civilization to Ashanínka children."

*"Since the priests were unable to gather together a large enough
school attendance," Don Javier told me, "they were forced to demand that
the Piro and other Indian enemies of the Ashanínka stage raids on the
borders of the Great Pajonal territory to ambush the Campa—not to kill
them, although many were in fact killed, but basically to steal their
children. With orphaned and kidnapped children, those Sons of God of
Puerto Ocopa filled their classrooms. All of them died, teachers and
pupils, Westerners and Ashanínkas—they all died on the day chosen by
the god Pachamakáite for the otorongo to fall into the universe."*

"Maestro Ino Moxo is gone," I hear Iván say as I wake up. "He has gone
into the forest alone, wearing his yellow cushma."

And avoiding my look, with a remembering gaze in his eyes, pretending
to watch the sunlight from the open door of the hut:

"He asked me to say good-bye to you. Maestro Ino Moxo asked me not to
wake you up until after he was gone."

*"One week before the appointed day, all of the animals of the
Pangoa and the Tambo wanted to warn us. I saw it with the eyes of my
most distant father," says Inganiteri. "Because exactly seven days before,
all of the fish became desperate. They fled the waters of the Tambo and
the Pangos with an agonizing speed, in tempests of panic, as if they were
abandoning two torrential fires. They surged against the currents, disputing the air of the raw waves, toward the creeks, the squalid canyons,
toward the fragile, transparent refuge of those pitiful, arid brooks that
narrow to nothing, their sides covered with stones. They died by the
thousands, attempting to warn us, and they died in vain."*

*"Be aware that before you reach Puerto Ocopa, two gigantic hills are
located on the sides of the Pangoa," says Don Javier. "The great otorongo
fell on those hills and pulled them together with its paws, blocking the way
of the current. The Franciscans, who were far away at the time and who
were thus saved by omission, said that it was an earthquake, not an
otorongo, and that it was God's decision, not that of the moon."*

"What do they know," says Inganiteri.

*"It was that black tiger which dispersed the Campa. It welded
together the two hills with colossal paws, and in the place of its embrace
the waters of the Pangoa became an ocean. The furor of those repressed*

seas fell like a wave without distance and without time, like a single wave of stones, fear, and mud, into the empty channel of the Pangoa, toward the uninhabited Perené, toward the useless Tambo. It traversed the skin of the Ucayali and made it a dagger of death and mud which offended the impossible: the Amazon."

"And that happened recently, in the third moon of 1947," says a face I remember but which I have never seen.

Still empowered and dizzy, under stress, I let myself be led by Félix Insapillo. We move through the brown mass of the Amawaka village. I remember mute children with big bellies, the two natives carefully keeping watch over our empty supply boxes, and a lively little dog we called Waskar, Admiral, or Blueblood, which accompanied us, jumping, rubbing against my legs, and fretting until we crossed that eternal bamboo wall. I remember the fragrance of the pomarrosa as I walked by leaning on Insapillo's arm, and I remember that maze of garabatokasha, beyond which vanished the chullachaki boyhood of Ino Moxo, the sorcerer.

When I retrieved my heart, we were already back in the Mapuya River, gathering fossils millions of years old, the memories of the seas this forest had once been: the great shells turned to stone, the remote medusas. I thought about the wapapa, and I thought I heard, far, far away, the sound of the shot with which I did not kill it. And we were again walking back on that hot, sinuous trail to the muddy shores of the Inuya. We untied our boat from the depth of the woods and pushed it, very tired, and returned it to the waters of the roaring Inuya.

"They say it happened recently, but what do they know," says Inganiteri, the witch doctor. "I know from the ancestors of my ancestors that it happened centuries ago, in the time some virakocha insist on calling the Universal Deluge."

"It was no deluge," affirms Don Juan Tuesta. "It was the wooden tiger that Narowé still animates in the bottom of the river."

"Because the time of times doesn't fit into our time," Don Javier tells me. "The cause of the disaster was death—the death of Ino Moxo. I was a child then, and that is why I could see it. For many days, I saw in front of Iquitos, where once the skin of the Amazon glistened, a crust of mud, which dragged monstrous corpses with it: great fish with the jaws of a

*wangána, giant snakes with three wings made of stone, two-headed boas,
creatures I had never seen and will never see again. There were creatures
like a turtle, like birds, wapapas with scales, and horses and white-haired
children, and floating rocks, the remains of houses filled with strange
women, hairless maidens without breasts, and logs, many logs, all of the
logs of the jungle floating by on the Amazon, and lizards with bulls' horns,
and a type of innocent, golden fish, singing better than all of the musics of
the world, slow open mouths telling us all that is in memory, saying
nothing on land."*

We navigated for three days, spending the nights on sand or pebble beaches
or on perfumed strips of land, under torn mosquito netting. It was almost dusk
when we came around the island stealthily hidden by grass pastures and sighted
the forlorn dock, the lanterns of the first houses, the misleading profile of the
city of Atalaya.

*Because you should know that in another time, in these same waters
of the Ucayali, thrived a race of yellow, singing fish. When Ino Moxo spoke
no more, everyone became mute, as if when the life of the Amawaka
sorcerer passed on—thank you—it also took away the lips of things, and
their golden languages.*

10

Via Crucis of the Black Otorongo

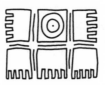

Two rows of oil lamps allowed us to sense the location of the dock and the approach to the boardwalk of planks encrusted on the side of the Ucayali River. We felt our way out of the boat, slid as we climbed the hill, and estimated the navigable stretches of the main street of Atalaya. I don't know how we finally arrived at the Central Square.

At one side of the darkness, the dim lights of the Grand Hotel de Souza appeared under the rain. Refusing the tenuous protection of rooms, totally exhausted, we collapsed before a table in the bar of the hotel and pleaded for beer and cigars. A young priest—a Jesuit, I believe—was sitting at a table near the door, not drinking or smoking anything, as if ready to leave forever. I stopped him in time and invited him simply to join us. He opened his eyes wide and gave a noble smile. He was almost blond and had a beard. He stood up to his full height, which was almost offensive and the envy of athletes, and accepted, whether from pleasure, curiosity, or just forgiveness. Later we found out he was not only a priest but also a child, the memory of a sage, a certain naive and malicious bible without crimes or masochistic saints, without incest and without punishment. He was one of us and all of us, and at the same time the opposite—not excessively joyful nor bitter in disdain, so much so that without intending to he forced us to be silent and listen to him.

"At that time I lived at the brow of the jungle," he said, "in a zone adjoining the mountains that lead to Cajamarca. Whenever my feet would not carry

196

me farther in those immense distances, someone would lend me a mule. On that particular day I was going to a small place called Polish, where I had been told one could find many rocks with carvings of very ancient and unusual animals. I'm telling you what I heard, because I never saw them. I could not enter Polish that day. As I was arriving, I was stopped by a shadow, a voice, a hand that picked up the reins of the mule."

"'Little father, are you Father Pedro?' asked the shadow. 'I am,' I answered.' 'Forgive me, little Father Pedro!' said the shadow, kneeling down in the darkness. I remained silent. The shadow seemed to grieve, and said, 'Last night I made a vow to kill you, little father. I have promised them I would kill you.'

"'What are you saying, son?' I was disconcerted, says Father Pedro.

"'Forgive me, little priest; give me your blessing.'

"'Has someone demanded that you kill me?'

"'Little father, forgive me.'

"'Who wants you to kill me, and why?'

"'Give me your blessing!'

"I had to bless him," he says. "I had to bless and forgive him so he would stop wailing. Only then did the shadow quiet down. That hand kissed my hand, he thanked me, and that voice forgave me:

"'Thank Heaven, little father, because if you had not forgiven and blessed me I would have had to kill you on this very spot.'

"And he insisted," says Father Pedro. "With strong entreaties he asked me not to enter the town. I still don't know whether the metallic flash in the hand of that man came from a machete or from something else. I leaned over, trying to get a better look. And just at that moment I recognized him. 'Insapillo,' I asked him, 'tell me what has come over you!'

And Félix Insapillo, seated to my right, here in the bar of the Grand Hotel de Souza in Atalaya, avoiding the questioning eyes of the priest:

"I could not tell you then; it wasn't my fault, but I can tell you now."

And raising his face, but not his eyes, toward the shape of Father Pedro in the dimly lit bar, Félix Insapillo was briefly silent and then continued:

"The night before your arrival, all of the inhabitants of Polish, including myself, gathered together at the cemetery, among the tombs and the old stones, and palisaded the town against you."

"Palisaded?"

"Just so," Insapillo confesses. "They gathered together in front of those centuries-old tombs and asked our dead to release their souls. And the souls of all time, the souls of all those who are dead, came out and surrounded the town. Just as if they were forming a palisade of planks or bamboos, the souls surrounded the town to prevent your entry. We made a palisade of souls so that you would never enter Polish again."

"It was no deluge; it was no flood," insists Don Javier. "It was a black otorongo. You must know that a black otorongo is never really black. It is black and aggressive only on certain occasions and at a certain distance. Near a fearless man without doubts, it becomes timid, afraid, and runs away. But by that time Ino Moxo was already dead. You must realize that, looked at closely, a black otorongo is quite different: it has soft, clear, gray spots all over its skin, especially near the mouth and under the bristles of its whiskers. I know why that is so, and at the same time why it isn't so. The black otorongo, almost from the moment of birth, is rejected by its own mother. It is the only being in the forest forced to look for its own sustenance from a very early age, when it still doesn't know what is food and what may be poison. You will feel even sadder if you realize that below every muyuna, below any of those river whirlpools, lies always a yakumama, a water snake. Where there is a whirlpool, there always also is a yakumama, a snake that nourishes it, a great boa that feeds the whirlpool, even if it is one thousand years old. Think of it! Think about the black otorongo! What would it feel, knowing as it does that even the most distant whirlpools, the muyunas in the rivers that no one has seen or will ever visit, those whirlpools that don't have even a fragile canoe to overturn, or even a floating log to amuse themselves with—what will the tiger think, knowing that even those deprived whirlpools have at least a mother!"

And the priest's look held back a nostalgia that was less than a lament and yet more, with the voice of the condemned, of blameless blame, convicted of a crime he did not commit, convicted of a crime that someone, in another life and another time, using his hands, committed. Soundlessly speaking, the priest, rising again, tired, pulled his hands away from the table as if they were being burned:

"Something happened every time I intended to visit that village. I suddenly would become ill without cause on the night before the journey, with chills and fevers that disappeared as soon as I returned to my parish. Now I understand. A hundred times I started out to go to Polish and I never made it there."

II

Juan González Walks Seven Days Along the Bottom of the Ucayali River

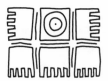

Back in Pucallpa, recovered from the winds that threatened us in the twin-engined plane, I often left my room in the Hotel Tariri to look in vain for Don Hildebrando. This made me accept Iván's invitation to visit the home of Juan González on the outskirts of town. Iván Calvo told me he was a magician of laughter and good times. Juan González states that resentments and anger are the cause of a shortened life. Happiness is the only thing that extends life. According to Iván Calvo, he believes that plants and icaros do not help unless there is happiness. "And Juan González cures troubles by spraying them with smiles," says Iván Calvo, as we see a silhouette in the door of the house.

"Come in," says Juan González, stretching out his arms in an adolescent's hug, giving us a beardless half smile, his stiff hair uselessly white, his face the face of a nobody. Nothing gives away his fame as a witch doctor, neither solemnity nor sympathy, and he speaks with a voice that sounds like two knives being sharpened:

"You have arrived just in time; we were getting started."

Once inside, we sense bodies all along the walls, moans kneeling down, vinegary clothes huddled in the darkness. The sorcerer led us to our places, and right away, without any preambles or ceremonies, he served ayawaskha in a cup we could hardly see. Before the oni xuma could become comfortable in my mind, or before I could get used to its mind, a voice with an undoubtable Campa inflexion moved close to Juan González.

"I have become ajuási," it said. "Some evil spell has turned me useless, incapable, forgotten. I go into the jungle to hunt and I always return empty-handed, with an empty bag, without any prey."

And with the color of supplication, the voice said in even darker and more rasping tones:

"Help me, shirimpiáre. I haven't lived for months; I live without will, without luck."

Juan González moved toward the voice. We never found out whether he had given it tobacco to chew, but immediately the voice began to vomit, trembling and moaning. I am unaware whether it was two hours later, or right away, since ayawaskha was already affecting my soul, but I could see everything clearly as if under the noon sun. Juan González was coming apart in the midst of convulsions, inaudible gestures and demands. He grimaced, he was bent, he was someone else. His arms flailed the shining, sharp air. I knew we were in the middle of the night, but he was transformed, scintillated like a red moon, like the Pisacq sun, the Pawkartampu sun. Juan González suddenly entered the repose of a Sun being, a High Priest of the Inkas, issuing blue and orange orders:

"Severo Quinchókeri!" he calmed the voice. "All of the animals are yours, Severo Quinchókeri!"

Iván assured us that when Juan González was really Juan González, before taking oni xuma, he had no knowledge of the name or of the problems of the voice. Nevertheless, this Juan González, after taking ayawaskha, seemed to know everything beforehand and was shouting out loudly:

"Yours is the forest! Yours is the jungle!"

And somewhat more calm, wavering between an icaro and a relentless shout:

"I give you all the animals! All the animals are yours, Severo Quinchókeri! You are their owner! I return them to you; you are the best son of Kaametza and Narowé! I am the Lone Soul, I am Elegguá, I am the son-in-law of the god Pachamakáite, I am a god, and I give you what has always been yours, all of the forest, all the beings and persons in the forest!"

After that my memories are blurred. Juan González closed his arms around himself, a terse white post in the center of the hut. He closed his eyes and levitated, floated half a meter above the floor, flew out over Federico Basadre Road. I think he returned with deer antlers in his hands—but it wasn't a deer and they were not antlers. It was just him, returning still shouting, his voice warm with blood and joy:

"Quinchókeri hasn't lost his luck," he told me. "He only has been taken over by the manchari. The manchari is a different fear, more difficult than the fear we all know, the one even animals can sense. The manchari enters like a soul into a body, and the person in that body becomes incapable. From that person, the manchari scares away anything alive—not only animals, as is happening to Severo Quinchókeri, but also will power, the love of things, the love for other persons, the unknown reason that vitalizes some existences. That and a lot more: everything is scared away by the manchari. It knows how to introduce itself like a body into a soul."

The intoxication lasted until the following day, and only Iván, Insapillo, Juan González, and I remained in the house. I still remember in a reddish haze how Iván was reminding the sorcerer about the time the latter was arrested by the police, following the accusation of a neighbor who was a doctor, probably because Juan González never charges for his cures.

"They wanted to make me angry," says Juan González, "but I didn't let them. 'Let's see, sorcerer, since you are a magician, let's see you escape from jail.'"

"He was in prison only one night," says Iván. "The next morning they found an empty cell."

"I was inside that cell all along," Juan González smiles. "It's only that the guards couldn't see me. I fixed their eyes. During the whole night I sang icaros to myself and chewed strong tobacco so that my material body would become invisible to the guards. It was easy. The policemen opened the locks and I walked out, next to them, quietly, disembodied, as if I really were not present."

"The chief of police received a telegram from Iquitos that morning," says Iván Calvo, "a telegram sent two days before in which Juan González announced he would be arriving in Pucallpa at dusk, on that same evening, and from Iquitos, which is several days' journey away, navigating in the ship *Mariana*."

"I sent that telegram in person," laughs Juan González. "And I arrived that evening, at dusk, aboard the *Mariana*—no lie. The police chief was at the dock waiting for me, bitterly awaiting me along with several policemen. They arrested me again, but only for a moment. They spoke with the engineer of the *Mariana* and they were afraid and set me free, the engineer having confirmed that I had come aboard his boat in Iquitos, at the port of Belén, one week earlier."

Casting off the last ayawaskha visions, I dared to ask:

"I don't understand, I didn't hear clearly, I believe I haven't understood you. You were in jail, and while in prison you boarded a ship hundreds of kilo-

meters away, far away in Iquitos, one week before, and yet you arrived in Pucallpa only a few hours after having left the jail?"

"On that same night, in the prison cell, I not only sang icaros," explains
Juan González naturally. "I also concentrated on having time without time return. Just after midnight, I made time turn back. I came down to the oldest time
and surrounded myself with it, drank its pollen before dawn, and increased
my power of seeing. Within that time, which is of no use in moving toward death
and is only good for producing joy, it was easy for me to travel several days
backward, to Iquitos."

"Return to the Urubamba!" exclaimed Jose Maria Arguedas, "going back
to walk over the river! Take me back with you upriver, advance four centuries,
go back four centuries along the Sacred River of the Inkas! Amazon, river-sea,
stop the landing of the barbarians!"

"It was easy," insists Juan González. "When one has sung the icaros, in
that special time, water is like the flap of a great mosquito net. I left the prison,
walked to the river, raised the flap of the Ucayali, entered, and started walking
without any danger, well protected by the cloth of the water, and surfaced in
the port of Belén in Iquitos. So that no one would see me, I was careful. I came
out of the water crouching and waited for the sun to dry the small spots where
my shirt was wet. Then I went to the telegraph office and sent the message to
that loud-mouthed police chief."

And again with a voice that I recognize, Juan González says:

"No jail can imprison us; no virakocha can do us harm or transform us
into evil! We have black blood, our time is another time, we descend from Urus,
and to Urus we ascend!"

I was going to insist, to persist, to doubt. I don't remember clearly when
I heard the noise of breaking foliage outside the house, I see steps that approach, I finally can see. A lean Indian appears in the doorway with neck-
laces of small stones, pink and green, blue and orange. His cushma is held
by a belt from which hang dozens of thin bones. His arms are adorned with
bracelets up to the beginning of the shoulders. His back is bent over by the
weight of something that looks like ice. I take a better look and see the half-
body of a native, and above him the half-body of a hornless deer, too young,
the forehead destroyed by shot, and I am surprised by the Winchester carbine in the hands of the native.

"Severo Quinchókeri!" Juan González warmly exclaims.

"I have come right away, shirimpiáre," says last night's voice.

"And it will always be this way, brother," the sorcerer comforts him. "This is the way it will be; I have told you that all of the inhabitants of the forest are yours, were always yours, this is the way it is. Yours is the forest: I have returned it to you. The existences of the forest are yours—you are seeing it! Every day you must go to the forest—never forget that! Remember that your brothers, our brothers, are already in such straits that if no one does anything, they are already being damaged."

"I don't know how to thank you, shirimpiáre," said the voice, depositing the half of the deer at one side of the room. Juan González stopped him:

"If thanks are needed, don't give them to me, Severo Quinchókeri. Be thankful to yourself because you are worthy of the great souls that are never mistaken! They cast that soul of fear out of your body! They removed the body of the manchari from your soul!"

And to me in a lower voice:

"The Ashanínka never kill a deer, much less eat it. For the Ashanínka and for the Campa, like Severo Quinchókeri, the deer is inhabited by the soul of a distant and very hostile relative. The Campa hunters have been afraid of deer for a very long time. They are more afraid of it than they are of the tiger, the otorongo. They fear it more than they fear the virakocha, more than they fear the white man! Do you understand?"

Back at the Hotel Tariri, while taking a quick shower, because we were leaving for Iquitos that very same afternoon, I discovered three scars on my chest that I had not noticed before, arranged in a deliberate triangle. I opened my eyes and pulled my body away from the cold shower. I looked at the scars, touched them, looked at them again. I didn't know what to think.

Iván Calvo's words drift in from the bedroom:

"Juan González made those marks on you so that his altar will accompany you forever on your chest, protecting you. Don Hildebrando asked me to tell you."

And I remember his words, return to the Mishawa River, reconstruct the beginning of our trip to see Ino Moxo, scan the tall bushes. I see Iván appear, dragging a deer behind him, bringing us the receptacle of a remote soul. He carves the deer, nourishes us with that chullachaki from who knows what era. Something that is son and father from another time pushes the dilapidated bathroom door with my hands, enters the bedroom, and faces Iván Calvo. But Iván Calvo, with his suspicious aloofness, suitable to those who live protecting some dream, ignores us and continues speaking to his voice:

"Maestro Ino Moxo cut you last night, with a bloodwood dagger I believe, or perhaps with a bone—a rib transformed into stone. He made three cuts on your chest as a shield, so that no one, not even you yourself, no one or nothing can bring you harm. So that it will protect you even against yourself. He asked me to tell you."

IV

THE
AWAKENING

3

Where One Will See That Masks Always Lie Under the Face

The squalid alley that begins on the left side of Huallaga Street, in Iquitos, penetrates into the space of a living room without walls, with a wicker sofa in one corner, a rope hammock, and four brown chairs. A floor extends dim blue tiles around a space of planted earth. Behind the small sprinkled garden, smelling of mint, to one side is a stairway leading to bedrooms on the second floor. To the other side, hidden by brown partitions, is the inscrutable laboratory where Manuel Córdova, the witch doctor, is awake, triturating petals, combining roots cut while fasting, pressing sweet and sour secrets. In that room where nothing is allowed to enter except dawns and sunsets, this "simple herbalist," as Manuel Córdova calls himself, spends entire nights as his innumerable patients require, sharpening the claws of his distant name, disciplined by the patience of a jungle shaman, and attacks disease from the heights of his wise man's forehead.

"This is a good time of day to talk," he says, chewing the bit of his rugged pipe, which gives fragrance to the passing time, already six o'clock in the evening. "People begin to arrive later on, and I have to help them. 'It hurts here, I cannot sleep,' they complain. 'I have diabetes, my bones creak, I have cancer.' Cancer? They diagnose themselves; they make themselves sick. Sometimes it is the doctors who make mistakes. Some doctors tell them, 'You have cancer, there is nothing to be done.' But they come to me, and with the help of things I learned in the jungle, I cure their cancer. Believe me. Many times

207

cancer is nothing but an inflammation, a severe inflammation of the tissues. It is curable at that stage."

Less than a month ago, I met Don Manuel Córdova, while strolling along July 28 Plaza, a few blocks away from his home. His expression changed as soon as he looked at my face:

"You have troubles with your ears, don't you?" he said. "You suffer from what some call sinusitis. I'm sure you've suffered it for many years and no one seems to be able to cure you, is that not so?"

And taking a few more steps on the tiles of July 28 Plaza, inconceivably limber, his feet almost one hundred years old, he turned to face me:

"I can cure you, if you wish. First I have to clean you inside and leave you as new, so that all the dirt one accumulates in the body, unknowingly, in those internal factories, will not interfere with the medication. Then I will give you something to drink. Don't let me down: drink a tablespoonful before anything else when you get up in the morning, and another before you go to bed. And I will give you drops. You don't need to put them inside your nose, just on the openings to it: the essence of the liquid will be sufficient."

The latest nasal radiographs astonished my doctor in Lima: not a trace of chronic sinusitis. Also, the pain in my joints that had bothered me for so many years is gone, perhaps following an ayawaskha vision, after I began using an ointment given to me by Don Manuel Córdova. I also found out that my uncle, Carlos Arana, also received from Don Manuel Córdova an infusion of certain roots that made his diabetes disappear. And that the Minstrel of the Jungle, Raul Vásquez, learned from Don Manuel how to capture musics that live in the air, how to sing without lips, with the memory of the heart.

"No, you do not have stomach ulcers." Don Manuel Córdova stops the anxieties of César.

"But the doctors in Paris . . ."

"What do they know. All you have is gastritis."

And César, refusing to abandon his ailment:

"Two days ago, I was bleeding again."

And Don Manuel Córdova, unmovable:

"It is only gastritis, acid stomach. I am going to cure you."

When later on in Lima, César verified that his ulcer was in the healed stage, I could confide in him:

"Don Manuel told me confidentially that you really had an ulcer, but he asked me not to tell you. The cause of the problem was located in your spiri-

tual body, in the stress in your soul. In order for him to cure you, it was absolutely necessary that you not know it."

So: very clean, and new inside.

But we haven't come—Iván Calvo, Félix Insapillo, and I—to chatter about
the sick or about magic, but to ask Don Manuel Córdova for the kindness to
invite us to drink ayawaskha, if possible with tohé added, and to have him watch
over us because the two drugs together require a master who knows how to
manage them and how to direct the inebriation of the participants along the
proper path. Don Manuel Córdova accepts, warning us that tonight we will ingest
black ayawaskha, the strongest kind. If we have eaten something, he warns us,
we should postpone the session, because the tohé will reject food of any kind,
tohé being the only ingredient that can maximize the insights and the powers
of oni xuma. We have fasted since last night, we are prepared, and we reassure
Don Manuel Córdova.

Doctor Oscar Riós had told me he met Don Manuel Córdova in 1960, when
he was working as a botanical plant collector for the Astoria Company. Manuel
Córdova had held that post until 1968. At that time, his salary was double that
of a doctor working in the hospital. I know that Don Manuel Córdova came to
Iquitos in 1917 and right away began to apply his knowledge about the medicinal properties of plants. A legal dispute with a certain local doctor made him
go to Brazil. There, he worked as a collector of plant species for analysis at
the San Sebastian Laboratory. He returned to Peru in 1947, shortly after the
Gran Pangoa earthquake, and was hired by the Astoria Company that same
year. He is now retired, and the pension received from that American company
for his services allows him to live comfortably, without having to collect fees
from his patients.

"What exactly did you do for the Astoria Company?" I asked him that afternoon in July 28 Plaza.

"Many things. An important part was to collect plant species for identification and investigation in the United States."

"How many species did you collect?"

"From the Alto Tapiche area alone, I brought back about three hundred,
each with a live sample, a photograph, and a detailed description. From each
plant I had leaves, flowers, fruit, and a small bottle of extract ready to use as
medicine. In all, I probably gave them about two thousand."

"Ayawaskha included?"

"Only the vine, not the potion, and not the additive plants with which it must be mixed. That I cannot do for anybody. I know that they were able to extract the active principle of the vine, called harmine, but used as an injection it does not have the same effect."

"When did you take ayawaskha for the first time?"

Don Manuel Córdova takes a deep puff and settles down in the wicker sofa. His look drifts to the small garden crowded on one side of the living room, near the door to his laboratory. He slowly returns:

"I was very young, only thirteen years old."

"Do you remember that experience clearly?"

"As if it took place yesterday."

"Was it pleasant?"

"It was beautiful."

"Could you tell me about it?"

"At first I heard a humming noise that seemed to float, rising to the crown of some espintana trees. My eyes tried to follow its ascent, and as my gaze drifted among the foliage, I discovered a beauty I could never have imagined, even in dreams. Each leaf shimmered with a green and golden hue. The nearby singing of birds, an urkutútu, and the irregular chirping of a sietecantos suddenly descended. I could look at their songs, I remember. Time appeared to be suspended, like a cloud of silvery pollen. There was only that very moment in which I was alive, and that moment had no limits: it was infinite. I could separate each dark note of the urkutútu, each and every note of the sietecantos, and taste the notes one by one."

Turning inward again, his eyes drifting back to the garden, Don Manuel Córdova said:

"When I closed my eyelids, something like arabesques appeared, complicated decorations of iridescent light and shadows, which gradually took on a green-blue tone as they changed their structure and design. They seemed to be animated, moving against a backdrop of geometric figures, pointed planets, great rocks carved with the outlines of ancient animals, an unending diversity of forms. Sometimes, in an instant, they resembled something familiar: cobwebs, wings of yellow and black butterflies. A gust of wind struck me, coming from deep in the forest, in the night, and moved my field of vision. The fresh air was something I could see, and sometimes a sound was like a texture of feathers that I could touch. All of my senses were one, communicated between themselves: I could listen with my fingers, touch with my eyes, sense those visions with my voice. The maestro who was directing me that first time sang in a low voice in the Amawaka language. He invented an initiatory icaro, because the icaros also do the work of producing the effects, the irreparable, carrying out the intentions of oni xuma."

Don Manuel returned to the living room, his teeth biting on his gray pipe:

"That master showed me everything I know about the plants. Some of it I passed on to the laboratories working for the Astoria Company. From some of the knowledge I transmitted, they later made bottled remedies, labeled, which they now sell to us in drugstores. For example, I know they manufacture a birth control preparation I told them about, and also a drug for diabetes, although it seems that the effect of these products is temporary, not complete as it is when I prepare them simply, without altering the purity or the confidence of the plant. That is the secret. That is what ayawaskha knows. What we give to our medicines is love, perhaps even more than powers. Because even the dead need love, and the sick need it even more: the sick await at the door, thin as fragile skin, as that transparent scale that separates day from night. We awaken the mothers of the plants. Each plant has a mother, the same as the muyunas, those whirlpools fed by giant serpents. Every plant also has a mother. We awaken the mothers so that they will augment the strength of the cure with their love. And when the mother of a plant is harmful, we cut the plant slowly and at night, so that its mother will not wake up. I am going to tell you more: the ayuma tree, which is similar to a chestnut, has an evil soul. Its mother is a perverse, headless man, and that is why the ayuma tree is used in revenges only to do harm. The mother of the white lupuna tree is also a man, but a generous one: a gentleman of a certain age, who always responds gently, with teachings that help cure when he is properly called upon. The mother of the red lupuna tree, however, is a very dangerous man: if he finds you in his territory, he makes your belly swell, and you die with destroyed intestines. The mother of the katáwa tree is the worst of all: it makes your body rot, it burns you from the inside, and if you poison a lake with its resin, the animals in that lake will float with burned eyes, all white—not only fish, but also alligators, boas, and eels run aground on the shores, blind, not even able to see that they are dead. The mother of the white chuchuwasha tree is a lady. That of the red chuchuwasha tree is a young man, very brave and virile. When you ingest white chuchuwasha, the mother of the tree appears, talks to you, and asks you why you have taken it. In your dreams it speaks to you and accompanies you all night. But that mother says: beware of not doing what I ask you to do. And if you take red chuchuwasha, the male will appear as well and ask you the same thing: why have you taken

211

me? And you cannot lie, no matter what. And then he will say: be confident, trust in me. And he orders you to follow a very strict diet—no chili peppers, no cigarettes, no women, no lard—for a strictly specified time. And if you follow it, everything works out beautifully, whether you took it to heal yourself from some ailment, or to obtain something, not only health, but also luck, and love. All things have their uses, their mother, the origin of their purpose and of their use for healing or for harming."

Forgetting his pipe on the small table to the right of the wicker sofa, Don Manuel Córdova turns to Iván and tells him:

"The only regret I have now is not having found someone to whom I could teach everything I learned in the forests. My sons, each following his own preferences, are professionals in other careers. It is worse with my grandsons: none of them are as interested in plants as I am. Surely I will leave no disciple. Even though I plan to live for quite a while."

And laughing loudly:

"After all, I'm only ninety-five years old."

Lowering his voice and his eyes, taking out a match, and scraping the clogged bottom of his pipe with it:

"That first time, before the visions I've told you about, I had some other equally clear visions," Don Manuel Córdova says again, looking at me. "There was a very special, clear one," he says. "The maestro who protected me during the intoxication cried out at a certain moment without forewarning me:

"'Visions, begin!'

"And a female panguana entered my field of vision. I was thirteen years old. The maestro ordered me to make appear a male panguana next to the female. I started to think, to fervently wish. I opened my eyes. The male panguana was right there, in front of us, in that clearing in the jungle surrounded by lighted torches! And the pair of partridges began to dance in courtship. 'Qespichiway!' shouted the male panguana, as if it were a human being, an Amawaka, in the Quechua language but with an Amawaka voice. 'Qespichiway!' which really contains two words: *qespi*, which means 'crystal,' and *chiway*, which is the coupling of birds when they want to reproduce. *Qespichiway* therefore means 'couple me with crystal, make me crystalline, make us have transparent offspring, free, as if born from crystal.' That is what the panguana said to his female in my vision. Its voice was large and yellow. A white nest appeared between the two partridges, made of hairy cotton of the type used to crown the blowgun darts, and five blue eggs shone in the nest. I had been unable to control my visions for quite a while, and in my visions I saw the male sit on the eggs as if he were going to hatch them. It is the male that always hatches the eggs, the maestro told me, and the panguana rose from the nest. And the blue eggs cracked open like the sky, and five pairs of panguanas issued forth, two from each blue egg, fully grown, the same size as their parents. And without my having any control over their appearance, the newly born panguanas left in pairs, dispersing along the four corners of my field of vision. I opened my eyes, but the mother partridge was not there. I closed them, and she wasn't there either. Only the male remained alone in the middle, as it crouched down, smaller and smaller. It seemed as if he were becoming an egg, because his color turned blue and his wings came apart. I saw it; I saw his wings say farewell to his body as they flew away by themselves, moving like smoke, and the male sank his beak into the ground, abandoned, like a human being crying."

2

And He Orders Me to Speak
from My Other Self

"It is black ayawaskha, the strongest kind," warns Don Manuel Córdova, as he pours the oni xuma mixed with tohé into a small cup, a rather yellow one, with its bottom darkened by close relatives of rust. He gets up from his couch, turns off the light, and sits down again. "Its effects will soon be noticed," he comforts us, gazing into the shadow with a serene look, to offer us confidence. All of us drink it one by one from that rusty cup. A few moments later I hear myself say something, already under the influence of the hallucinogen: a surprising whiff invades my words. It has occupied the room more as a color than as an odor, a colorless breath of dead earth, of forests handcuffed with the vine of the soul, a cold, quiet wind, a mirror raised against the forest, which the night has suddenly surrounded. I can see my voice come out of the mirror, replete with trees, and it slowly descends, like colored smoke, wrapping itself around the trunk of a machimango tree, then advancing to the shimmering grass that invades the floor of the open room. I close my eyes and see: we are in Don Manuel Córdova's house. Everything is all right in Huallaga Street in Iquitos. Everything is fine. The sorcerer smokes while contemplating me from the wicker sofa, and Félix Insapillo is on the floor to my right, and Iván is a little farther away, with closed eyelids, his wooden outline detailed by the fresh dim light. I hear myself repeat something. I open my eyes, the voice is mine. I'm looking at that voice, which slowly creeps toward my cousin César. But César isn't there. Only in this instant do I discover that there never was anyone in my cousin César's place. Bewildered, yet not bewildered, I look and look again at my hands and my face, I look at myself with my hands. Don Manuel Córdova teeters between compassion and satisfaction. "You're already feeling the oni xuma, aren't you?" he smiles. "It's just that this is the strongest kind. You'll know that there are two kinds of ayawaskha." His words move further away from my life; I can see them hissing in the air:

"There are two types of vine, identical on the outside, with equal color and thickness. But if you shear through their stems, you will see that one has three round strands and the other five. The black one is not any thicker, but it contains more and therefore has stronger effects."

And he rises from the espintana log. Everything is all right in this forest, which is no longer mirror and which occupies the room with greater conviction than a real forest. Absolutely everything is fine, smelling like a forest, sounding like a forest. Don Manuel Córdova comes across the clearing. Without surprise, I see him reach over the neck of his cushma and extract a bottle of Florida water. He unscrews the cap and the cap unfurls wings and flies away sparkling. Later he comes close and sprinkles me with the music that pours from the open bottle. The other hand of Don Manuel Córdova holds my sweating forehead. I feel fine, then I hear my cousin César, speaking through me, say that everything is all right. I feel fine, it repeats. The sorcerer wets my head with a dash of camphored alcohol and later concentrates on the neck and chest of my brother Iván. Everything is fine. He moves to Félix Insapillo, pushing colored bamboos out of the way, tanrilla leg bones, achúni penises, a palisade of souls. He himself rubs his head, pouring drops of fragrant music through the neck opening of his cushma. The glare from torches paints, erases, paralyzes his face, his faces, those three profiles blossoming over his hair like moons, crowns of yellow and red lupuna leaves. I see them from a distance, far away, vanishing as I vanish.

Among the farewells of the tohé and of the night, after the stubbornness of the oni xuma, a rumor of steps, voices, movements of early risers, automobile horns penetrates the room. "How did this session go for you?" Don Manuel Córdova asks Félix Insapillo. "Well," he answers. "What visions did you have?" and Félix says: "There was a moment in which I saw my body from a distance, and I thought if someone were to whip that body sitting there, who is myself, neither it nor I would feel pain. I tried to smoke; I couldn't. I took the little box of matches and began to laugh inwardly, without my mouth laughing, because the matchbox was the skull of a deer. How could I light a cigarette with the skull of a deer, I thought, knowing that it really was a matchbox. The same with the top of that small tree next to the wall: it was a canoe that was beached there. But at the same time, in the same way, it was just the top of the small tree! Some time later, I became lost inside an enormous machine of slow colors, in the middle of huge iron gears turning noiselessly yet motionless, with pink screws, great nuts of bland colors, and pulleys. It was a fearful machine, and I was in the middle of it, in the middle of those monsters, gyrating full of yellow and violet spikes. My body was pierced by them without feeling any pain, without any bleeding."

"And my godson Iván Calvo?" asks Don Manuel Córdova. "What visions has my godson seen?" His voice—I recognize it—brings me back from the depths of the inebriation. A tiredness that doesn't belong to my body makes it collapse on the chair.

"What I have seen is not for telling," says Iván with irritation.

Don Manuel Córdova looks at him tenderly, and still smiling turns his face to me:

"And young César Calvo, perhaps not so young? Can you tell what you have seen, or have you seen the same things as your brother Iván?"

While still stuck in my visions again, still inside the night that refuses to leave, I tell him:

"I had a very strange dream, as if I had watched a film while being drunk. At the beginning, I saw here in your living room a forest against a mirror fogged by kindness, raised against the face, against the breath of a sleeping boy. I closed my eyes and opened them, and nothing changed in the vision. Everything proceeded normally, naturally, within the dream. I dreamed that I was, and at the same time that I wasn't, and that the two of us that were I traveled from Lima to Pucallpa, and from Pucallpa to Atalaya, and I dreamed that we rented a canoe with an outboard motor in Atalaya. I dreamed that we went on the Ucayali River to the Urubamba River, and from the Urubamba to the mouth of the Inuya River. In my dream we navigated against the current several days to the Mapuya River, where we gathered marine fossils, stone shells, medusas millions of years old. I dreamed there was a man-eating wapapa, entire villages floating like fish in a poisoned lake, inside my vision."

Don Manuel Córdova pretends to fuss with his pipe, goes to light it, prefers to focus on the match he uses to remove the ashes in it. "And then?" he asks with a voice I have watched before. I decide to say nothing, but fidget in the chair and don't follow my resolve:

"I saw colors, only colors, for quite a while. But the dream suddenly returned. The same dream returned and picked up where it had stopped before. We continued the journey. An Amawaka boy led us. We left the Mapuya River behind and went into the jungle. I turned back and took aim at the wapapa with my gun. I don't know what made me change my mind. The dream kept going on with great clarity. I dreamed that I was not César Calvo but César Soriano, a cousin of mine who lives In Cajamarca: he inhabited my body without my ceasing to be me. I lived in both persons ambling through those woods, persisting in walking next to Iván. And the boy you had sent to guide us was in front. Because I dreamed that we were walking and suffering and forcing ourselves only to be able to reach you. And I dreamed that you were the chief of the Amawaka. You were called something like Ino Moxo. Yes, I remember clearly: you were called Ino Moxo, but you were not Ino Moxo, you were Don Manuel Córdova. It was you—the light skin, the same eyes, the voice, the gestures, everything. Finally, after traversing on foot some bushy foothills, we reached the Mishawa River and you received us. Ino Moxo welcomed us, I dreamed. We spoke at length, for four days, seated on the shores of the Mishawa River. Later, without warning, coming back from an ayawaskha and tohé session identical to the one in your house tonight, Iván told me that Ino Moxo had donned his yellow cushma and entered the forest, disappearing while spewing smoke. I recall that during that inebriation, with the ayawaskha you gave me in your hut in the Mishawa, I dreamed the exact same dream I have dreamed here in your house in Iquitos, in Huallaga Street, just as if it were a dream within a dream. I had the vision of being in Atalaya with Iván, and with Félix Insapillo, and with myself—that is to say, with César Calvo—and that we navigated the Ucayali River, and the Urubamba, and the Inuya. Just as in a vision that died stillborn and never ended, like a journey ending in its beginning, which was looking at itself in my vision. Here it is still, in my head, a recently lived one, that journey that your oni xuma has made me dream."

And Don Manuel Córdova, smiling, and placing his pipe upon the side table:

"The Ashanínka say that dreaming is like conversing with the air, that during the dream one wakes up to life in another time, to one of the lives of the time of this life. What one sees with oni xuma is as real or even more real. Don't ever doubt it. Last night you really traveled, even though not in the conventional way."

217

And talking to himself, inwardly:

"One of the several masks of this same reality."

And his face changing, with an unforgettable voice:

"The whole journey in your dream is true for me, in my life, and it should be the same for you, a very real journey in its totality."

And weighing my doubts:

"There, on the shores of the Mishawa River, in your dream, was there a big renaco tree in the middle of the waters, or not?"

Redirecting his gestures, turning his eyes to Félix Insapillo and to my brother Iván:

"They will no longer be what they have been up to yesterday, up to the time we took oni xuma and tohé. In an imperceptible manner, but in a very real one, they too have been nourished by your visions, they have journeyed with you to their souls. Although they may not yet know it in the thinking of their hearts, beyond their memories, neither of them will ever be the same again."

And sharpening the claws of his Amawaka namesake, falling upon me from the height of his wise man's forehead:

"I know. You have not come from Lima only to have me heal your material body. And you did not come last night only to drink oni xuma mixed with tohé. I know it. That is why I dictated what you were to see in your dream. I dictated each one of the visions you saw, every one of them. That is also why I could not dictate them to you yourself, but only to your double, to one of the bodies of your shadow. Some day, if all goes well, I may confide in you. I may find out why I was not able to do it directly to you, why I made you travel inside your relative, by his side, as a stranger, why I made you travel as your other self in your visions."

The morning was becoming hot, and patients were beginning to arrive, a line of anxious and haggard faces. Abandoning the wicker sofa and saying farewells, Don Manuel Córdova gave orders that I, not César Calvo but my other César, be the one to tell, for the benefit of others, the stories of this journey I thought I had dreamed. That journey of sixty years ago, or of sixty million years in the future, in timeless time, which led me to an encounter with Ino Moxo, Black Panther of the Amawaka.

"Now go and rest," said a tired Don Manuel Córdova, sounding like a convalescent, very slowly accompanying us to the door. "But do not alter the reality of the dream; do not divorce the magic of the story or the vitality of the myth. Do not forget that rivers can exist without water but not without shores. Believe me: reality means nothing unless we can verify it in dreams."

The trembling of a net enveloped me it was not a dream it was a lake I saw Kaametza on the third shore over the black blood of the stabbed otorongo I tried to approach her and the net returned me to the waters darker and darker warmer clearer, qespichiway! I shouted and it was not a lake it was a river, qespichiway! I invoked Kaametza, couple me with crystal let us have children who are transparent and free! the dream heard me shout that out in Quechua but did not listen, Kaametza continued on the shore absorbed and Narowé awakened, the tentacles of the net became looser, loosened lied persisted took hold of me once more. And it wasn't a net. It was a hand that was shaking me, two hands grabbing my shoulders: Roosevelt Guzmán was waking me up apologetically, saying that everyone had left the house worried about my nightmare and that it was almost dusk.

I have slept all day long, here, in this house facing July 28 Plaza, in Aguirre Street, in Iquitos, precisely in the same room where I spent my school vacations twenty years ago. The wind has not come through. I am now facing the same shutters that my father, the painter Calvo de Araújo, pushed open with fingers full of tobacco and turpentine and brushes, gathering joys and colors, and joys and angers, giving it all to the tripod where another window was waiting. Has the wind come through yet? I know very well that Don Daniel Guzmán Cepeda is not in the house, that this is no longer his house or mine, that he left together with my father, stepping on tender branches as they went, that their bodies disappeared spewing smoke. If I could only continue the dream, I say quietly, seeing, but a sudden downpour wakes me up fully. Thick drops slide down the window. I get up and close it in vain, my eyes fixed on the rain. Because the wind has come through like willows. Yes, it has come this way: mango, pomarrosa trees, devastating generous medlar trees, unforgettable eternal trees, accomplices in my life. And there is no one in the square or in the house. I ask Roosevelt to say there is no one at home, that if someone is looking for me to say that I am not at home, to tell them that I have left as well, that I left four hundred years ago. I set up a white sheet of paper, then a black one, then another white one, in the dilapidated typewriter.

And I write:

THE THREE HALVES OF INO MOXO

by César Calvo

"That is how it is when someone tells the truth," the voice of Don Manuel Córdova reverberates in my memory. "If only one existence listens to it and takes it into consideration, then you don't even have to tell the truth. In telling other things, you will invariably tell the truth as well, even if you or the truth wish otherwise."

"The first man was not a man," Don Javier tells me, entangled in deep laughter. "The first man was a woman. . . ."

I

Some Personalities
and Landscapes from Dreams

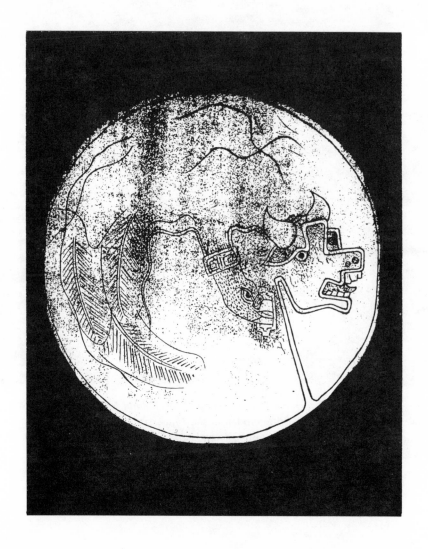

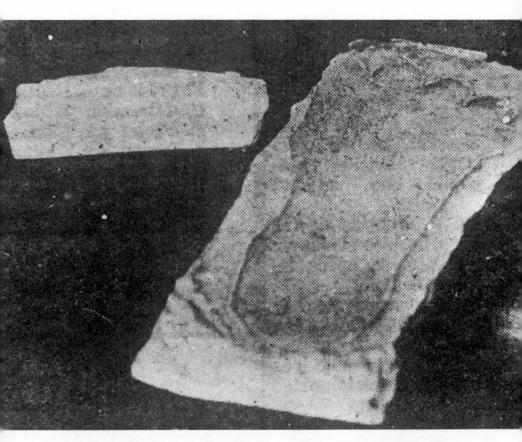

The first man wasn't a man. I am referring to the human footprint found in the Ascope area. Professor Jack Evernden of the University of California has found that the rock in which the footprint is embedded is more than sixty million years old.

Don Javier speaks to me in the lobby of the Hotel Tariri in Pucallpa, emerging from the walls tattooed with imitations of the portraits of souls painted by the natives.

With Iván's hands . . .

. . . and from the Mapuya River, we extracted the remote medusas, the marine shells converted to stone.

Not the Inka Manko Kalli, but Don Hildebrando, appears in a great glow holding a timeless vase.

"I don't like to talk about that, but I'm going to tell you only because Don Juan Tuesta wants me to," says Ruth Cárdenas, Don Javier's wife, in the city of Iquitos. "I'll tell you how they kidnapped my little brother Aroldo and how they turned him into a chullachaki."

"It's just that things are not as they are but as what they are,"
explained Don Juan Tuesta on Muyuy Island.

I saw myself at the foot of a mountain, a summit cloaked in eternal snow. "Qoylluriti!" they shouted. "Star of the Snow!" they shouted.

And only the young men with great chunks of ice on their backs began the ascent of the inaccessible Qoylluriti.

Not the largest but the most distinct one: we figured Ino Moxo's hut was the center of the Amawaka village.

"When I think about Fitzcarrald and his mercenaries," said Ino Moxo, "when I think those genocidal people were men, I feel I'd rather be a snake."

"Give me your blessing, Father Pedro!" begged Félix Insapillo, hiding a machete, while urging the priest not to return to Polish.

Not the largest but the most sought after: the house of Ino Moxo, today Manuel Córdova, on Huallaga Street in Iquitos.

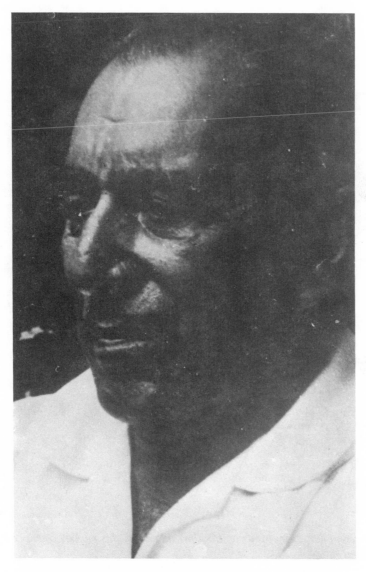

"Because I was Ino Moxo," reveals Don Manuel Córdova, "for many years I was the Black Panther of the Amawaka, obeying the great Maestro Ximu ever since being kidnapped."

And he commanded me to write, from my other self, this journey ordained by the sacred drug.

The journey led me to the first man who was a man and is again beginning to be one, becoming a man again for men, rising.

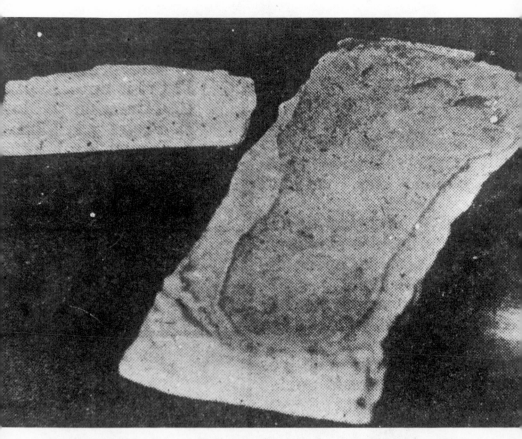

Walking toward the river's shore and entering the Amazon, becoming entangled in curling waves . . .

Glossary

Abigeo A mixture of avenger and cattle thief. Rebellious by nature and a farmer without land, he is and he isn't a cattle thief. He really doesn't steal—he recovers. In the highlands, he is called a qorilazo, a word combining Keshwa and Spanish that means "golden bow," referring no doubt to the infallibility with which abigeos, even in the most hostile darkness, can tie up and seduce cows and horses.

Abuta Although hardly noticed, this tree, imposing in thickness and height, prefers to grow in flat jungle. Its reddish black roots, chipped and boiled in water, lend strength to a drink that lowers blood sugar.

Acarawasú A type of fish that prefers small creeks and lagoons and does not live in the larger rivers. It can weigh up to three kilos and rarely exceeds a length of fifty centimeters. It is used in the cities for the ornaments of its skin and in the villages for the flavorful meat. The facts are that for some reason, besieged by either hunger or the aquariums, the acarawasú barely

lives: it is close to the point of extinction.

Achiote *Bixa orellana*. A seed forming a red powder when ground, used in flour or as a paste for culinary, ritual, or simply decorative uses. In the most civilized and demanding kitchens, achiote has become indispensable as a seasoning. But the natives insist on ignoring its other virtues, except that of an efficient, magical paint: its color keeps away fierce animals, dangerous men, and contrary souls. Achiote makes us invulnerable to attack from any visible or invisible enemy.

Achúni A medium-sized, nervous, four-legged animal. Only at close range, and often only by ascertaining the hairiness of its tail and its languid ears, can one tell it apart from a fox. In spite of its well-known indifference toward chickens, the eager hunters continue to confuse them both.

Afanínga This snake usually lives anonymously in the protection of the prairies. It differs from other snakes in that it changes color not for hunting purposes but simply out of

237

shyness. It does not strike back even when attacked. It protects itself only by twisting its tail, hiding behind a whirlpool of innocent lashings.

Aguajal An area of swampy or wet lowlands, where a certain palm grows, called aguaje, the same name used for its fruit. There are two equally valid explanations for the origin of the name. Some say the aguajal is named after the palm tree growing in it; others say the aguaje palm is so called because it grows only in flooded lands. (In Spanish, *agua* means "water.")

Aguaje Giant palm tree, which prefers flooded lands or sites next to rivers or lagoons. The fruit of this palm, also called aguaje, is a sort of small, reddish pineapple. Under a difficult, scaly skin, which people peel away with their teeth, the aguaje hides an oily pulp, nutritious and delectable, although not plentiful.

Aguaje-machácuy A peaceful water snake, which owes its name to the resemblance of the color and texture of its skin to the aguaje fruit. *Machácuy* is the Spanish version of the Keshwa word *mach'aqway*, referring to common serpents and snakes. Would it be necessary to point out that *amaru*, another Keshwa word meaning "serpent," or more specifically "great serpent," "boa," or "anaconda," was and is reserved only for the God-serpent, one of the minor Inka divinities?

Ajuási Refers to a useless man rather than a lazy one: to the one whose soul, moved by irrevocable disability, leads him to a stubborn destiny of failure. Ajuási is not necessarily the man who refuses to take action, but rather the one who always takes the wrong action.

Allpaka Peaceful animal, smaller and more fragile than a burro. It is less esteemed for its flesh than for its fur, highly productive of copious and silky wool. The allpaka is one of four animals of the camel family native to the South American mountain ranges. It is related to the other three: the wanaku, the vikuña, and the llama.

Allqoruna *Allqo,* dog; *runa,* man. Many natives of the Peruvian ranges and jungles use this word to refer to the white man, to the virakocha, with all of the insult that it implies: not-a-man, inhuman, exploiter, bastard, thief, liar—all that and more, depending on how the word is pronounced.

Ama sua, ama llula, ama qella In Keshwa, "Do not be a thief, do not be a liar, do not be lazy." The Inkas used this phrase instead of our impoverished "good day." In response, the person addressed would reply, "Ch'eynallataq q'ampas," meaning "I wish you the same."

Amawaka The term used to designate the Yora nation since the Spanish conquest, as well as the natives constituting it. The main territory of the Amawakas, or Yoras, where Ino Moxo's wisdom became famous, still lies in the proximity of the Mishawa River, between the Inuya and the Mapuya Rivers, which feed the sacred river of the Inkas, the grand Urubamba.

Andiroba A tree with very hard wood, almost as hard as wakapú wood, used to provide beams for housing.

Anima Spirit, soul, apparition, ghost. Also strength, that essence which inhabits and gives life, which gives breath, which animates human beings, animals, plants, and things. Used by Amazonian sorcerers, the expression "great souls" may refer to the superior spirits who once occupied a material body, as well as to the powerful deities who create and destroy creation in recreating it in their daily existence. Anima is also what comes forth from the dying person and continues to live after he is dead, visiting the places and the loves of the deceased, eternally in search of its end. That is why in the jungle, as well as in the superstitions of villagers, whenever something unexplainable happens—a noise, a gust of wind, an unforeseen movement or silence—someone will always explain: "It is a soul (anima), it is an anima following the dead man's footsteps."

Anona (anon.) One of the most nutritious and tasty tropical fruits. The discolored, rough, green skin hides a pulp that is almost too white and sweet.

Añashúa A fish about forty centimeters long and never above two kilos in weight, which compensates for its small size with transparent flesh and with a taste as undescribable as the colors of its skin.

Añaz This animal, no bigger than a lapdog, has the vivacity of a fox in dire straits. Few natives consider it edible; most of them find it laughable and hunt it only when they have nothing else to play with.

Añuje Although the añuje is one of the smallest rodents of the Peruvian jungle, it has the strength of two rabbits. The coarseness of its fur is deceiving: the meat is tastier and tenderer than that of two rabbits as well.

Apasharáma Tree with a strong and rugged bark, used in tanning fine pelts.

Apashira Small chameleon, very flighty. Some natives crave its translucent, sticky flesh as a luxury. The apashira moves very quickly and has the miraculous ability to blend into any background. Its capture is the reward and privilege of the luckiest hunters, not of the most able ones. In the vernacular, *apashira* also means a woman's vagina.

Aqllawasi House-of-the-Selected-Women; name used by the Inkas to designate the dwelling of the maidens who performed worship rites to Inti, the Father-God.

Arambasa Fierce black bee. People fear it and seek it. Arambasa honey, slightly acidic and more golden than syrupy, is highly regarded for its tonic properties.

Aripasa Tree with variable girth and thickness of leaf. It produces gray fruits, round and flat; they are not edible.

Ashanínka Name used to denote their nation by the natives who inhabit the Great Pajonal and its surroundings, an area comprising more than one hundred thousand square kilometers; they are also known as Campa. In their language, Ashanínka means "man." To them, outsiders are either choris (mountain people, Quechuas, or mestizos), or virakocha (usurpers, whites, invaders). In that limitless, high jungle plateau known as the Great Pajonal, which is still their country, the Ashanínka do not allow police stations or schools in the Western style, nor churches, nor soldiers' barracks. Nevertheless, they are extremely hospitable, but only toward those who visit them in peace. With others they are merciless. Their indomitable warrior nature not only stopped the Inka conquerors and the Spanish conquerors but continues to defy the new barbarians.

Ashipa Mealy tuber of dubious sweetness. It is perhaps the only one that can be eaten raw in its natural freshness, without cooking, as if it were a fruit.

239

Ayañawi *Ñawi* means "eye" in Keshwa. *Aya* is "soul," "dead," "spirit-of-the-dead." *Ayañawi*, therefore, means "eye-of-the-dead," "eye-of-the-soul," the Keshwa name for the firefly.

Ayaymáman Onomatopoeic name of a bird. Its inconsolable, wailing song is heard only in the night. No one claims to have seen an ayaymáman. That is why the jungle inhabitants continue to give credence to a legend about two children, a boy and a girl, whose parents came to the realization that starvation would lead them to a sure death, and therefore preferred to lead their children deep into the woods and abandon them there. The little ones had to become birds in order to survive. Ever since, they have wept "ayay maman!" calling their mother, their father, any human being who can look at them. People can barely hear their song through the leaves in darkness. For centuries, the children have wept and sung all night long until daybreak. Country people, in their unarguable and innocent simplicity, say that the ayaymáman could recover their original form and soul only if they were to be seen by a human being.

Ayawaskha Vine-of-the-dead, vine-of-the-soul. Keshwa term for a hallucinogenic vine, which Humboldt renamed *Banisteria caapi*. Recently scientists were able to isolate its active component, an alkaloid they named harmine. They have used it in experiments, almost always unsatisfactorily whenever they have ignored the other plants mixed with it by Amazon sorcerers until the potion reaches the medicinal and divinatory powers that give rise to its fame as infallible.

Ayúmpari An Ashanínka who establishes or accepts an interchange of gifts with a fellow countryman. The ashanínka consider this ancient custom to be a sacred institution. It is not a matter of giving in order to receive—it is a matter of breathing. Life is in the air; it doesn't belong to anyone but to everyone. If I am worthy of being your ayúmpari and I give you something—arrows, handfuls of salt, achiote paste—I am not giving you life; I am returning it to myself. Objects, gifts, presents—all of them are created, as air is created, by our Father-God Pachamakáite, and they are finally mine when they cease to be mine. Everything belongs to everybody—but only among the Ashanínka. No white, no mestizo, not even a member of another Amazon nation is ever accepted by an Ashanínka as his ayúmpari, because the interchange of gifts, that sacred exchange, not only binds the two ayúmparis who execute it for the rest of their lives but also provides cohesion and strength to their whole nation.

Awíwa A multicolored, edible worm, normally about ten centimeters long.

Balata Latex from the tree of the same name. Those who extract latex from this tree, a relative of the rubber tree, are called balateros. The painter Calvo de Araújo sketched them, with more candor than color, in a song that truly reflects popular feelings:

You have loved me, deceiver,
* deceiver,*
When I had lots of money,
* lots of money,*
I have worked as a shiringuero,
* as a balatero,*
And that money I've given to you,
* given to you.*

Banda Shore, edge. The shore of a river or creek.

Barbasco A plant containing large amounts of a dangerous substance, rotenone. Fishermen, even though they also use the latex of the barbasco, prefer the venom extracted from its roots. They mash the plant (smashing it to release the rotenone), then scatter it over water and instantly gather the fish agonizing on the surface.

Bayuca Name applied to several species of poisonous caterpillars, all of them covered by multicolored, irritating hairs.

Bloodwood In Spanish, palosangre, a tree with impenetrable red wood.

Bora Name of an Amazon nation or any of its members.

Bocholócho This bird is longer and more alert than a pigeon, with a monotonous, melodious, monotonous, monotonous, monotonous song that repeats its name: "Bocholooooochooo! Bocholoooochooooooo!"

Bubinzana A magical song, also called an icaro. An invocation. A musical prayer sung by sorcerers in certain ceremonies while they smoke.

Bufeo, bujéo. A river dolphin. A water mammal reaching the size of a man. Some of the native women, when they are pregnant or menstruating, avoid embarking on a fragile boat. They know that the bufeos get very excited by their odor and will ram the boat, trying to overturn it. Frequently there are cases of women who have drowned, not because of the over-turning but because the bufeos dragged them to the bottom and fornicated with them. There are also many stories from fishermen who have captured female bufeos; they say that no woman can compare to them in the skills or passion of sex. The female red bufeo is the most sought after. The

sorcerers cut out the ring around its vagina, empower it by means of fasts, sing icaros to it, and with that ring make a pusanga, which is infallible in affairs of love. It is also well known that male bufeos can, if they wish, transform themselves into human shape. Disguised as such, they come out of the rivers, especially during holidays and feasts, when they are protected by the noise, confusion, and dancing, and they court maidens and steal them. The bufeos can assume any shape better than any trained human being. But along with the powers of a chullachaki, they also have their weak points: no matter what they do or how they appear, bufeos are doomed to always carry a hat. In the same way that a chullachaki disguised as a human being is revealed by the deer or tiger tracks it leaves with its right foot, the chullachaki bufeo is forced to breathe by that unavoidable orifice in its head. To recognize them and scare them away, all one has to do is remove the hat.

Cahuára Kawára. A fish. Its incredible length disguises very tasty flesh.

Caimito A fruit that resembles the breast of a maiden, with a round, nippled shape, intense colors, and an excellent white, rubbery pulp. The best-known story about the caimito involves a woodcutter who punished the infidelity of his wife by amputating her breasts and burying them near the river's shore, in the most distant area from his land, precisely on the spot where a certain tree would grow whose branches were heavy with abundant, shimmering fruit. Such a macabre origin perhaps accounts for the yearning texture, the soul of its flesh, that sweetness of the caimito that exalts it to excess.

Cajón A type of wooden hand drum common in eastern Peru, made in the shape of a hollow box about 1 x 1 x 2 feet, with an opening in one side. *Trans.*

Campa *See* Ashanínka.

Camucámu A semiaquatic bush. It has sweet-and-sour small fruits.

Camúnguy A chicken-like bird with an onomatopoeic name. The enormity of its manners and the color of its feathers make it a relative of the wild turkey. It is a pity that its flesh is totally devoid of any flavor.

Canela-muwena Canela-mohena. A tree with cinnamon-colored wood, intensely fragrant and very hard.

Canero A fish whose voracity, strength, and slipperiness are disconcerting. A permanent phlegm covers its length of barely twenty centimeters. It doesn't have teeth and therefore feeds strictly by suction. The most feared canero is the smallest one, and with good reason: its hunger, always unstoppable, becomes lethal when the canero enters the anus or vagina of an unfortunate human being.

Capirona Tree with a wood so impenetrable and fibrous that it is famous as a producer of the best firewood and longest-lasting charcoal.

Carachama Karachama. Antediluvian fish, which inhabits the bottoms of lakes and eats mud. An articulated immensity of thick scales protects it better than armor. It survives too many days out of water. Its flesh is not a frequent guest at baronial tables. The males of the Chama nation, whose only known occupation is fishing, consider it a matter of great pride to capture a karachama. Their satisfaction is greatest if they capture one without hooks, arrows, or nets. They dive incessantly, for so

long that when they have been given up as drowned, they suddenly surface with the prized prey. The young ones carry them in their hands, and the experts bring them out between their teeth.

Cassava Yuca. *See* Masato.

Catáhua Katawa. Giant tree covered with thorns. It grows in lowlands. Its sap is a powerful poison used by men as well as animals. Some natives bathe the tips of their arrows in catáhua sap. Carnivorous birds (the famous wapapa, for example) dip their wings in catáhua sap and then submerge themselves in quiet waters to deposit the poison, and wait. They don't have to wait long: soon they devour fish killed by the catáhua sap and stranded on the shores.

Cetico Some errant herbalists classify this tree as a bush because of its lean opulence of fan-shaped branches. The cetico is nevertheless a tree, a semiaquatic one. The interior of the trunk, more bark than wood, is rich in cellulose, a luxury desired by paper manufacturers. Our natives, driven to practice the art of fishing not for pleasure but rather to dispel hunger, have degraded the cetico by using it as wood for constructing emergency rafts.

Chacchar To chew coca leaves.

Chacra A small farm.

Chamáiro A vegetable ash used to replace lime in chewing coca leaves.

Chambira A palm tree, the fruit of which, arguably sweet, can be eaten depending on one's discretion. It does not have a massive trunk, but very high up it develops an unending freshness of shade from vast expanses of fibrous, persistent leaves. Not especially fit to thatch roofs, the chambira leaves are exclusively used as tightropes. Thinned out, woven with dexterity, rolled up, and braided again, they have never disappointed—their fame is unbreakable. Inexplicably, chambira is also the name given to a fish with ill-tempered spines and repellent teeth, which is nevertheless quite edible.

Charge, to charge This verb complements the verb *to cure* in the usage of shamans. A sorcerer can charge with evil spells anything previously destined to kindness, and vice versa—and also neither. For example, an innocent handkerchief can be charged so that it will bring about good fortune or a curse, happiness or death. Charging, in the minds of the uninitiated, gets confused with healing, healing gets confused with bewitching and with haunting, even though those words cannot fully encompass all of the meanings and resonances of charging.

Charicuelo A tree with an irrelevant crown, high, compact in leaf, and with high branches. It has sweet-and-sour fruit, rarely abundant but quite tolerable.

Chicoza A type of reed or big pasturage. As a nutrient for cattle, this plant has justifiably gained the rank of the miraculous.

Chicozal A place that is usually sandy and full of chicoza.

Chimicúa Tree that obtains revenge on its facile and useless branches, which break at the slightest gust, by producing red, persistent fruit, so attached to their source, so intricate to remove, and so unable to exist in isolation, that few hunters can claim truthfully to have sampled them.

Chinchilejo Dragonfly. Also irresponsibly known as syringe-sucker. An inevitable nickname of squalid and sickly youths.

Chirisanango A tasty tonic prepared by shamans by blending the energies and the juices of several plants.

Chonta Heart of palm. The edible interior of several palm trees: wasái, shebón, cinámi, pijoayo, hunguráhui. The pulp of a palm called pona. A hard wood used in arrowheads or dartheads.

Chori A man of the Andes, a mestizo or Quechua from the high sierra.

Choshna A nocturnal monkey. In spite of its size, there is no evidence that it is violent or aggressive. Its nocturnal screams in the height of the jungle, and its jumps, which sometimes break heavy limbs, may confuse us and cause alarm, but as is well known, that is not the choshna's intention.

Chuchuwasha A tree whose roots, when chopped up and macerated in rum, give power and prestige to a medicinal drink, an aphrodisiac or tonic, equally called chuchuwasha or chuchuwasi: the former Keshwa word could mean "back of the breast" or "breast that turns," and the latter would be "house of the breast."

Chullachaki From the Keshwa *ch'ullan chaki*, meaning "single foot" or "sole foot." A mythological being, a demon, a goblin. It has been proved that any chullachaki, even if he adopts the most outlandish appearance, can never disguise one of his feet. Usually the right one refuses to assume a human shape and insists on taking the shape of a jaguar's paw or a deer's hoof. The chullachaki is therefore not betrayed, but rather given away unwillingly by one of his extremities. In Brazil, it is known under the dubious and insolent name of *curupira*.

Chullakaqla Uneven jawbone. A fish totally devoid of scales, endowed with enormous and poisonous spines.

Chushpi An insignificant mosquito, whose bite, however ,is not only disturbing but also infectious.

Chushúpe Chushúpi. A thick snake, with coarse skin, almost bony. It is extremely poisonous. It has a special habit that triples its danger: among all of the members of its tribe, it is the only one that pursues its victim, even after biting it once. If it can, it will bite again and again, tirelessly. Perhaps it is the only animal other than the human being that is fierce beyond all limits. It is surprising to know that the majaz, for many the most flavorful inhabitant of the jungle, lives under the protection of the chushúpe, within the latter's nest. The hunters and river people say that they often find somewhere in the body of a majaz a cartilage whose shape closely resembles that of a chushúpe fang.

Citarácuy Huge ant whose bite does not hurt and carries no poison. The word is also used to denote a style of dance, and it is the country custom to accompany it with fifes, drums, and hand-clapping. During the dance, the couples imitate, with pinches and insinuating gestures, the counterproductive wriggling of the ants and their empty aggressiveness, fatal in its evasiveness and deadly in its lovemaking.

Coca Bush used to obtain cocaine hydrochloride. Andean peoples chew (chacchar) the coca. They make a bolus of leaves in the mouth and chew it with added lime, the latter aiding in the release of the active ingredients that produce the vitalizing effects of this plant. The Quechuas have always used it for divination. If the coca tastes sweet in the lips, good fortune is to be expected and one must continue with the path one has started. If the coca is bitter, this is a bad sign and one must postpone the path embarked on. Amazonian sorcerers only rarely add coca to ayawaskha. They also consider coca as a help in divination.

Cocha Kocha. A Keshwa word. Depending on how it is used, it may mean "lake," "lagoon," "back-water," "quiet water," "pond," or "ocean."

Cocona The average appearance and size of this plant hides the large leaves and the fruit with a cracked, sour, yellow-green sweetness.

Comején Termite, a highly destructive insect. It will eat any wood and immediately secrete a brown, porous substance, which soon hardens. This secretion, emerging from the ruins, is used by the insect to construct its home.

Coto-machácuy Koto-machácuy. A mythological animal. Giant serpent with two heads, which inhabits the bottoms of large lakes.

Cumaceba A hardwood tree, not especially notable.

Cumala A softwood tree, of no particular significance.

Cupiso Cupisu, a small turtle, amphibious and elongated. Its eggs, which carry the same name, are more in demand than its flesh.

Cure, to cure This verb changes its content and meaning when used by sorcerers. To cure any object is to provide it with powers, to give it strengths, to endow it with purposes previously ignored by the object, which would not have been placed there originally by habits or from birth.

Curuínce One of the large ants. Lacking venom, it is provided with formidable pincers. With them it cuts the tremendous leaves from which (after the darkness and humidity the ferment of which forms time in the

244

subsoil) will sprout the decay of fungus upon which the ant feeds.

Cushma A woven tunic decorated with various dyes; a sort of large poncho with sleeves, sewn together from armpits to feet, worn by both males and females.

Demento-chállua Nonedible fish, small and decorative, which can fly. Its name, "mad fish," derives from its excessive behavior, without limits, both in and out of the water.

Doncella A large fish. There are no scales in its skin, which is framed by endless black stripes. They are generous; some doncellas weigh more than thirty kilos, and their flesh has no spines.

Dorado Also called zúngaro. The head of this fish alone takes up more than half the size of its body, which is scaleless and spineless and usually weighs more than fifty kilos.

Elegguá The Separate Soul, an African divinity often mistakenly confused with Ekué, Death, in the ageless enthusiasm of some of its South American devotees. It would then refer to a Separate Soul not separate at all, more desired than revered, since the Ekué adepts are not alone in considering death to be a relief, a blessing that releases them from the humiliations and suffering of this life. Our black ancestors, when slaveowners prohibited their religion as well and pushed them into Catholicism, masked their gods with the identities of Christian saints in order to continue adoring their own without mentioning them. They covered them with foreign tunics in the secrecy of distant memories. Why did they select Christ specifically as a mask for Ekué, and Ekué specifically as a mask for Elegguá?

They must have had their reasons. The truth is that they invested him with the trappings of death, as no less a person than the resurrected and immortal Jesus of Nazareth.

Espintana A straight tree, with compact bark, highly desired for beams in the construction of houses. It is known that the mother, the spirit of the espintana, is really two persons: an old lady and a young woman, who converse and talk at sunset.

Evil One The Evil Spirit. The greatest and most feared of all evil souls. Not *a* devil, or *a* demon, but *The Devil.*

Fasácuy In spite of its abundance in lakes and lagoons as well as in tame backwaters, it is not easy to fish the fasácuy. It possesses a set of teeth that parallel its rapacity, and its protective scales are always covered with a whirling gray slime. Its four kilos, distributed along sixty centimeters, lack any fat or small spines.

Firirín A type of partridge, but smaller in volume and with more tender flesh.

Fitzcarrald Family name of two unforgettable genocidal criminals of the Peruvian jungle. Time and the Huaraz tongue, not yet accustomed to the English language, apparently disfigured the ancestral *Fitzgerald,* transforming it into the French-Amazonian *Fitzcarrald.* The boundless ambition of Fermin and Delfin Fitzcarrald, natives of Huaraz, encouraged by the laws and authorities at the beginning of the century, exterminated the population of vast regions of the Amazon by blood and fire. Fermin and Delfin organized and led the mercenary armies, disguised as colonizers and rubber workers, that exterminated entire nations— thousands and thousands of natives—only to take possession of their lands and extract the rubber that abounded in those regions. In spite of this, certain historians insist on considering the Fitzcarrald brothers and their accomplices as "pioneers of civilization and progress." A number of important towns in the Peruvian west have more than one street, square, or avenue still burdened with the name "Fermin Fitzcarrald." Fermin, who surpassed Delfin in age, fame, impiety, and fortune, was also the first to die. Obeying the spells of the great Amawaka witch doctor Ximu, a whirlpool trapped Fermin Fitzcarrald's boat and wrecked it in the bottom of the Urubamba, the sacred river of the Inkas. Days later, floating amid branches and slime in a backwater, they found his corpse, visibly reduced by the hunger of fish. They buried him on the spot, with more haste and fear than ceremony, in that bank of the Inuya River. Later, by the time other Amawakas, following Ino Moxo's orders, had executed Delfin Fitzcarrald in the Purus River, torrential rains and creeping jungle had already disposed of the older brother's tomb.

Flautero This little bird asserts itself in its name—"flutist," in Spanish: it victoriously compensates for its small size with the extreme and nostalgic sweetness of its song.

Gamitana The capture of this thirty-kilo fish, one meter long and of an incredible width, is a celebration that involves and entertains a whole village. Jungle hunters avoid capturing more than one gamitana in a day, since the richness of a single one is enough to satisfy the urgent demands of lean river dwellers.

Garabatokasha A creeping plant with a thin, firm stem, interrupted fre-

quently along its length by rough knots that produce a curved spike. The uses of garabatokasha are as many as the ways in which sorcerers prepare its roots or mix its bark or direct its sap, the zig-zagging and wisdom of its spikes.

Haraweq A Keshwa word used to designate a poet, musician, or singer. The closest English equivalent would be "minstrel."

Harmine Alkaloid extracted from ayawaskha.

Hiporúru Also called *para-pára*, a bush with terse, testy leaves. When wrinkled, they always return to their original shape as if they were made of rubber. When macerated in alcohol, they produce a tonic whose powers, in addition to expelling weaknesses of the blood or the heart and overcoming diabetes, enjoy an invaluable efficacy: the tonic returns sexual youthfulness to the dispirited and to old men.

Huacapú Wakapú. Tree with an immovable heart, stubborn and very difficult to saw. As a support for houses or buildings, wakapú has properties that approach those of steel. But it is useless in provi-ding cover or food: the hard wood slows down campfires and rankles kitch-ens. Even its slivers, insensitive as stalactites, will become extinguished without ever producing light.

Huacapurana Wakapurana. Tree with fibrous wood, quick to dry and with a pressing inclination to become firewood.

Huacra-pona Waqrapona. A palm tree with an enlarged trunk, wrinkled, as if pregnant on all sides.

Huairanga Wayranga. *Wayra* is "wind" in Keshwa. This wasp never alights on the floor and remains in the air. Its sting discharges a poison, which instantly expands under the skin. The resulting pain, although short-lived, is beyond description. It is also deceitful: the torment passes quickly, only to be followed by high fever and dreadful, recurring dizziness.

Hualo Wálo. A toad of agreeable flesh and spasmodic, impudent, and hoarse screams. It usually weighs about one kilo.

Huancáhui Wankáwi. Large, strong bird of prey, with an onomatopoeic name. It sings only upon the approach of a human being, as if announcing him or denouncing him, warning about the greatest danger to the denizens of the jungle.

Huangana Wangána. One of the two kinds of wild boars that inhabit our forests. Different from the pacific and vegetarian sajino, a wild pig that barely resists and lives in pairs, the carnivorous huangana lives in noisy, morbid, tumultuous herds, hundreds and hundreds of fangs tirelessly depredating the wilderness.

Huapapa Wapapa, a carnivorous, web-footed, dark brown bird. With three spikes that sprout from the elbow of its wings, it tears the bark of the noxious katáwa tree wets its feathers in the sap, flies, finds the backwater of a creek, dives in, and expertly flushes, spreads the poison in the water, and waits. On the shore, motionless, it waits for the poisoned fish to rise to the surface and then gathers them up and devours them without haste or anxiety: a piece from this one, a piece from that one. It always kills more than its appetite desires, and it does so slowly, resignedly, as if it needed to complete that premeditated, unnecessary, and bloody ceremony out of duty, not from hunger in life, but from death of satiety. The wapapa, absorbed in those trances, abstracted from

everything and everyone, would be an easier hunter's prey than any of the dead fish if that were the desire of any hunter as blind as the wapapa itself. The wapapa gives the impression of being a corpse undeservedly resurrected, a sleep-walker, reduced to follow the dictates of an immemorial perversion.

Huicungu Wikungu. A palm tree, protected by colossal, very strong black spines. That makes the fruits of the wikungu more desirable for the difficulties involved in securing them rather than for their delicacy.

Huito Wito. A medicinal fruit particularly rich in iodine and saccharine, miraculous against any disease of the respiratory system. When it is still green, people call it "jagua" and extract from it that blackened and indelible tincture used by women to clean their faces and by males to prevent insect and vermin bites.

Hunguráhui Unqurawi, a palm tree producing yellow, mealy fruit, afflicted with infinite numbers of tiny black seeds. The fruit of this palm, also known as "hunguráhui," distills a precious oil. Bald people use it as an ointment in massage, and their deprived heads inevitably become thickly covered with hair again.

Icaro Magical song. *See* Bubinzana.

Inkarri Mythological being. His enemies captured him through deceit and quartered him in the central square of Cusco. They buried the remains in distant places to avoid their later rejoining and inevitable resurrection. Today's Quechuas affirm that the dispersed corpse of Inkarri every year advances underground toward Cusco, where the head was buried, and that one day the divine remains will become welded to the head. Then Inkarri will return intact, and the "Indians of the Kingdom of Peru" will again rebel under his leadership, expel the invaders, and recover the freedoms and dominance of their lost empire.

Isango Microscopic animal, living in pastures, which penetrates under human skin and nests there, producing an unbearable itch. Local people combat it with poultices of various vegetables. Others wait until the end of the interminable summer, as cold is the natural enemy of the isango.

Ishinshími An imposing ant, which nests high up on trees and bushes. Its bite does not produce pain or inflammation, but men flee from it. They are afraid not so much of the ishinshími itself, even though this ant has a preference for biting genital parts. What threatens them is the stink that attaches to anything it touches.

Isula A lethally poisonous ant, which reaches five centimeters in length. It wounds with its powerful claws, and its posterior sting inoculates a poison that generates fevers and aches lasting several days. Four isulas are enough to kill a man.

Itahúba Tree with a fine, compact wood.

Itininga Lean palm tree, not very high and with a frail appearance. A dull and sickly vine, a creeper without known purpose or use, it also has the name "itininga," a word originating perhaps in the Keshwa term *tilingo* (or *itilingo*), which means squalid, sickly, useless.

Ivénki The Ashanínka term for a herb chock-full of incontrovertible magical and medicinal properties. Natives of other nations call it "piri-piri."

Jagua Fruit of the huito tree. According to its age, it possesses two names and uses: Still green, it is called "jagua," and its pulp produces a black, indelible dye. When already ripe, it is called "huito" like its parent tree and only then is elevated by the farmers to the status of edible fruit, and by sorcerers to that of a medicine.

Jergón Proverbially fierce and poisonous snake.

Jíbaro A member of a nation of the same name. Jíbaro warriors remove and shrink the heads of their enemies, but only the most skillful and indomitable—those whom the Jíbaro overcame fighting on equal terms, in an honest fight, face to face, in a planned battle, and with identical arms. Not all males return to their village with the bleeding trophy in their hands. As soon as they arrive the sorcerer gathers them together and directs them in the job of taking over the soul and the virtues of the decapitated men, a rite that concludes with the shrinking of the enemy heads to the size of a closed fist. Each privileged warrior then cuts off the hair of his booty, adding it to similar ones he wears around his waist. Because they remain loyal to this ancestral ceremony, the Jíbaros have acquired an unjust reputation. Our civilized people fear them without motive (there is not a single case of a white man's head worthy of having been considered by a Jíbaro) and they are irresponsibly called "headhunters."

Kaápa Every Ashanínka chief—that is to say, every head of a family—builds two homes: first the kaápa for his guests, and then the tantoótzi for his children and wives.

Kamalonga An indispensable bush in some prepared potions. Its principal ingredient is ayawaskha. The sorcerers attribute divinatory powers to the leaves, and to a lesser degree to the roots, of kamalonga, comparable to those of coca.

Karawiro Carahuiro. A dye made from a mixture of various seed and root extracts. Many natives adorn themselves with it over their arms, chest, and cheeks. The Tzipíbo also dye or draw designs on their clothing with karawiro.

Katáwa *See* Catáhua.

Katziboréri A term for sorcerer, herbalist, magus, wizard, healer, etc., which includes the more precise one: *shirimpiáre*. To state it simply, *katziboréri* would apply to a general medical practitioner, while *shirimpiáre* applies to the specialist in "sucking tobacco," or "smoking witch doctor" who knows the enigmas of smoke and can direct them against specific diseases and spells.

Killa Moon, Mother Moon. Her condition as wife to the Sun God made the Inkas revere her almost as another one of their divinities.

Killka A sign carved into stone. Probably a hieroglyphic writing carved by Inkas in the stones of their temples or in their immediate vicinity. Curious Westerners have yet to discover their significance.

Kocha *See* Cocha.

Kosho A container made by hollowing out a piece of wood into the shape of a small canoe. The Ashanínka use it to prepare and ferment the cassava beverage called masato.

Koto-machácuy *See* Coto-machácuy.

Locrero Medium-sized bird, with blue plumage, more black than blue: the color of the sea at night as if it were in blue mourning.

Lupuna The Amazon does not know a taller tree. In order to support that huge immensity, the lupuna spreads the base of its trunk in several giant buttresses. Lupunas grow in two families, one white and the other pink, both similar in appearance and in size although inhabited and directed by different mothers and possessed by different souls. Ino Moxo says: "The mother of the white lupuna is a generous gentleman who when properly invoked will always respond with gentleness, with healing teachings. On the other hand, the mother of the red lupuna is a very dangerous man, and will inflate your belly if he catches you in his territory. You die from destroyed intestines."

Machácuy From the Keshwa *mach'aqway*, serpent or snake; a generic term.

Machiguenga An Amazonian Indian nation, or a member of it.

Machimango High and solid tree, recognizable by its imposing aspect as well as by the sharp, excessive perfume of its branches in fruit.

Maestro Great sorcerer or great magician, recognized by his powers, by the proven efficacy of his wisdom, by other motives that here remain a mystery, and by his exclusive ability to prolong in his disciples the intuitions and knowledge that were entrusted to him for his use or stewardship.

Majaz Huge, semiamphibious rodent, with gray hair spotted with white. The fortunate hunters who have tasted the flesh of the majaz swear without hesitation that it is the most delicious of all—that of men included.

Makána River fish covered by thick, rusty scales, long and solid like an ancient sword. The Inka warriors called one of their favorite weapons, a massive club with a heavy star of metal or stone inserted on its end, a makána. In the Amazon today, some natives call a sort of very hard, wooden sword a makána. There is no connection with a derogatory and slimy meaning given to this word by certain Latin Americans.

Makisapa Black monkey with large limbs, each endowed with four fingers. With its very long, hairy tail, the makisapa swings among the high branches of trees. *Maki* means "hand" in Keshwa; *sapa* means "large," "huge," "out of proportion."

Mamántziki Wife of Pachamakáite, the Father-God of the Ashanínka, Son of the Sun, creator and maker of everything that exists and of what doesn't exist.

Manacarácuy Small, fierce fowl, usually black. To balance its small size, it evidences a boundlessly bad temperament and an impious, uncontrolled, and permanently combative disposition, which forms the base of its fame as invincible.

Manitóa A fish one meter long, weighing twenty kilos. It moves very quickly and camouflages itself by mimesis. Only the enormous shining orange mouth reveals its presence in those turbid streams. Fishhooks give it no rest—certainly not on account of its flesh, I believe, because even though it is devoid of spines and scales, still it is very far from being appetizing.

Manguaré Percussion instrument made from a hollowed, dried log. Natives give it life and sound by striking the bark with a beater covered with tarred rags. The manguaré is played in several ways, depending on coded rhythms the knowledge of which belongs exclusively to the chief sorcerer and his associates. Generally it is used to send messages and warn of dangers, at other times to gather for war, or yet at other times

to invoke deities or great souls or to wake up the spirits of ancestors about to fall asleep, giving up and no longer protecting us. Mostly it is used to issue joyous invitations to celebrations and games. It is known that once upon a time, the Moon was a piece of white lupuna, a hollow log made of ash. Pachamakáite had not yet taught it to shine. The Ashanínka say that Narowé, the first man, furious because the koto-machácuy had stolen his woman, flung a lance at the sky and struck the Moon. The Moon reeled, fell, and came to a halt at the feet of Narowé. At that very moment, a bolt of lightning flashed. Narowé caught it and used it to beat the Moon again and again. And the log of the Moon, Manguaré, resonated. Manguaré! Manguaré! it rang as far as the remotest parts of the Moon, that piece of white lupuna, the first manguaré to be heard on our globe.

Manshako Mansháku. A stork as tall as a tall man. It wears wide feathers, smooth and silvery gray.

Mantablanca This insect, as small as the track of the foot of an insect, feeds on blood, more particularly human blood, and more specifically on that blood which flows beneath hairs. If we add that hare-brained nutritional preference to the diminutive, invisible size of its body, able to traverse all mosquito nets, then the result is a confirmation of the mantablanca as belonging to the category of impossible torment.

Mantona Decorative snake. Its ten-meter length scares only the foreigner, because it never attacks a human being and has no poison.

Maparate River fish with no spines and no scales. It weighs less than a kilo and is less than one-half meter long. Its flesh is not especially tasty or especially disagreeable. It has no attraction or importance. Really, it should have no place in this vocabulary.

Marakána Medium-sized parrot, with green-blue plumage, nothing more.

Mareación Inebriation, intoxication.

Mariquiña Wild duck, harmless and not very big. Red-black feathers cover the tasteless and tender meat.

Mariquita Multicolored flower, endowed with stinging, sweet aromas. It opens its corolla only when the light has gone, when it is assured that no one can see it, on dark nights.

Masato Alcoholic drink based on cassava (yuca), a large cylindrical tuber with a dark surface and white pulp, a drink to be reckoned with. Native women split the pulp with their teeth, chew it, and spit it into a wooden container called a kosho. This product of cassava, fermented by saliva and time, has no equal among aboriginal preferences. Some spice it with a powder made from scrapings of the bones of their ancestors.

Mashko A member of the Amazon nation of the same name.

Mitayero Hunter and/or fisherman.

Mitayo Game.

Mokambo Makambo. A tree with wide leaves and oval fruit like a human head. Also, the fruit of that tree. The inside is full of seeds which when toasted, without anything else deing added, develop an appetizing odor and are much in demand.

Montete A running bird with an onomatopoeic name. It sings without moving the beak, inside itself and perhaps only for itself. Its chest inflates with hoarse music, and vibrations rather than songs come out—resonances that overcome flesh, traverse feathers, and can transcend further and be heard very far away, filling up the air. The montete, known elsewhere as trompetero, feathered in black or brown, always displays a yellow expanse in its forehead. The firm, long legs, enfolded by green, imitating the beak, impose upon this bird the aspect of a clever heron. Once, in the area of the Utuquinia River, I stole two montete eggs and camouflaged them in the nest of a distracted hen. In that way I discovered that the trompetero, not the dog, is man's best friend. My two kidnapped birds guarded the house night and day, protected the children and played with them, acted as sentinels in the corrals, quickly warned us of any danger— whether customary dangers such as foxes, tigers, and sudden storms, or less common dangers such as visitors. They accomplished errands; they understood everything with overwhelming intelligence and skill. There was only one matter in which they refused to listen to reason: their unbounded attraction to chicks led them to take possession of all of those around them in the coops, with sectarian zeal, and to administer merciless beatings to any mothers who dared come close. Our montetes, misappropriating human destinies and habits, abandoned themselves to the contagion: the kidnapped of the past became the kidnappers of the present. Born under the wings of another species, the trompeteros believed themselves to be hens. Such a classic and irrevocable mistaking of identities pursued them, however, only until old age. "And this, which is nothing, is everything," says Ino Moxo. It was then that the trompeteros, for nothing, recovered everything. They recovered their persons only to part with them. They recovered their voices only to become finally silent. Having a premonition of the closeness of the far away, and not having been able to live as they could have lived, they decided to die as they should have died: they converted their forcibly adopted offspring into forced orphans. They advanced, breathless. They went into the night, froze motionless, and discovered that they had always lived surrounded by wire nets. For the first, only, and last time, they flew: they entered the forest, radiant, with closed beaks, singing darkly in the wilderness. I am certain of it. Because between dreams, I heard in the shadows, far away in the bush and even farther away in clearings, a muffled song bouncing in the air, mirroring other singing in my soul and then dying out. This happened last night, and today, dawn came to an empty world with no one in it.

Motelo Land turtle, which hunters classify into two groups. The common motelo never exceeds eighty centimeters in length and is the most sought after. The flesh varies in tenderness and flavor depending on the part of the body it comes from. The other motelo, the giant one, is one meter long and two meters in diameter. The irreducible hardness of its arid flesh makes it disdained even by the hungry.

Muwena Muena, mohena. A tree with extremely resistant wood.

Muyuna Whirlpool, a circular current, which rivers encourage especially in their ninety-degree turns.

Naka-naka Black, lean reptile, small and deadly. It lives in bucolic ravines and unsuspected creeks.

Ñejilla A type of destitute palm tree,

stubby, spiny, and with sweet-and-sour fruit. It occupies only lowlands, exposed to the most imperceptible drizzles. Always on the banks of rivers or lagoons, the ñejilla, poor tree squashed by the sky, imagines itself growing at water level. But droughts return it from its dreams, and dreams return it from reality: the extended ñejilla was a reflection of what the ñejilla is no more.

Ojé A giant tree, common in lowlands. Its sap, effective as a tonic and strengthener, overcomes the most obstinate parasitic infections.

Oni xuma Ayawaskha, in the Yora (Amawaka) language.

Otorongo From the Keshwa *uturunqu*: puma, tiger, panther, jaguar. Most commonly, the skin of this animal tends to be yellow-green spotted with gray. The darker its color, the more it is feared. Only some humans can equal it in fierceness. This animal, therefore, is the only one that lives and dies alone.

Pachamakáite The Father-God, the *pawa* (great Father) of the Ashanínka nation. Son of the highest Sun, the Noon Sun. Husband of Mamántziki. Creator and sustainer of all that passes over or remains on the surface of the earth.

Paiche An aquatic mammal with an imposing, tubular, blackish body, more than three meters long and weighing two hundred kilos. It has bony lips. Its tongue, also bony and serrated along its thirty centimeter length, is used as a file to polish wooden objects. The paiche has a flesh similar to that of cod in texture but superior to it in flavor and in protein content. It is the most prized inhabitant of Amazonian rivers.

Palometa Fish, which unfortunately

Palometa Fish, which unfortunately weighs only one kilo, having small silvery scales and priceless meat. Because of that and also because of its shape, a flat roundedness the palometa must descend from an ancestral relative of the sole. A woman's genitals are also called palometa.

Pamacari A curved, small roof, similar to the upper half of a tunnel, made of palm leaves interwoven into the hardness of a shield to form a compact barrier, which when placed over the decks of canoes protects the travelers from the sun's fury, from rains, and from other threats. Pamacaris are wise: they cover only transitory dwellings.

Panguana The panguana is superior to any other partridge in the South American jungles in delicacy of meat, in quality of song, and in deceits to avoid capture.

Papási A coleopterous insect, born from the mortal remains of an edible worm, the suri. In turn, the suri is born from the eggs deposited by the papási in the bark of aguaje palms.

Para-pára *See* hiporúru.

Parinári A tree with elongated, red fruits, sweeter than they are peppery, known as *súpay-oqóte* in Keshwa, meaning "devil's ass."

Pashako An almost high, almost thick, almost useless tree. The crown of lean leaves does not provide shade. The feeble, damp wood does not know how to burn. The pashako is barely saved by its bark: when squeezed it produces a juice used in the tanning of leather.

Paujil Wild turkey with mourning plumage, which contrasts with the incendiary red of its beak.

Páwkar Páucar. A bird with showy feathers, black and yellow. The páwkar imitates to perfection the songs and whistles of absolutely all the birds of the forest.

Peje-torre Fish with yellow skin and black polka dots. When inflated with air, it floats as a buoy on the surface of large rivers. The body of anyone who eats the peje-torre instantly becomes covered with persistent gray spots. Some birds allow themselves to eat the peje-torre; one can recognize them because their plumage is discolored forever.

Piraña Paña (in Caribe). Depending on voracity and size, this carnivorous fish has been classified into seven species. The most fearful one measures up to fifty centimeters in length and carries three rows of triangular teeth, sharp in their points and sides. All pirañas go into a frenzy when they sense the proximity of blood.

Piri-piri Hollow herb, tubular and lengthy, growing at the edges of swamps and lakes. In sorcery there are infinite uses for piri-piri. The Ashanínka call it *ivénki,* the magical herb par excellence, and include it in that class of plants that need not be combined with any others, or magnetized, or charged in order for them to reach their maximum efficacy. Actually, piri-piri is a generic name for an unmeasurable family of dissimilar tubers. Sorcerers apply them according to their shape. The piri-piri shaped like a penis is used against infertility or impotence, even though, logically, the shape of each tuber may depend more on the sighting of the sorcerer than on the tuber itself.

Piro Native from the tribe of the same name. They are loyal allies of the rubber collectors, against their brothers from other regions of the Amazon. This is why even today jungle people use *piro* to mean "coward" or "traitor."

Pisonay Tree with unembraceable trunk. The foliage in its giant crown explodes in small, red flowers. It is hard to find a pisonay in the Amazon jungle and less improbable in the jungle outskirts. Only the Andean valleys rejoice in its abundant presence.

Piurí A fowl as big as a turkey. Except for the whiteness of the breast and the red of the beak, all of the piurí is black, including the halo of tiny, shining feathers cresting over the forehead. The piurí is the most prized game bird in the forest; the juicy, delicious meat, along with its pride, condemn it to perdition.

Pomarrosa A tree, *Syzygium malacciensis,* myrtaceae, "mamey."

Pona Black, hard palm tree. A justifiable custom makes the pona the inevitable flooring for houses on stilts.

Pucaquiro Pukakiru. In Keshwa, "red tooth." A tree with inflexible, red heartwood. Also an enormous and feared ant, whose red, powerful jaws are more painful than poisonous.

Pukuna Pucuna, a blow gun.

Punguyo Punqúyu. A leafy, medium-sized tree. It thrives isolated, alone, in the middle of a lifeless space. Nothing survives under the shade of a punguyo. The green leaves expel a venom without appeal.

Pusanga Spell, witchcraft. A drink or talisman that has been charged to dominate or attract someone sexually.

Q'enqo Zigzag, labyrinth. Name used to designate the Temple of the Puma God, a rock located in the heights surrounding the city of Cusco. The Inkas carved a zigzag trough on its top. Pouring a corn beverage, chicha, on it—and, less frequently, the blood of a vicuña—our ancestors forecasted the future in ceremonies now lost forever.

Q'ero Ceremonial wooden vase, preferably carved out of a piece of dark wood. Also the name of a farming community near the summit of the town of Pawkartampu, inside the jungles that surround those mountains. The members of that community have indefatigably refused even the slightest "benefits of civilization" imposed by the Spanish conquerors. Behind the boundaries of their customs and their territories, the people of Q'ero to this day dress like Inkas, converse like Inkas, and live like Inkas, inaccessible to the time of the virakochas. More than four hundred years have been defeated by the still vital tenacity of the Q'ero people.

Qespichiway In Keshwa, *qespi* is "crystal," "transparent," "pristine," and therefore "free." *Chiway* is the coupling of birds for reproductive purposes exclusively. "Qespichiway!" uttered thus, with an edge of pleading, of invocation, would literally mean "Let me couple with crystal like birds who would procreate!" Or else "Couple with me, let us marry the crystal, let us marry that which is pristine, let us have free and transparent sons!" The Cusco poet Angel Avendano, supported by Jose Maria Arguedas, considers Keshwa as more easily expressed by pictures than by concepts. He does not exaggerate or miss the point when he translates (or reduces) "Qespichiway!" as "Free me!"

Qoylluriti *Qoyllur,* star; *riti,* snow. Keshwa name of a mountain crowned with perpetual ice.

Quichagarza Kichagarza. *Kicha:* Soft excrement, diarrhea. The kichagarza is a small, gray, elongated heron, which owes its name to the insistence and frivolity of its fecal deposits.

Quillu-avispa Yellow wasp.

Quinilla Behind its indecisive appearance, fainthearted in girth as in altitude, the modest quinilla tree hides not only consistent wood and sweet fruits but also curative powers diversified according to the afflictions against which it is used, and distributed among leaves, petals, root, bark, and sap. Common mortals nevertheless fear the quinilla. Only the great sorcerers, the authorized people, dare approach it. The anima, the mother who rules the affairs of this tree, is a young, long-haired maiden who sings among the rocks surrounding waterfalls. Her songs are healing; her lips are deadly. Natives affirm that the quinilla is "a plant to listen to but not to touch."

Raymiyáwar *Raymi.* feast, celebration; *yawar.* blood. A blood celebration.

Renaco An enormous tree, with gorged branches, twisted toward infinity. It grows without end at ground level until it occupies a whole forest. It is well known that the sap of the renaco is a powerful coagulant.

Renaquílla Parasite plant, of mediocre size, with branches that extend in a thicket similar to those of the renaco. With them, the renaquilla wraps around, and eventually strangles, the tree that supports it.

Ronsoco The largest rodent in nature. When mature, it approaches 120 centimeters in length and one hundred kilos in weight. Thick gray hairs cover its body. Hunters pursue this animal only on land. If it manages to escape into water, the webbed feet make it truly unreachable.

Runasimi *Simi*, language; *runa*, man. The language of man. Inkas called their language *Runasimi* instead of the term *Quechua* used by the Spanish conquerors, for reasons that have yet to be determined.

Sachavaca Wild cow, tapir, danta. A ruminant of great strength and even greater timidity, absolutely harmless.

Sachamáma A type of boa. Gigantic anaconda, mistaken by some for the yakumama. They coincide in strength and length; they are both as thick as a thick tree. But the yakumama lives in the water as exclusively as the sachamáma lives on the ground. Furthermore, the latter has a fin on each side of its head, resembling ears.

Sajino Wild boar collared with a stripe of white hairs, the rest of its body being gray. This wild pig, unlike its closest relative, the huangana, does not move in herds but in pairs, flees instead of attacking, and is hopelessly frightened and vegetarian.

Saltón Giant fish without scales, teeth, or spines. In spite of the two meters that host the one hundred kilos of its body, the saltón habitually jumps—almost flies up to five meters above the surface of rivers.

Sapote An inordinately high tree. Also the fruit of the same tree, whose tender, sweet pulp lies, unsuspected and white, underneath a corrugated, shadow-green skin.

Saqsawma Gray Head, Speckled Stone Head. The name of a fortress in Cusco, which the Spanish conquerors mistook for Sacsayhuaman: Hawk Head. The original Cusco, then sacred in its essence by being the capital of the Inkas, of the Sons of the Father Sun God, was also sacred in its shape: the city exactly filled the outlines of a puma, of an otorongo, one of the divinities of the Inka Empire. Cusco was Qosqo, Navel of the World; it was also Puma God, Uturunqu God, Stone Otorongo. The chest of the sacred city was occupied by the Wakaypata, the present central square, and Pumakurku Street (vertebral column of the

255

puma) leads to the Saqsawma Fortress, Gray Head, Speckled Head of the City of the Puma God. The tail of that sacred stone tiger was made of water—the frothy tail of the puma was the Watanay River.

Shánsho Small fowl with an onomato-poeic name. It is as out of tune in its song as it is delicate in the flavor of its meat.

Shapája A palm tree disproportionate in girth, height, leaves, and branches. It fruits in numerous and disorderly almonds, not very useful in their pulp, discrete in taste and protein content, more helpful by the airy fuel produced from its oil. Shapája leaves roof a house better than anything else. The wide leaves, interwoven with tight and resistant fibers, are invulnerable to the cutting edge of the sun or the insidiousness of torrential rains.

Shapra A native of the nation of the same name. A widely diffused Western lie affirms that the Shapra are more than polygamous—that the wives belong unrestrainedly to all of the males in the community.

Shapshico Devil, goblin, apparition, demon.

Shebón Tall palm. Its fruits, with pleasant pulp and heavy skin, weigh down large but fragile branches. Perhaps because of that, the leaves of the shebón are used to build pamacaris to serve as roofs for boats but not for dwellings.

Shibé A beverage prepared from cassava flour dissolved in water, sometimes with added sugar.

Shirimpiáre *See* Shirikaipi.

Shiringa Rubber.

Shirikaipi Homemade cigarette, put together wholly or partially with wild tobacco leaves. The general sorcerers of the Amazon are called katziboréri, but the specialists in

smoking shirikaipis—those who appeal to smoked tobacco in their healings and rituals—are known as shirimpiáre.

Shiripira Even though apparently easy to capture because of its weight and size (under two kilos and sixty centimeters), this denizen of the large rivers, with pleasant-tasting flesh and a total absence of scales or spines, also displays along its back three bony blades, sharp spikes that give rise to despair in the neediest and most persistent fishermen.

Shirúi Protected by a rough and impenetrable shell, this fish inhabits only lakes and swamps. Three times smaller than the shiripira, it is usually mistaken for it because of its yellow flesh.

Shuyu Shuyo. Famous for its voracity, sharp teeth, and scaly armor, this fish prefers to live in the bottom of isolated lakes and swamps sur-rounded by hostile wilderness. It is capable of walking over the ground for several days, sliding along like a snake and leaving behind a mess of dull yellowish phlegm.

Sitúlli A banana-like plant, fruiting in bunches of great red flowers.

Songárinchi A very long flute made of blackened wood, producing abrupt and ear-splitting dissonances, used by Amawaka warriors to gain courage in battles and joy in celebrations.

Súpay-oqóte Devil's ass. An elongated, red fruit growing amid wide dark leaves on the parinári tree.

Suri Edible worm, which is born inside, and is nourished by, the tender shoots of several palm trees. Actually, the suri is born from the eggs laid by a coleopterous insect, the papási, which inserts them in the bark of palm trees, preferably the aguaje palm. When the suri dies, the papási is born from its corpse. The papási is born from the remains of the suri and lays the eggs from which the suri is born. . . .

Tabaquerillo Diminutive woodpecker, proclaimed by a flash of smoky yellow feathers, the color of sun-ripened tobacco.

Tágua The fruit of the yarina palm tree. The whitish insides, remote and translucent, have become famous as the vegetable marble of the yarina.

Tampu Mach'ay Water temple in the Cusco area, beyond the Saqsawma Fortress and beyond the Q'enqo, Temple of the Puma God. The virakocha conquerors christened this site the Bath of the Princess. They did worse with the Waka Qollana in Lima (*waka:* sacred place; *qollana:* principal), which is known even today as the Huaca Juliana.

Tangarana Large and merciless red ant, extremely poisonous, which inhabits the inside of a tree that is also called tangarana. The wardens of jungle prisons use it as an instrument of punishment. In the El Sepa Penal Colony, on the shores of the Urubamba, the prisoners call the tangarana the torture tree. Countless prisoners, nearly always political ones, know that death is preferable to the tangarana. The executioners disrobe the prisoner, cover him with honey, tie him to the tree, and strike the trunk with a club. Thousands of voracious red jaws surge from the cracks in the bark and suffocate the body and the shrieks of the victim. The victim is immediately untied and removed from the stings. The jailers know full well that the punishment has just begun: an infinite number of black and oozing sores will torment the condemned man for months to come.

Tantoótzi One of the two houses built by all Ashanínka families. The chief and his wives and children live in the tantoótzi. The other dwelling, the kaápa, is built first and is destined exclusively for guests.

Taperibá Giant plum, with sweet-and-sour pulp and a spiny center, called by many the most delicious fruit produced by nature.

Taráwi Tarahui. Notwithstanding its curved beak, the color of bleached gold, and the black plumage with which this bird attempts to hide the fruity freshness of its flesh, this fowl feeds only on snails.

Taricaya Very fast, lean turtle of medium size. The eggs and meat are edible.

Tatatáo Medium-sized bird of prey. During the day it opens its beak and wings only to eat. After sunset, though not always, it sings "Ta-ta-taooo! Ta-ta-taoooo!" That is why absent-minded tribesmen, not remembering the bird's true and original name, temporarily call it by using the sound of its song.

Tibe A white bird with long legs, either a miniature heron or a river gull—take your choice.

Tiríri Generic name of seven varieties of small fat fish, covered with a gray armor, living in swamps and lagoons.

Tiwakuru Small bird with an onomato-poeic name and black feathers that are lighter in color only on its chest. The beak displays all shades of red. It prefers to nest in the crowns of wimbra trees in summer, and it favors all types of ants as food in any season.

Tohé Generic name for several solana-ceous plants with hallucinogenic sap and large, marble-like, bell-shaped flowers. The most common is *Datura speciosa,* or *Tohé mullaca.* Other varieties have been variously called *Solanum bicolor, Cornutia odorata,* and/or *Datura insignis.* Amazonian sorcerers add the potency of tohé to the beverages based on the juices of ayawaskha.

Tokón Large monkey with a large, strong, hairy tail. It depends on the latter more than on its limbs to move about or defend itself, grabbing a branch and swinging to another one, almost flying from tree to tree.

Tortuga-kaspi Turtle tree, so called because of its gray and rough bark.

Trompetero *See* Montete.

Túnchi Small nocturnal songbird. Few have seen it; many have heard it; everyone fears it. When a túnchi sings, it is only because someone has died or will inevitably die somewhere nearby that night.

Tupac Amaru Shining Serpent God; in Keshwa and in Runasimi. Name of one of the Inka emperors. One of his descendants, Jose Gabriel Condorcanqui, adopted the name of Tupac Amaru II and in 1781 led one of the biggest rebellions against the Spanish conquerors. Once the revolt was put down, Tupac Amaru was tortured and quartered in the Wakaypata, now the central square in Cusco. His head was buried near the sacred city, and the other parts of his body were dispersed and buried in lands along the boundaries of the ancient empire of his ancestors.

Tuta-cuchillo Knife-of-the-night. Nocturnal monkey. In the presence of danger, meaning man, it cuts branches and sticks and throws them down at the intruder in the darkness.

Tzangapilla Zangapilla. A bush that flowers only once and does not know how to flower more than once. Also, the flower of that bush, whose gigantic orange petals, boldly colored and perfumed, emit such heat as to make it untouchable. The tzangapilla

flower can survive several days after it is cut from a branch. Usually on the seventh day the petals lose their color and their aroma and suddenly fall off, cold, like small dead animals.

Tzího Buzzard, in the Ashanínka language.

Tzipíbo Shipibo. Native of the Amazon nation of the same name.

Ucuashéro Diminutive songbird with an onomatopoeic name.

Uchusanango Peppery sanango. A slightly alcoholic beverage prepared by sorcerers by macerating, in various ways, a diversity of vegetables, following the needs of each special case: as a tonic, as a medicine, or to cast a spell.

Unchala Bird of the same size as a large pigeon. It has a harmonious and persistent song, and dark red feathers.

Urkutútu Owl.

Urus Uros. Members of a nation of the same name, now totally extinct, who inhabited the high plateau where Lake Titicaca remains today. It is said that they were the founders of the city of Cusco and that the first Inka emperors, Manko Kapaq and Mama Oqllo, belonged to the Uru nation.

Valdez, Zacarías Rubber collector who worked for Fermin Fitzcarrald, and author of the booklet "The Real Fitzcarrald in History," published in 1944. As he proceeds along the pages, as full of arrogance as they are replete with spelling errors, he describes some of the crimes and misdemeanors committed by his accomplices, the "pioneers" of their time, under the pretext of taking progress and civilization to the natives.

Varayoq Mayor, the principal authority in Inka communities, or *Ayllus*, which are scattered over the Peruvian Andes Mountains.

Virakocha White person. *Trans.*

Virote Very small poisoned dart, capable of abandoning and resuming its material shape in order to traverse any distance; any time; any wall, shield, or protection; to nail itself in enemy flesh and to reach the target selected by the sorcerer who gave it form and then animated that form, endowing it with destiny and transcendence. A spell of mostly lethal consequences.

Wacamayu Macaw.

Wakapú *See* Huacapú.

Wakapúrana *See* Huacapurana.

Wálo *See* Hualo.

Wanakawre Mountain upon which lies the city of Cusco. The siblings Manko Kapaq and Mama Oqllo, born and raised in the nation of the Urus, left Lake Titicaca under orders of the Sun God, carrying a golden staff. They were to establish a city, Qosqo, in the place where the staff would ground itself effortlessly. The city was destined to be the heart of a limitless empire. Manko Kapaq and his sister/wife meandered from the high plateau to the Andes ranges, seeking in vain the site selected by the Sun. Almost hopeless, they tried the summit of Mount Wanakawre. The golden staff sank in at the first attempt and disappeared.

Wapapa *See* Huapapa.

Waqaypata Place where one weeps. Inka name for the central square in Cusco, where the conquerors executed Tupac Amaru.

Waqrapona *See Huacra-pona.*

Wayranga *See* Huairanga.

Wikungu *See* Huicungu.

Willaq Umu High priest of the Inkas. The highest religious authority, presiding over principal ceremonies.

Willkamayu Sacred river. Inka name for the Urubamba River, which joins the Tambo River to form the Ucayali River. The latter, in turn, unites with the Marañón River to form the Amazon, river-sea of the South American jungles.

Wimbra Huimbra. A lanky tree with an emerald bark, which opens up into a smallish crown, superficial and noisy. Nests of a whistling, nervous bird, the tiwakuru, are often found on the branches of the wimbra.

Witoto Huitoto. Member of the nation of the same name.

Yaku-jergón A river snake.

Yakumama Giant snake living in the rivers. Mother of the waters.

Yanaboa Anaconda, black boa.

Yarina Palm tree producing fruits called tágua or vegetable marble.

Yora Member of an Amazon nation of the same name. For unknown reasons, Westerners call them Amawakas instead of Yoras.

Yuca Cassava. *See* Masato.

Yungurúru Giant partridge, whose sky-blue eggs are identical to those produced by chickens.

Zui-zúi Small songbird with an onomatopoeic name and sky-blue plumage.

Zúngaro Name given to any river fish that is large, that has a head of the same size as the rest of its body, and that is spineless and scaleless.

Zúri *See* Suri.